A Woven Book of Knowledge

Woman from Umasbamba, Chinchero, wearing her traditional dress.

A Woven Book of Knowledge

Textile Iconography of Cuzco, Peru

by

GAIL P. SILVERMAN

THE UNIVERSITY OF UTAH PRESS
Salt Lake City

The Defiance House Man colophon is a registered trademark of the
University of Utah Press. It is based upon a four-foot-tall, Ancient Puebloan
pictograph (late PIII) near Glen Canyon, Utah

12 11 10 09 08   1 2 3 4 5

LIBRARY OF CONGRESS CATALOGING-IN-PUBLICATION DATA

Silverman, Gail P.
  A woven book of knowledge : textile iconography of Cuzco, Peru / by Gail P. Silverman.
      p. cm.
  Includes bibliographical references and index.
  ISBN 978-0-87480-909-1 (pbk. : alk. paper) 1. Q'ero Indians—Material culture—
Peru—Cuzco. 2. Indian textile fabrics—Peru—Cuzco. 3. Textile design—Peru—Cusco—
Classification. 4. Cuzco (Peru)—Social life and customs. I. Title.
    F3430.1.Q47S55 2008
    746.1'408998323—dc22   2008021227

Printed and bound by Sheridan Books, Inc., Ann Arbor, Michigan.

To my father,

Joseph Silverman

Contents

Illustrations

Color Plates
(following page 122)

Tables

Foreword

The last twenty years have witnessed a notable advance in the study of precontact American writing systems, especially from Mesoamerica. Maya writing, for example, has been 80 percent deciphered. Research in this field for the Andean area, however, is still in its infancy. This is due in part to the unusual material support that was used and continues to be used in the Andes, mainly textiles.

The Incas used textiles to make the quipu, the knotted string recording device, and to produce cloth. The finest textiles were decorated with geometric motifs circumscribed inside rectangles, known as *tocapus*. In ancient times members of the nobility had the privilege of using these sumptuous textiles. Today members of the Cuzco communities, descendants of the Incas, preserve that predominantly Inca tradition and many of its motifs.

Gail Silverman holds a doctorate from the Sorbonne, where her mentor was Georges Balandier. Trained in one of the best methodological currents in scientific investigation, Silverman went to Peru in the 1970s. She was the first anthropologist to carry out detailed and prolonged anthropological studies of the modern textiles woven in the northeast-northwest area of Cuzco, especially among the Q'ero, an ethnic group from the province of Paucartambo. Silverman has lived in Cuzco for almost thirty years. In order to conduct her fieldwork, she learned Quechua before Spanish, and she still speaks Quechua daily with the weavers with whom she interacts either in her Cuzco home or in their villages. Silverman also learned to weave, both to better enter into dialogue with the weavers and to comprehend by her own experience their weaving techniques, writing, and cosmology.

The Peruvian Victoria de la Jara was the first to believe that the tocapus produced on Inca and pre-Inca textiles could have the purpose of transmitting ideas, and in the 1960s she tried to interest anthropologists in finding proof for her hypothesis. More than fifty years later, Gail Silverman has achieved the task of that pioneer, assembling a lexicon of modern tocapus based on those from the prehispanic period, all of them with meaning. Her contribution is thus exceedingly valuable because it illuminates not only Cuzco ethnology but also the study of Andean notation systems.

Silverman situates this iconography in both its technological and cultural context in the Cuzco area, going back to the Inca era. She includes semantic data for each motif, enriched by the perspectives of Quechua speakers, whose words Silverman has been very careful to reproduce as accurately as possible. Her mastery of Quechua means that her work not only emphasizes the viewpoint of the Quechua speakers but also provides anthropological validity.

This book, for the first time available in an English edition, for which I have the honor of writing the prologue, presents the knowledge that persists in the Cuzco area about cosmology, agriculture, and history, knowledge that is stored in the textile iconography. Similar studies exist for Bolivia and Chile, carried out by Verónica Cereceda, but not until now for Peru. Thus the author's contribution is extremely valuable. Gail Silverman has become for Cuzco textiles what Verónica Cereceda is for the study of the textiles of Jalca and Tarabuco, Bolivia, and Isluga, Chile: a lifetime of dedication.

CARMEN ARELLANO HOFFMANN

Acknowledgments

I am deeply grateful to my Quechua-speaking friends in Q'ero, Chinchero, Calca, Pisac, Paucartambo, Huancarani, Markapata, Kauri, Ccatcca, Choque-cancha, Kachin, Willoq, Pitumarka, and Parubamba. Without their assistance, this book would never have been written.

My expeditions to Q'ero and the other Cuzco-area communities were financed by numerous institutions: Fulbright Hays, 1979-1980; the Universidad de Santa María de Arequipa, Arequipa, Peru, for 1984; and the French Ministry of Education, for an Aires Culturelles grant for 1985. In 1989 I received financial assistance from the Editorial Fund of the Banco Central de Reserva del Perú and in 1989, 1990, and 1991 from the Ministerio de la Presidencia, Consejo Nacional de Ciencia y Tecnología (CONCYTEC), Lima, Peru, for fieldwork undertaken outside Q'ero.

During my fieldwork in 1985 and 1986, I was guided by Georges Balandier of the Université de Paris V, Sciences Humaines, Sorbonne, Paris, and I thank him for his unwavering support. I also thank the Peruvian Central Reserve Bank in the persons of Santiago Antúñez de Mayolo and Javier de la Rocha Marie for understanding the importance of this work, and Blanca Varela, director of the Fondo de Cultura Económica, Peru, for publishing an earlier version of this book so it could reach an international audience.

Many institutions sponsored the exhibits I have given over the years concerning the Cuzco-area textile tradition. I am grateful to the Casa Cabrera, the Banco de los Andes, and the Universidad de Cuzco for sponsoring my first exhibit in Cuzco in 1988; the Escuela de Bellas Artes, for exhibits given in 1990 and 1991; the Biblioteca Nacional del Perú, Lima, Martha Fernandez, and the Coca-Cola Company for an exhibit in 1996; and the Instituto Nacional de Cultura, Lima, and Sarah Acevedo for an exhibit given at the Museo Nacional de la Cultura, Lima, in 1995.

Earlier versions of this book were published in Spanish in 1994 and 1998; Chapters 1 and 9 are updated here. Early versions of Chapter 3 were published in the catalog to my first Cuzco exhibit (1988) and in *Antropológica* in 1994. The material in Chapter 4 was presented for the first time at the Junius Bird Andean Textile Conference at the Textile Museum, Washington, D.C., in 1984; early versions were published in 1986 in the *Boletín de Lima* and presented in 1987 in *Dialogo Andino*. Chapter 6 was published in early versions in 1991 in the *Boletín de Lima* and in 1995 in the exhibition catalog *Leyendo el tejido cusqueño*. Early versions of Chapter 7 were published in 1986 in the *Boletín de Lima* and in 1999 in *Tejidos milenarios del Perú/Ancient Peruvian Textiles*. The graphic dictionary in Chapter 8 appeared in an earlier form in 1991 and 1993 in *Awani wasi del Cusco*, vols. 1-3. Quechua terms are based on Antonio Cusihuamán's *Diccionario Quechua: Cuzco-Collao* (1976). Unless otherwise noted, all translations and photographs are my own.

Fernando Pinedo and Julio Lara Lavalle invited me to Chicago twice to raise scholarship monies for the Peruvian American Medical Society in 1995. I also express my gratitude to the Peruvian consulates in Miami and Chicago for their invitations to present the Spanish version of this book in those cities in 1995. In 1997 I presented an earlier version of this book to the Danish Ministry of Culture and the Copenhagen National Museum, and in 1995 in La Paz, Bolivia, at the invitation of the Instituto de Estudios Bolivianos.

Many colleagues read portions of this book, and I thank them for their comments: Joseph Bastien, Carmen Arellano Hoffmann, Ramiro Matos, Karen Mohr-Chávez and Sergio Chávez, Federico Kauffmann-Doig, Manuel Chávez Ballón, Cristina Bubba, Odi Gonzáles, and Blenda Femeninas. In addition, many provided assistance in other ways: Tom Zuidema, Jorge Flores Ochoa, Juan Ossio, Iña Rosing, Verónica Cereceda, Laura Laurencich Minelli, Victoria Solanilla, Carmen Escalante, Ricardo Valderrama, Italo Oberti, and Luis and Mary Vásquez. I also thank members of the staff of the University of Utah Press for their support and expertise.

Finally, I am indebted to my Cuzco family, Lucha, Antonio, and Catalina, who lived this experience with me and gave me the strength and encouragement to continue on this long and arduous road.

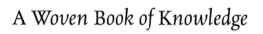

A Woven Book of Knowledge

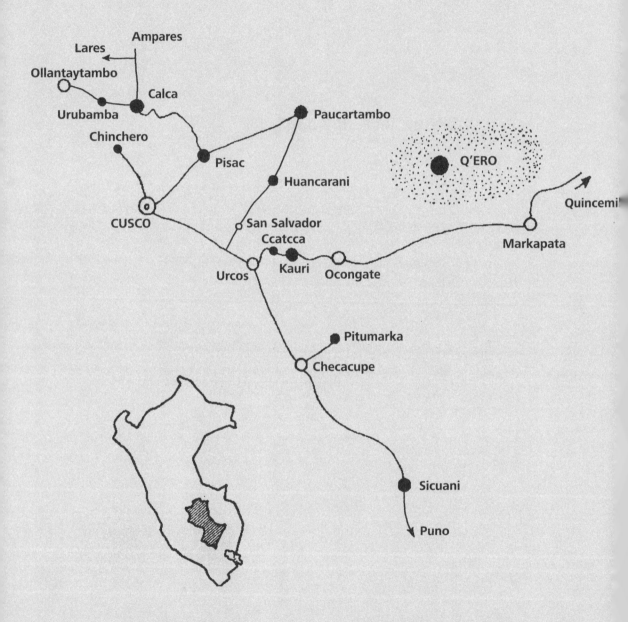

Map 1. Peru.

Q'ero

A Window on the Inca World

I first heard about the traditional community of Q'ero from my Quechua teacher at the University of Paris VIII, Abdon Yaranga Valderrama, who was a Peruvian from Ayacucho and knew both his country and the anthropological literature on the Andes well. I wanted to test my hypothesis that the Incas had nonalphabetic writing, and Abdon suggested that only two sites in Peru were relatively unharmed by the encroachment of modernity: Cangallo, in Ayacucho, and Q'ero, high in the mountains to the east of Cuzco. I chose the latter as my study site because it was close to the ancient capital of the Incas, and because its geographical remoteness was ideal for testing my hypothesis.

Q'ero is situated approximately 190 kilometers northeast of Cuzco (Champi Ccasa 2005:427). It has eight principal communities: Hatun Q'ero, Q'ero Totorani, K'allakancha, Markachea, Pukara, Q'achupata, Kiko, and Hapu. These villages are distributed in four main valleys that range in altitude from 1,800 to 4,600 meters and overlook the upper tributaries of the Madre de Dios River. The entire Q'ero region measures just over 914 square kilometers (Champi Ccasa 2005:427; Núñez del Prado 1970; Webster 1972:7).[1]

Figure 1.1. A Q'ero woman wearing a ceremonial hat and a lliklla with the ch'unchu Type III motif. K'allakancha, 1985.

[1]

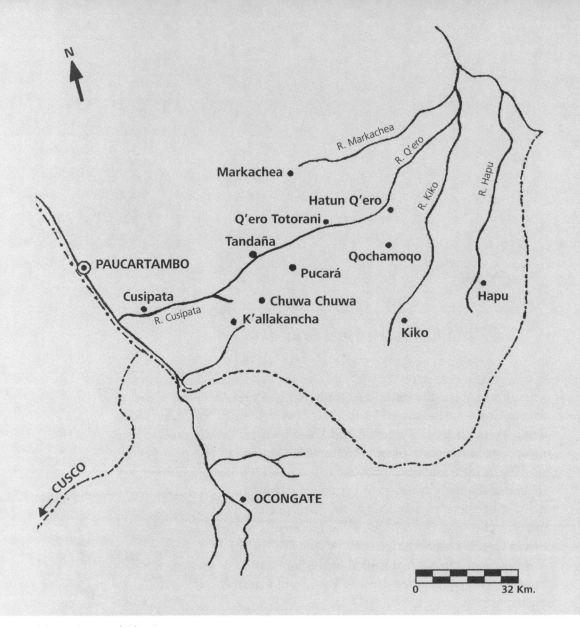

Map 2. Cuzco and Q'ero.

According to Steven Webster (1972:1), in 1969-1970 the Q'ero had 376 people distributed in 82 families. The 1981 census carried out by the Cuzco Ministerio de la Vivienda (1983) notes 651 people, and the 2004 census lists 628 Q'ero families for a total of 3,786 people (Champi Ccasa 2005:427).

In many ways Q'ero appears to be like the hundreds of other Quechua-speaking peasant communities in the Cuzco highlands, but because of both geographical remoteness and specific circumstances, the Q'ero have

Figure 1.2. The unoccupied ceremonial center of Hatun Q'ero, 1979.

conserved more Inca lifeways than their mestizo neighbors (Flores Ochoa 1989; Núñez del Prado Bejar 2005; Schevill et al. 1991:103).[2]

Because of the community's geographic isolation, there is no evidence of a former Spanish presence in Q'ero with a central plaza occupied by both church and government buildings. To date, no Sunday Mass has ever been said in Q'ero (Padre Orihuela, personal communication 1985; Título Privado 1851; Silverman-Proust 1987a:385-429). In contrast, Q'ero sheds light on an Inca settlement pattern, indicated by the presence of four unoccupied ceremonial centers—Hatun Q'ero, Q'ero Totorani, Hatun Kiko, and Hatun Hapu—each of which has only a small adobe church surrounded by houses and dirt roads arranged in a haphazard manner. These ceremonial centers contain large stone houses that shelter extended families when they come down to assist at the yearly festivals of Carnival and Corpus Christi or travel to and from the lowlands.[3]

The Q'ero exploit three ecological zones, the *puna*, *qheswa*, and *monte* or *yunga*, which I treat in more detail in Chapters 3 and 6. The puna is located at an elevation of 3,500 to 4,600 meters and is the site of their permanent residences.[4] They grow the *ruk'i* potato and graze their alpacas on *ichhu* and *khunkuna* grasses. In the qheswa, located between 2,800 and 3,500 meters, they cultivate potatoes and other crops, and in the monte, at about

Figure 1.3. A wall-less shelter in the Q'ero yunga, 1980.

Figure 1.4. Sunday market in Pisac, 1980.

1,800 meters, they plant corn, as well as pumpkins and peppers. Throughout the year the Q'ero travel up and down between these zones to carry out the different tasks necessary to harvest potatoes and corn. According to Oscar Núñez del Prado (1983, 2005:100), they are constantly going down to the yunga cornfields, up to the permanent residences in the puna, down to the qheswa potato fields, back again to the yunga cornfields, up to the qheswa potato fields, and so on, throughout the month and indeed during the entire year. Added to this are their yearly festivals of Corpus and Carnival, when they abandon their permanent residences in the puna for their ceremonial centers in the qheswa, leaving an elderly woman or a few small children to watch the herds.

Unlike Pisac, Calca, and Chinchero, each of which has an important Sunday market where potatoes are sold or bartered for nontraditional goods such as sugar, fruit, and liquor, there is no Sunday market in Q'ero. Instead, during the shearing season, as they have for generations, the Q'ero barter their alpaca fleece for cash, coca, bread, and salt with traders from Ocongate and Paucartambo. There are no stores in any of the Q'ero villages, unlike Calca, Pisac and Chinchero, which have numerous stores, important agents of cultural change (Allen 1988).

Q'ero is a center for religious specialists, who are ranked according to their skill and knowledge in healing (Rozas Alvarez 1983, 1989, 2005; Yabar 2005; Yabar et al. 1994). They intercede between humanity and the spiritual world, in which the sacred mountains (Apu) and Mother Earth (Pacha Mama) play a pivotal part (Rosing 1990, 1991). In 1979 there was at least one *altamesayoq*, the highest religious specialist, living in Chuwa Chuwa, as well as several *pampamesayoqs*, *hampeqs*, and *watoqs* (lesser specialists). At least one woman fulfilled the position of hampeq. In contrast, only one person carries out offerings in Pisac and one in the Lauramarka highlands (field notes,

Figure 1.6. A varayoq from a highland Paucartambo village, 1979.

Figure 1.5. A religious specialist living in Chuwa Chuwa, 1985.

1979, 2005), neither of whom is an altamesayoq.

In addition, the Q'ero still preserve the position of *varayoq* (he who carries the staff), a community official from Inca times, along with a community mayor and other officials borrowed from the Spanish colonial political system (Pérez-Galan 2002; Rasnake 1989).

At the time of my fieldwork (1979-1991), no Q'ero in the memory of the community had married outside the Q'ero nation.

Figure 1.7. María Pauccar Quispe of K'allakancha, 1980.

According to Webster (1983, 2005:111), exogamy between the high Q'ero valleys "is greater than 50 percent but is less than 20 percent for the entire Q'ero region since none of the diverse ecological zones in an isolated way is capable of supporting the community." This pattern is in sharp contrast to the fluidity with which other Quechua-speaking peasants marry outside their villages. In fact, it was not until 1986 that María Pauccar Quispe, of K'allakancha, had to marry outside because she did not know how to weave the two-faced cloth called Q'ero *pallay*.[5]

In 1955 Oscar Núñez del Prado, of the University of Cuzco, carried out the first anthropological study of the Q'ero and discovered two Inca legacies thought to have long disappeared. First, he came upon a quipu-kamayoq using a quipu, the knotted string counting device, to keep track of the haci-

Figure 1.8. Q'ero men playing their flutes in Hatun Q'ero, 1980.

enda owner's herds. Second, he discovered a special flute that did not exist outside Q'ero (Túpac Yupanqui 1955b).

Finally, the way Don Luis Ángel Yabar, owner of the Cusipata hacienda and much of the Q'ero lands, treated the Q'ero also helped them maintain more Inca lifeways than their mestizo neighbors.[6] First, Don Yabar prohibited the Q'ero from fulfilling their national military service. Second, he kept them from attending school, and when one family went against this rule, he expelled it from the hacienda (Prefectura de Paucartambo 1957b:Of. No. 81:21). Influenced by military service and the introduction of schools in Calca, Pisac, and Chinchero in the early twentieth century, the Quechua peasants became bilingual Quechua Spanish speakers who cast off their traditional costumes for modern dress and little by little shed their Inca ways.

In 1955, at the time of the first scientific expedition to Q'ero, no schools were located there, which meant that the Q'ero were monolingual Quechua speakers. And when schools were established, they were placed in the unoccupied ceremonial centers of Hatun Q'ero, Hatun Totorani, Hatun Kiko, and Hatun Hapu, one to two days' walk away, so that few children could attend. But if the Q'ero did not know how to write in Spanish, they did know how to write the Inca way, because they had conserved Inca ways of recording knowledge with the use of two Inca cloth types as well as various Inca weaving techniques.

The Q'ero still wear the sleeveless tunic, called *uncu*, which was the garment commonly worn by Inca men and which has disappeared from Cuzco (Flores Ochoa 1983:10, 13; Flores Ochoa and Fries 1989:34, 38, 42-43, 44, 55; Silverman 1998:59, Fig. 2.7). The uncu is formed with a single piece of cloth, woven of black alpaca wool and devoid of geometric motifs. A plain red stripe runs down the sides, which are joined by red sewing threads. Colonial paintings show the male Quechua peasant wearing

Figure 1.9. Q'ero boy wearing an Inca uncu.

Figure 1.10. Q'ero woman with baby, Wañunapampa, 1980.

Figure 1.11. The Q'ero wayako evolved from the quipu maker's bag.

such a garment (Dean 2002; Gisbert 1999). They also wear the *llaqolla* head covering, which was used during Inca times for ceremonial occasions (Phipps 2004, 2005).

In addition to the uncu and the llaqolla, the Q'ero weave a small rectangular bag, or *wayako*, that is very similar to the bag used to store their quipu in 1955. This bag, which I discuss in Chapter 6, is decorated with multicolored striped panels that are probably related to the Inca quipu.

In addition to these two textile types, the Q'ero use weaving techniques that are tied to the Incas. According to the Spanish chroniclers (Polo de Ondegardo [1585] 1916:85; Acosta [1590] 1979, book 4, chap. 41:136; Garcilaso [1609] 1960:155; Cobo [1653] 1956:259), the Incas wove two types of cloth, called *awasqa* and *cumbi*. Awasqa was a coarse, single-colored cloth devoid of geometric motifs, whereas cumbi was described as a two-faced cloth decorated with geometric motifs set into square or rectangular frames.

The Incas used different weaving techniques to create the two-faced cumbi cloth: tapestry weave, warp-faced plain weave, warp-faced stripes, warp-faced stripes plied to the left and to the right, double cloth, discontinuous warp weave, and three-color complementary warp-weaving technique. All but the tapestry weave and double cloth are woven by the Q'ero.

Figure 1.12. A Q'ero ceremonial poncho woven with warp-faced stripes and the three-color complementary warp weave.

Finally, instead of using a pen and paper to write, the Q'ero use colored threads to weave geometric motifs that have names and meanings. In fact, the Q'ero compare their textile motifs to "books" that can be read in this way, as one of my informants indicated:

Q: Imarayku awanku pallaykunata llikllapi, ch'uspapi, ponchopi?
[Why do you weave motifs in the *lliklla* (shawl), in the *ch'uspa* (ceremonial coca bag), and in the poncho?]

A: Hinapuni. Qan hina yachayku leyeta hinata.
[It's like that. They know how to read like that.]

Q: Imataq leyenki?
[What do you read?]

A: Ch'unchullata intiwan.
[Only Ch'unchu (a motif representing Inkarri, founder of the Incas) with the sun.]

(Lorenzo Quispe Yapura, Chuwa Chuwa, 1985)

Lorenzo added: "It is like a study for the women. They study the myth of Manco Cápac and Mama Ocllo."

❊ Andean Textile Studies ❊

A study of Q'ero textiles in relation to those woven in a broad geographical area of Cuzco is important because it not only creates verifiable data about a tradition that has not been described in the anthropological literature before, but also explicates a tradition that is tied to the Incas and therefore can help in the decipherment of the Inca geometric (*tocapu*) motifs.

Teresa Gisbert, Silvia Arze, and Martha Cajias (1987) were the first to publish a preliminary description of modern Cuzco-area textiles. They identified ten textile types based on weaving technique and motifs:

> "(1) Cuzco viceregal Spanish garments, floral baroque decoration with silver threads. (2) Laura marka [Lauramarka], including Ocongate, Calca-Pisac, and Chinchero, potato flower, scissors, eyes. (3) Lares, which includes Choquecancha and Cachin, horses, Tupac Amaru, diamonds, hooks, and zigzags. (4) Pitumarca, Checacupe, Chilca, *Chunchos* [*ch'unchus*], baroque decoration, Inca geometric decoration, diamonds. (5) Tinta, floral baroque decoration in ponchos, machine-made trims. (6) Vilcabamba, black *pampa*, little decoration, balanced warp and weft. (7) Chumbivilcas, geometric decoration, use of cochineal. (8) Cotabambas, geometric decoration, (9) Quero (Q'ero), serge, geometric decoration, *lloque* in the *pampa* [*lloq'e pañamanta*]. *Inti* and *Chunchos* [*ch'unchus*]. And (10) Paratia, geometric decoration. Discontinuous weft."[7]

In the late 1960s two studies paved the way for others: Junius Bird's (1969) focus on contemporary Cuzco spinning techniques and Louis Girault's (1969) ethnographic investigation of Charazani (Bolivia) textiles and their iconography, which included the reproduction of the entire motif repertory. Additional spinning and braiding techniques were described by Elayne Zorn (1980), Grace Goodell (1969), Anna Gayton (1961), and Edward Franquemont (1986), and the reproduction of both precolumbian and contemporary weaving techniques was detailed by Adele Cahlander and Susan Baizerman (1985), Cahlander (1983), Marjorie Cason and Adele Cahlander (1976), Ann Pollard Rowe (1975, 1977), and Zorn (1979).

Investigations also concerned textiles as indicators of ethnic identity (Matos Mar et al. 1984; Meisch 1991; Medlin 1983; Prochaska 1988; Wasserman and Hill 1981; and Adelson and Tracht 1983). Linda Seligmann (1978) studied the socioeconomic function of textiles woven in Santa Barbara and Ayapata in Sicuani (Cuzco), Peru, and Zorn (1983) conducted a similar study for Taquile (Puno), Peru, and investigated their impact on community development (2004).

Descriptions of Cuzco textile iconography were conducted by C. Franquemont (1986), E. Franquemont et al. 1992, and Martina Munsters (1986) for Chinchero, by Gertrude Solari (1980, 1982, 1983) and Rita Prochaska (1988) for Taquile, by Katherine Seibold (1992) for Choquecancha, and by Andrea Heckmann (2003) for the Ocongate area of Cuzco.

In the ethnographic study of both Bolivian and Chilean textiles, Verónica Cereceda (1978, 1987; Cereceda et al. 1993; Davalos et al. 1992) focused on the semiotic aspects, and Denise Arnold and Juan de Dios Yapita (2000) investigated the textiles woven in Qaqachaka, Bolivia. Eva Fischer (2002a, b) looked to those of Upinhuaya, Joseph Bastien (1978) to those of Kaata, and Jaime López, Willer Flores, and Catherine Letourneux (1992, 1993) to the textiles woven in Laymi and Chayantakas, Potosí, Bolivia. Mary Ann Medlin (1991) described Calcha textiles, and Lynn Ann Meisch (1988) studied those woven in Tarabuco, Bolivia. Finally, Lee Anne Wilson (1990) described the ch'unchu motif woven in Cuzco.

Liliana Torres Ulloa and Vivian Gavilan Vega (1992) proposed a methodology for the study of contemporary textiles, and Penny Dransart (2002) investigated animal husbandry in Chile as well as focusing on the symbolism of Isluga textiles. Lindsey Crickmay (1997) studied the spatial organization of contemporary textiles. Finally, Jesús Ruiz Durand (2004) reproduced iconography from the precolumbian period as well as contemporary textiles from Q'ero and Taquile, Peru, creating the first dictionary of textile iconography spanning thousands of years.

Before my arrival in Q'ero in 1979, almost nothing had been written about its textile tradition. In his 1957 unpublished master's thesis, John Cohen listed four Q'ero motifs—"*inti, ch'unchu, qocha,* and *chili*"— and wrote a brief description of Q'ero textiles as well as those from other Cuzco-area villages. In 1970 Oscar Núñez del Prado listed eight Q'ero motifs: "*ch'unchu, inti, mut'u ch'unchu, ch'usu inti, pilliy, chili, puntas,* and *k'eraqe.*" Webster (1970, 1972) listed two: "*inti* and *ch'unchu.*" In 1976 Medlin described Q'ero motifs based on museum collections. It should be mentioned that Cohen focused on Q'ero music, and both Núñez del Prado and Webster examined Q'ero social organization; none of them specialized in Q'ero textile iconography. Recently, however, Rowe and Cohen (2002) published a descriptive catalog for an exhibit of Q'ero textiles, basing their work on that of Núñez del Prado and Webster.[8]

My contribution to the study of the Cuzco-area textile tradition is fivefold. First, I conducted a detailed description of the textile iconography woven in a single Cuzco community, Q'ero. In this book I describe the textile forms, weaving techniques, and resulting motifs woven in the entire Q'ero nation. In 1980, for a period of four months, I walked from Hatun Q'ero to Hapu, staying along the way in the villages of Qochamoqo, Kolpakuchu, Chuwa Chuwa, Tandaña, Palcabamba, Wañunapampa, and Kiko, as well as numerous hamlets such as Yana Orqo, Qulluyllu, and Chawpi Wasi. I stayed for as little as a few days to as long as two weeks in each of these villages and wove motif samplers on thin belts with several weavers. I also gathered informal, nontaped data concerning motif identification and loom and textile types, as well as the names of the persons with whom I worked. That trip permitted me to verify the uniformity in the Q'ero textile tradition.[9]

Second, this study compares Q'ero textiles with those woven to the northeast-northwest of Cuzco, an area that encompasses Calca to the west, Markapata to the east, and Ocongate to the south. In 1982 I worked for three months (June to August) in Calca, Pisac, and Markapata in order to identify textile types, motifs, and looms. In 1984 I carried out the same research in Ccatcca, Kauri, Ocongate, Pitumarka, Checacupe, and Uchu Llucllu. In 1989, 1990, and 1991 I organized a research team of my students from the University of Cuzco and conducted the same study in Chinchero, Huancarani, Kauri, and Pisac.[10]

Third, I identified two motif types woven in Q'ero. The first is called *Q'ero pallay* (Q'ero motif) and is produced with the *kinsamanta iskay uya* (from three [threads], two faces) weaving technique, which is called in the Western literature three-color complementary warp weaving. This technique creates a two-faced cloth (*iskay uya*) in which the design woven on the front of the textile appears on the back of the same fabric but in reverse. It is usually woven with white, black, and cranberry threads.

The second motif type, *qheswa pallay* (valley motif), is produced not only in Q'ero but also in such communities as Calca and Pisac, located southwest of Q'ero; Markapata to the southeast; Paucartambo and Huancarani

Figure 1.13. Q'ero pallay woven in a ceremonial poncho.

to the west; and Ccatcca, Kauri, and Ocongate to the south. Qheswa pallay is fabricated using the *iskaymanta hoq uya* (from two [threads], one face) weaving technique, called in the Western literature two-color supplementary warp weaving, in which only two contrasting colors are used, producing a one-faced cloth (*hoq uya*) in which no motif is woven on the opposite face of the textile (Silverman-Proust 1986a, 1988a, 1988b). It is usually woven with red and white threads.

According to Q'ero weavers, Q'ero and qheswa pallay differ significantly. The latter, they say, is "worthless," whereas the former, the two-faced cloth, is "valuable": "Hoq uyayoq mana valinchu. Iskay uyayoq valin" (taped, 1985). [A one-faced cloth is worthless. A two-faced cloth is valuable.] What precisely makes Q'ero pallay valuable? Woven with the kinsamanta technique, Q'ero pallay, as we shall see throughout this book, symbolizes the cosmological beliefs of the contemporary Q'ero because it records spatial and temporal

Figure 1.14. Qheswa pallay woven in a lliklla from the Calca highlands.

concepts based on observations of sunlight and shadow. Qheswa pallay, in contrast, depicts only spatial concepts because the iconography fabricated with iskaymanta lacks the graphic elements necessary to represent ideas about sunlight and shadow (Silverman-Proust 1988a).

My study of these two motif types as used in Q'ero and in the wider Cuzco area is confirmed by Rowe's pioneering work *Warp-Patterned Weaves of the Andes* (1977), in which she notes that the three-color complementary warp-weave technique is the oldest known for Cuzco, being found in the "Ocucaje material dating to the end of the Early Horizon (1977:69)." The two-color supplementary warp weave is not "very common in pre Columbian textiles," she says, but in modern times "there are few parts of the Cuzco area where this technique is not known, but it is the most common decorative technique in the villages to the east of the town of Pisac and north at least to Calca and in the towns between Ccatcca and Lauramarka (1977:40, F40, 41, F41, 42, F42)."[11]

Fourth, both Q'ero and non-Q'ero villagers read their own textile iconography. In order to accomplish this myself, I studied Quechua in Paris in the mid-1970s, before my first field trip to Q'ero, and then in 1982 and 1983, before living for two years in Q'ero (1985 and 1986).

In addition to studying Quechua, I learned how to weave. In Paris I studied Bolivian weaving using Majorie Cason and Adele Cahlander's book *The Art of Bolivian Highland Weaving* (1976). Before entering Q'ero I stayed in Chinchero, where I learned to spin and ply with Rosalio Callañaupa of Ayllu Pongo and to weave with Cipriana Quispe of Ayllu Cuper. Finally, I also learned how to barter potatoes for products such as coca, fruit, and bread. In this way, I could present myself to the Q'ero as a Quechua-speaking weaver who also knew how to barter.

Last, I created a graphic dictionary of the motifs showing their forms, names, and meanings (Silverman-Proust 1986a, 1988a; Silverman 1994a, 1998; Silverman, ed. 1991a, 1995). In addition, I published a study of the changes in form of the Chinchero textile tradition and identified three motif periods: *ñawpa pallay*, ancient motifs, which show a relation to the Q'ero motifs with their use of the three-color complementary warp-weave technique; *mestizo pallay*, newer motifs that were introduced with the opening of schools in Chinchero in the 1920s; and *kunan pallay*, present motifs, introduced by the Chinchero textile merchants who had been buying and selling textiles since the mid-1960s (Silverman, ed. 1991b). I also published a distribution study of the ch'unchu motif (Silverman, ed. 1993) showing that three types of it were common throughout the Cuzco region before 1950.

I carried out fieldwork in the Q'ero villages of Tandaña, K'allakancha, and Chuwa Chuwa for twenty-two months, as well as in the other Cuzco villages mentioned above, for a total of forty-three months of fieldwork.

⁜ Methodology ⁜

I used numerous methodologies to test my hypothesis that textile iconography functions as nonalphabetic writing. First, I carried out a weaving apprenticeship in all the Q'ero and non-Q'ero villages where I studied. This meant that I wove almost exclusively with female weavers.

I wove all the Q'ero and qheswa motif types as motif samplers on thin belts. I paid the weavers with coca and with plastic hair beads called *piliminis*, which were so popular that I never lacked for a weaving teacher. I made repeated visits to weave with the same woman and through time asked her to identify the motif's name, color, and meaning. This method gave me preliminary data on the motifs.

Much later in my fieldwork I conducted formal, tape-recorded interviews in Quechua with both Q'ero and non-Q'ero men and women concerning motif identification, weaving technique, color, and meaning. I showed them both Q'ero and qheswa pallay textiles, including the *lliklla* (woman's shawl), the ceremonial poncho, a small bag called *talega* or *wayako*, and the *ch'uspa* (coca bag). In addition, I showed them color photographs of these same textiles and always asked the simple question, What is it? (*¿Imas chay?*) (Silverman-Proust 1987a:293-312, 321-323, 324-327). These interviews were carried out with 55 Q'ero men and women, as well as numerous people in Kauri, Ccatcca, Huancarani, Chinchero, Pisac, Calac, Paucartambo, and Markapata. With the help of my research team, composed of my University of Cuzco archaeology students, Filomena Juárez, Sergia Chaucca, Santusa Fernández, and Jorge Calanche, I conducted formal, taped interviews in 1989, 1990, and 1991 regarding the meaning of the Q'ero motifs, which I drew with black pen on white paper, as well as my colored photographs of Q'ero textiles. We interviewed 52 men and women in Chinchero, 93 in Huancarani, 50 in Pisac, and 53 in Kauri. We also asked the weaver's husbands to draw their village, the sky, their fields, and their mythic history.

These tape-recorded interviews gave me a data base concerning the identification and significance of the two motif types, but once this data base had been established, I needed another methodology in order to control these verbal statements. I did this in two ways. First, I wanted to see if the same structural principles that formed the motifs would be intelligible to the informants if removed from cloth, so I drew ten Q'ero motifs with a black felt pen on white paper and again asked, What is it? (Silverman-Proust 1987a:281–291). This method furnished some of the same answers as for the motifs woven in textiles. Second, I asked both Q'ero and non-Q'ero men to draw their world by handing them colored felt pens and white paper. This was my best method for confirming that the same graphic elements that form their motifs also composed their drawings of village and celestial space, daily and seasonal time, mythic history, and their crops and animals.[12]

Although I asked both men and women, young and old, to draw for me, it was always the men who obliged, while the women told me that they had never used a pen and did not know how to draw. In fact, in the twenty-two months I stayed in Q'ero in 1985 and 1986, I could find only one girl, twelve-year-old Juliana Samanta, from the Tandaña hamlet of Chawpi Wasi, who felt she could draw because she had attended school.

I asked Ramón Salas of Tandaña to draw his village and left him with colored pens and white paper (see Chapter 3). After consulting awhile with his brother, Benito, off he went to pasture and it was not until late afternoon, returning with the llamas and sheep, that he handed his paper to me. Bordering both sides was a series of repeating triangles he called *orqo puntas*, "mountain peaks."[13] In the middle of the paper, he drew a doubled vertical line that he named Tandaña Mayu, the Tandaña River. Last, on both sides of the paper he drew a series of horizontal lines; those on the right were short, yellow, and black while those on the left were long and black. These lines depicted the Q'ero fields and the sun's shadow and sunlight. A series of repeating triangles, a long vertical line, and different-colored short and long radiating lines are the graphic elements that form the Q'ero hatun inti (midday sun) motif.

Ramón's brother, Benito Salas, used almost the same geometry to depict the Tandaña sky (see Chapter 5). Repeating triangles represented the mountain peaks on both sides of the paper, while in the center was a very long, penciled, doubled horizontal line that divided the sky into halves and was called Mayu, "River" (Milky Way). On the left was a huge partial circle that Benito called *la mar* (the sea). Most important, he depicted two rising and two setting suns to represent the June and December solstices.

Both these drawings showed that the same graphic elements that compose the Q'ero world also are used to form their textile motifs. In this way, I had proved that the verbal statements given by the Q'ero concerning the meaning of their motifs were valid.

It was not easy getting these drawings, as they took almost an entire day to do, and so, later in my stay in Q'ero, more and more men would run away when they saw me coming with my colored pens and paper, saying they were busy. I also collected both songs and myths from the Q'ero and found that they registered information that was not recorded in their cloth (Silverman-Proust 1987a:328-378).

Last, I attempted to work with men of knowledge, known as *yachachiq*, but this was impossible in Q'ero, and it was not until 1998 that I was able to work with two of them. However, I worked with three shamans in Kauri: Prudencio Hakawaya, Francisco Lara, and Benito Nina. They provided invaluable, detailed answers about the significance of motifs.

❊ The Q'ero People ❊

I first went to Q'ero in April 1980, traveling from Cuzco to Paucartambo by truck and proceeding over the rugged terrain on horseback for several days with a guide. After some false starts and perilous misadventures, I settled in the village of Qochamoqo for a time and then went on to work in many other Q'ero villages for a period of four months.

I first met Tomasa Pauccar in Tandaña when I stayed in her patio for about an hour on my way to Hatun Q'ero. I was to stay with her and her family in Tandaña in 1985 and 1986 for about ten months.

For most of those months, I slept off to the side of the house while Miguel, Tomasa, their son Benito, and their granddaughter Lorenza slept in a row in front of the fireplace. I decided that the only way I was going to get good

Figure 1.15. K'allakancha men greeting my arrival in 1980.

Figure 1.16. The road to Wilkakunka, 1980.

Figure 1.17. Weaving a motif on a belt sampler in Hatun Q'ero, 1980.

Figure 1.18. Tomasa and Miguel. Tandaña, 1980.

Figure 1.19. Tomasa and Miguel's granddaughter, Lorenza, 1985.

Figure 1.20. Santiago Salas. Tandaña, 1985.

data was to "steal Tomasa's heart," and I did that by being indispensable to her. Early in the morning when I first heard her getting out of bed to begin the morning breakfast, I too put on my boots, grabbed two buckets, and went down to the Tandaña River to bring up water. I then sat across from her in front of the fireplace and helped with the cooking. After eating our meal of boiled potatoes and a soup of potato and llama or alpaca meat, we would go out and sit against the wall of the house to chew coca and take in the sun's warmth.

Tomasa taught me how to cook, weave, collect dung, take care of the potatoes and corn in her storehouse (*taqe*), and even cook tamales and pumpkin soup when I went down with her to the corn harvest. Finally, I was invited to sleep beside her because she had decided that I was her reincarnated sister (field notes, 1986).

I had an even better relationship with Santiago, Tomasa's oldest son, and his wife, Rosa Chura. Every time Tomasa had to go down to a lower field, I was taken to live with them. I would weave with Rosa in the morning and in the early afternoon set off to weave with one of the others living in Tandaña. At night we would share their radio, using my batteries, listening to Radio Tawantinsuyu for 30 minutes and then either Voice of America or France Culture. In my other trips to Q'ero it was always Santiago who brought horses down to meet me in Paucartambo to take me back up.

Miguel Salas, the head of the household, was another matter. He was a complete authoritarian, and we were at his mercy when he was back from his months-long absences taking the alpaca herds up to the pastures, located at an elevation of over 5,500 meters. When he was present, we would obey his every command: "Santiago, you'll be down at the qheswa preparing the fields; Tomasa, you pasture the alpaca; Benito, you take out the llama and sheep; 'María,' you weave with Rosa."[14]

His second son, Benito, was nearly as difficult. I had thought that by fetching water in the early morning, usually his job now that his first wife had died in childbirth, he would be appreciative, but no, he always gave me a hard time by not keeping his word or not wanting to draw or answer questions for me. Finally, I found a connection with him because he wanted to learn Spanish, and so every afternoon, I gave him a 30-minute lesson and he gradually became more cooperative with my work. But Benito always had to come out ahead, and before I left, he had appropriated my Quechua-Spanish dictionaries, my Chinese teapot, my alarm clock, and lots of used clothes.

I left Q'ero in 1986 and have never gone back. But my Q'ero "brothers" always come to Cuzco to look for tourists in order to conduct offerings for them or to sell their textiles to the Cuzco merchants, and when they have finished, they come to see me. In 1997 my entire Q'ero extended family came to stay with me for a week, even Tomasa, who had never been to Paucartambo, let alone Cuzco.

❧ The Q'ero through Time ❧

Very little information is available for the Q'ero during the Inca and colonial periods. There is evidence of Inca constructions in Q'ero: stairs carved out of rock, a doorway leading down to the Inca road that goes to the lowlands, stone-walled terraces (Luis Barredo Murillo (2005:43, 46-49), and an Inca platform.

Archival data from the colonial period indicates that when the Q'ero were incorporated into the hacienda system, they had to fulfill their *mit'a*, or forced labor, despite the fact that the system had been abolished in 1824 by Simón Bolívar. The Q'ero had to work 180 to 250 days per year for the hacienda, leaving little time to attend their own fields and animals. In addition, the Q'ero worked as *pongos*, or servants, in Cuzco and the other houses of the hacienda owner (field notes, 1980, 1985). It was not until anthropologist Oscar Núñez del Prado met them in 1955 and helped them purchase their lands from the hacienda owner in 1968 that they became free.

During the rise of Shining Path in Peru in the 1980s I never saw or heard about this group in Q'ero, probably because of its geographical remoteness. But if Sendero stayed out of Q'ero, anthropologists, ethnomusicologists, tourists, and merchants flocked to Q'ero with their money and factory goods.

So the Q'ero have become "shamans," looking for the tourist dollar, sitting on the steps of the Cuzco Cathedral and in the markets waiting for clients. They have also become guides for the tourist groups that pass through Q'ero on their way to the Ausangate sacred mountain.

Modernity has also begun to arrive in Q'ero. In the 1990s two new roads were built; one goes from Paucartambo to K'allakancha, and the other from a turnoff of the Urcos–Quince Mil–Puerto Maldonaldo Road to Hapu (Champi Ccasa 2005:428). Windows have been put in the houses in Hapu and Kiko through the efforts of the Ocongate priest (personal communication 1985), and now K'allakancha is full of stores, considered impossible in the early 1980s.

Anthropologists are still working in Q'ero. Holly Wissler (2005), for example, is investigating the changes in Q'ero music, and the Cuzco branch of the National Cultural Institute has elaborated a development plan for the area (Champi Ccasa 2005).

Today the Q'ero know they are caught between two worlds, a situation that has created psychological problems for some of them. Some want to leave Q'ero and live permanently in the Sacred Valley so they can grow corn and work with tourists. Others are now living in the Pueblo Jovenes of Cuzco or have put their young daughters into the houses of Cuzqueños so they can attend school.

But they are also concerned about the loss of their sacred knowledge, and in 1998 two Q'ero men approached me to say that they wanted me to record what they remembered of their textile motifs so it would not be lost. Now we have created a dialogue instead of being in a strictly anthropologist/informant relationship.

❊ Questions of Theory ❊

This book is important for its implications with regard to two theoretical orientations that were developed in the 1980s and 1990s. First, beginning with the publication of the *Esquisse d'un tableau historique des progrès de l'esprit humain* in 1795 by the Marquis de Condorcet (see Harris 1968), rational contemplation was considered the foundation on which civilization was constructed. "Primitive cultures," in contrast, were believed to be cloaked in mythical and magical thought (Harris 1968:24). This distinction between the types of thought processes used in the construction of culture was intimately related to the way in which knowledge was transmitted, hence the birth of the Great Divide Theory.

The Great Divide Theory was proposed by Havelock (1976), Ong (1982), Goody and Watt (1963), and Goody (1977, 1987). Numerous studies have situated this theory in relation to anthropology, cognition, linguistics, and philosophy, generating important themes that are beyond the scope of this book, but my interest lies in how it was expressed by Jack Goody.

In *The Domestication of the Savage Mind* (1977) Goody described alphabetic writing as superior to oral language as a way of transmitting knowledge because only writing leads to the gradual accumulation of information, forming a permanent record. Since this knowledge existed in a permanent way, Goody believed that it could be scrutinized and studied, thereby leading to the development of scientific, rational thought. Primitive cultures, in contrast, were believed to transmit their knowledge through language only in the form of songs and myths. Because these were not permanent, they could not be studied and scrutinized, and they thereby led to mythical and magical thought.

Although Goody corrected his omission of the graphic arts in the development of pre-alphabetic writing systems in a later work (1987), he still ignored the case of the Incas. It was Tom Zuidema (1982b) who was the first to use the case of the Incas to refute Goody's thesis, showing how the Incas used graphic art to record ritual and calendrics as well as their social, political, and economic organization. My contribution to this debate has been to demonstrate how the graphic arts, in the form of contemporary textile iconography, continue to serve as a method for storing knowledge (Silverman-Proust 1983, 1984, 1986a, 1986b, 1988a, 1988b; Silverman 1994a, 1994b, 1995a, 1995b, 1998, 1999) because this iconography functions as pictographic writing.

In addition, my study of the Q'ero textile tradition allows me to refute the Goody thesis on two points. First, the Great Divide Theory maintains that it is technology that enables writing to lead to the development of scientific, logical thought. Goody bases his argument on three points: writing creates a permanent record, it uses an external technology to create the text, and the text can change through time. I argue in these pages that this technological determinist argument can also be applied to the Q'ero textile motifs. First, like writing, Q'ero cloth creates a permanent record in the form of woven cloth that is decorated with geometric motifs and colors, which function as nonalphabetic writing. Second, an external technology is used to create the text in the form of the spindles used to turn raw wool into thread and the use of wooden poles and stakes to which the threads are tied as they are turned into fabric and motifs. Third, the Q'ero text woven in cloth also changes because the motifs change form over time and space.

A second argument of the Goody thesis is that only alphabetic writing leads to the development of logical thought. But as we see in Chapter 9, both binary and trinary logic are represented in the Q'ero and qheswa motifs. These two motifs and their weaving techniques not only signify different types of logic but also symbolize differences in cosmology and world view.

❀ The Evolution of Writing from Graphic Art ❀

The second theoretical orientation that was very important in the 1990s, and continues today, is the study of writing systems in the Americas. Before that date, there was an absence of academic interest in the possible existence of writing in the Andes, though much study had been dedicated to the writing systems of the Old World.

Seven principal systems of writing evolved in the Old World: Sumerian, Proto-Elamite, Proto-Indus, Egyptian, Cretan, Hittite, and Chinese. The development of these writing systems entailed a process of symbolization that was tied to the arts (Durbin 1968; Gelb 1963; Schmandt-Besserat 1990; Daniels and Bright 1996; Haas 1976; Harris 1986). Marshall Durbin (1968:28), for example, described writing as simply the "unconscious incorporation of linguistic information (phonological, syntactic, semantic) into an art style over a long period of time." Thus the study of the evolution of writing must also include a study of this symbolization process.

During the Renaissance, writing was believed to have developed from representational art (Gelb 1963; Schmandt-Besserat 1990). Art was first thought to denote words, then abstract ideas, and finally to stand for a sound in language. These differences in the development of writing from art were called pictographs, ideographs, and hieroglyphs, respectively.

In the Old World the earliest symbols used to convey a message were tokens. Used as counting devices, they were found in sites in Syria and Iran from 8000 B.C. (Schmandt-Besserat 1990). These tokens, made of clay, were modeled into geometric shapes that sometimes included markings. Three hundred such tokens in ten shapes were uncovered: "spheres, discs,

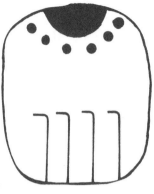

Figure 1.21.
The Maya day sign Imix.

cones, tetrahedrons, ovoids, cylinders, triangles, rectangles, T-shapes, and animal heads" (Schmandt-Besserat 1992:72). These shapes were the precursors of cuneiform writing.

The tokens functioned as word signs, their specific shapes indicating a commodity. For example, "jars of oils were counted with ovoids, small measures of grain with cones, and large measures of grain with spheres" (Schmandt-Besserat 1992:6). Tokens developed into pictographs, which were "stylized symbols of a picture" used to convey a message (Jackson 1981:13). This stage was very cumbersome because one would need literally thousands of pictographs to record historical and statistical data, so an idea evolved in which one could use a symbol for an object that sounded similar. This is called the phonogram stage, in which, for example, the picture of a bee could be used not only to represent a bee but also to depict all the words that sound like "B." Much later came the rebus system, in which "two or more phonograms were used to make up a word" (Jackson 1981:19).[15]

In the New World, specifically Mesoamerica, four major systems developed from graphic art: Maya, Uto-Aztec, Zapotec, and Mixtec (Coe 1995, 2001; Jansen 1988; León-Portilla 1996; Marcus 1992). The Maya wrote their hieroglyphic texts in bark paper books and carved them on "buildings, stone monuments, jade and bone" (Schele et al. 1999:18). These glyphs were used to write their calendar and to record historical data and ritual events of the Maya kings (Schele et al. 1999:547). The simplest glyphs were oval forms decorated with markings such as the Imix day sign (Gates 1931:1).

Maya hieroglyphic writing has been described as being similar to both cuneiform and Egyptian hieroglyphs because it is a "mixed system composed of full word signs combined with signs representing the sounds of syllables" (Schele et al. 1999:49).

In the case of the Andes, in the 1920s Rafael Larco Hoyle (2001) was the first to postulate the existence of nonalphabetic writing. Focusing on the Moche culture, he saw the dots and lines painted on Moche beans as depicting ideographic writing. Much later, in the 1960s and 1970s, Victoria de la Jara (1965, 1967) was the first to postulate the use of writing by the Incas, who decorated textiles, ceramics, stone, wood, and adobe with geometric shapes and colors. Influenced by the French semiotics of her time, and lacking a scientific methodology, de la Jara postulated the relation between the tocapu motifs and pictographic or ideographic writing. Then Thomas Barthel (1971) gathered de la Jara's 294 tocapu motifs and created 24 types, giving them phonetic values.

William Burns (1981, 1990, 2002) planted the seed connecting the tocapus drawn by the Andean chronicler Guamán Poma and the ten numbers and letters of the Quechua alphabet. Recently, Elizabeth Hill Boone and Walter Mignolo (1994), Carmen Arellano (1999; et al. 2002), Rocio Quispe Agnoli (2002), Lydia Fossa (2005), and Galen Brokaw (2005) have argued for the inclusion of the quipu and the tocapu motifs as Andean writing. Laura Laurencich-Minelli (1996) has published a colonial document that sheds light on colonial tocapus and their meaning, and Martii Parssinen (1992; Parssinen and Kiviharju 2005) has published the transcription of 20 quipus in relation to both ideographic and alphabetic writing.

Regarding the contribution of anthropology to the study of Andean notation systems, Verónica Cereceda (1978) has shown the multiple layers of texts woven in the Isluga talega. Denise Arnold and Juan de Dios Yapita (2000) have described the texts woven in the Aymara quipu and the significance of their motifs from the native perspective, as has Nelson Pimentel (2005). Gary Urton (1997; Urton et al. 2003) has studied the binary logic stored in the Inca quipu, and Frank Salomon (2004) has demonstrated the social use of the contemporary quipus made in Tupicocha, Peru.

This book presents an iconographic repertory of 58 textile motifs, their names and meaning as read by both Q'ero and non-Q'ero informants. Thus I have created a data base that can help us begin to study the Inca tocapu motifs as a system of nonalphabetic writing. Chapter 2 describes the technology involved in textile production and compares iconographic content in order to identify differences in the motif repertory. This brings me to eliciting the meaning of the motifs and graphic elements of both Q'ero and qheswa pallay as they refer to space (Chapter 3), daily and seasonal time (Chapters 4 and 5), classificatory systems (Chapter 6), and mythohistory (Chapter 7). Chapter 8 reproduces the entire motif inventory woven in the northeast-northwest region of Cuzco, and finally, Chapter 9 describes the types of logic found in both textile motif types and discusses the implications of this book for Andean cosmology, gender and knowledge studies, and the relation between Andean textile iconography and Inca motifs as nonalphabetic writing.

2

Weaving the Book

✳ Raw Materials ✳

Along with subsistence farming, the principal activity of the Q'ero, as in all Cuzco highland communities, is the pasturing of their herds of llamas (*Lama glama*), alpacas (*Lama pacos*), and sheep. These animals provide not only an important source of protein in an otherwise largely carbohydrate diet but also the fleece and bone tools necessary for cloth production. Llama, alpaca, and sheep fibers are classified according to texture, color, age, sex, fiber strength, and other physical characteristics.

Two textures of alpaca and llama fibers are distinguished in Q'ero: *suri* and *wakayo*. According to Jorge Flores Ochoa (1978:1007), suri is "silky, long, and brilliant," and wakayo is "less silky, with short locks, and not as brilliant."

A second classification system for alpaca and llama wool is based on color. These fibers are available in the natural colors of white (*yuraq*), black (*yana*), brown (*chumpi*), and gray (*oqe*). In addition, according to various male Q'ero informants, red (*puka*), yellow (*q'ellu*), and blue (*anqas*) also exist as natural colors (see Chapter 6).

Combinations of these colors create more than three thousand colors (Flores Ochoa 1978:1015). As we see in Chapter 6, Santiago Salas, from Tandaña, drew a picture of 27 llamas with different color combinations. Physical traits and size are some of the characteristics that determine which animals will be used to increase the herd and which will be sacrificed. Interestingly, Santiago mentioned only the two most prized fibers, *suri* and the rare *vicuña*, and he often used the terms *alqa*, *muru*, and *wallata*, all of which refer to various kinds of spots on either a white or dark-colored coat.[1]

Figure 2.1. Santiago Salas with his flock. Tandaña, 1985.

<h2 style="text-align:center">✤ Spinning Techniques ✤</h2>

Both Q'ero men and women, and all Quechua-speakers in the Department of Cuzco, spin shorn alpaca, llama, and sheep wool into yarn. They use a wooden spindle, or *phuskay*, which is composed of a wooden shaft called *tissi* and a rounded whorl called *peliku*.[2]

Two different spinning methods are used, depending on the quality of the desired yarn. To make weaving yarn, the spinner takes some unspun wool, called *millma* or *willma*, and spreads it into a thin sheet with her fingers. Then she rolls it between her hands to form a long, loose string that she winds around her left hand, ready for spinning. Next she takes the beginning strand of the millma and attaches it to the top of her phuskay using a slip knot. Then, holding the millma in her left hand and the phuskay in her right, she brings her hands together and twirls the phuskay between them toward the right, letting the spindle drop at the same time. While the phuskay is still spinning, she takes the unspun yarn up onto her right hand, where she winds it between her thumb and baby finger. Last, she detaches the slip knot from the phuskay, winds the spun thread up and down the spindle shaft, and makes a new slip knot with some unspun millma at the top of the spindle, and the spinning process is repeated until the spindle is once again completely full of spun yarn.[3]

Figure 2.2. Spinning in Q'ero. Tandaña, 1985.

Figure 2.3. Cipriana Quispe prepares the yarns for plying. Ayllu Cuper, Chinchero, 1979.

The Q'ero prefer spinning a thin yarn, called *nañu q'ayto*, as opposed to a coarsely spun yarn, called *rakhu q'ayto*, which is considered to be of poor quality, easily broken, and a demonstration of poor spinning skills. An additional method is performed by Q'ero men to make a coarse yarn used in the fabrication of slings and rope. With this method a short thick stick, called *soqo*, is used to shape the unspun wool, which is twisted and pulled around the stick until a very thick yarn is formed.

At least two phuskays full of newly spun yarn are needed in order to ply.

❊ Plying ❊

Two balls of q'ayto are put together to form a two-ply yarn. This process is called *q'antiy*. First, the spinner takes the two spindles that are full of q'ayto and unrolls them together, forming a giant ball. Then she sticks the two spindle shafts into the ground or between her toes to hold them stable during the winding process. Next she performs the same movements for plying as she did for spinning, except that instead of turning the spindle shaft toward the right, she spins it toward the left. This process creates a "S" twist yarn and makes it stronger.

Before the actual plying and warping takes place, natural or chemical dyes are applied to the natural white-colored q'ayto to create a multitude of colors.

❊ Dyes ❊

Until as recently as 1955, natural dyes were used in Q'ero in order to obtain a wide range of colors. Oscar Núñez del Prado (1970:274) lists six plants used at that date for natural dyes: *k'uchu k'uchu*, green; *chapi*, red; *hatun ch'illka*, yellow; *punki*, yellow-orange; *waqra waqra*, bright yellow; and *luma ch'illka*, black.

At the time of my fieldwork, very little dyeing with plants was done because it is much easier, and relatively inexpensive, to use the aniline dyes that are sold in Paucartambo and Ocongate. Chemical dyes are sold by the spoonful, one large tablespoon selling for 1,000 soles in 1985 (6,241 soles = US$1) and 30 intis in 1986 (14 intis = US$1). Anilines were developed in England in 1856 and quickly spread throughout the world (Silverman 1999).

Figure 2.4. Grinding a plant for dyeing. Parubamba, 1997.

The following names are used for the colors found in synthetic yarns and those obtained with anilines: black, *yana*; gray, *oqe*; pink, *panti*; brown, *chumpi*; white, *yuraq*; green, *q'omer*; red, *puka*; blue, *anqas*; violet, *sani*; orange, *q'ellucha*; and yellow, *q'ellu*.

Today everyone is returning to natural dyes, thanks to the encouragement of the Cuzco-operated nongovernmental organizations. For example, the Association of Parubamba Weavers began dyeing with plants in 1997 because they produce colors that are resistant to sunlight and water (Silverman 2005b). Plants such as *chapi* (*Relbienium microphyllum*), as well as the cochineal insect (*Dactilopius coccus*) (Chirinos 1999:82), are first ground and then thrown in boiling water with alpaca yarn to obtain a wide range of colors, including pink, green, blue, orange, and purple. Lemon juice and aluminum, as well as other minerals, are combined with plants to give different hues. In addition, fermented human urine turns the threads dyed with the cochineal insect into red. Fireplace ashes are also used.[4]

❦ Looms ❦

Three principal types of looms are used in Q'ero and throughout the Department of Cuzco: the body loom, the backstrap loom, and the four-stake horizontal ground loom (Gisbert et al. 1987; Heckman 2003; Rowe 1977; Rowe and Cohen 2002).[5]

The Body Loom

The body loom uses the weaver's left foot and hand as an anchor for the warped threads. First, holding the yarn with her left thumb, the weaver makes a loop around the big toe of her right foot; then she winds the yarn in a figure-eight manner between this toe and her left hand. When she has the desired number of warp threads fixed between her foot and hand, she inserts two small sticks, called *mumura k'aspi*, into the two openings made by the crossed warp threads. The first stick, located closer to the weaver, serves as the heddle stick (*illawa*) and the second one serves to hold the shed stick (*kawalla*) in place.

Next, in order to make the heddles, the weaver takes a thickly spun yarn and inserts it from right to left into the first shed opening. Using her left thumb, she wraps one loop around each warp thread until there is a single loop around each warp thread in this shed. Now she cuts this thread, leaving a long enough piece at the right to be able to tuck it back into the loops

Figure 2.5. Weaving on the body loom. Kauri, 1990.

from right to left. The thread that remains at the left is then inserted into
the opening in the same way. Both
ends are then brought up to the top
of the heddles and tied in the middle. There is always some string left
over after the heddles are made, and
this is twisted and then inserted into
the stick shed opening, from left to
right, out the other side, and then
tied tightly back onto the twisted
string that is joined to the heddles.
This creates the second shed.

Weaving commences with al-
ternately opening the heddles and
stick shed in order to form crossed
warp threads. The weaver begins by
holding the warps in her left hand,
using her right hand to open each

Figure 2.6. Warping with the body loom.
Uchu Llucllu, Pitumarka, 1982.

shed and insert the weft, called *mini*. As soon as a few rows have been woven, she pins the weaving to the waistband of her skirt with a needle (*yawri*), thus freeing her hand for warp pickup.

The body loom is used in the fabrication of small thin bands called *watanas*, which are used for hat straps. They are also used for the *awapan*, or borders, that finish a lliklla (shawl). I learned how to weave many motifs in Q'ero and in other communities using this loom.

The Backstrap Loom

There are at least three methods of warping the backstrap loom. In the first one, the backstrap loom can be viewed as evolving from the body loom because the toe used to hold the warp threads in the body loom is replaced by a single wooden stake (*takarpu*), which is pounded into the ground. In the second case, two stakes are pounded into the ground, thereby replacing the weaver's left toe and hand for better warp pickup and tension control.

While I was living in K'allakancha, I warped the *ch'isin ñawi* (night star-eye) motif with Victoria Quispe, using the two-stake warping loom, and then proceeded to weave on a backstrap loom.[6] First, Victoria pounded two small stakes into the ground, aligned directly in front of each other at a distance of about one foot. Tying one white thread and one green thread together at the top of the stake nearer her, she began winding this yarn between the two stakes in a figure-eight manner. When she had warped the desired number of threads around these poles, she wound them around the stake placed closer to her in order to fix it into place. Next she placed her hands in the two openings, or cross, and bringing her hands together, she began changing the warp order in the following way: the first shed, all green threads, the second shed, all white threads. Then she inserted a kawalla stick into each opening in order to secure them. Next she made another all-green shed, followed by another all-white shed.

Her next step was to fashion the heddles, or illawa. First, she inserted a doubled yarn into the first shed opening from right to left and tied a loose knot at the end, leaving some yarn left over. Then with her yawri (needle), she made a loop around each warp thread. When the last heddle loop was made, she inserted the leftover string back into the heddle loops from right to left. Then, taking up the leftover string at the left side, she proceeded to insert that from left to right back into the opening at the top of the heddles. These two ends were then brought up and over the heddles, where they were tied in the middle. She made the stick shed by inserting a doubled

Figure 2.7. Using multiple heddles to weave a skirt trim. K'allakancha, 1980.

yarn into its opening and tied it into a large loop. This loop was then attached to the heddle string, which was on the top of the heddles.

In order to weave with this loom, Victoria untied the yarn from the stake placed closer to her and began weaving by holding the warp threads with her left hand, which also held the cross open. At the same time, she used her right hand to pick up the pattern. When she had completed several rows of weaving, she pinned this strap to her skirt, thus freeing both hands for weaving.

The Q'ero also use the multiple-heddle backstrap loom to weave thin skirts and jacket trims. For example, Juliana Flores, of K'allakancha, wove a trim for her skirt with a multiple-heddle loom called *tukuru*, which is fashioned of bamboo. First, the weaver must pick up the pattern with her fingers, and when that is completed, she puts the appropriate threads into the heddles. After the heddles are formed, all she has to do is open up the shed and weave, alternating the appropriate heddles with the shed, instead of picking up the pattern with her fingers. Using multiple heddles, the weaver can make a very long skirt border in just a couple of days. Outside Q'ero, in places such as Kauri, Parubamba, and Calca, I have seen weavers replace the bamboo heddles with string heddles, which are made in the same way as just described.

The Four-Stake Horizontal Ground Loom

Warping on a four-stake horizontal ground loom requires the help of a second person. I observed Rosa Chura Flores and Juliana Pauccar, both of Tandaña, warp a daily-wear poncho on this loom.

Rosa began by pounding a stake into the ground. Then she took a measuring string, called *tupu*, and aligned it with a second stake, which was placed at the desired width and pounded into the ground. Next Juliana took another stake, and measuring it to the one at Rosa's left, she also pounded it into the ground. She then proceeded to do the same thing with another stake. In this way, Rosa and Juliana had horizontally aligned four stakes in the ground, forming the frame for the loom.

The next step consisted of attaching an *awa k'aspi*, or weaving pole, horizontally to the stakes with a braided rope (*warak'a*) called *awa watana*. The two women now had formed a rectangular frame composed of horizontally aligned poles with which they would warp vertically aligned threads.

In order to warp these vertically aligned threads, Rosa attached previously selected yarn to the left of the awa k'aspi and then rolled it over to Juliana, who wound it over the awa k'aspi and then rolled it back to Rosa. This process was repeated across the entire loom width until all the required threads were warped. To change colors, Rosa just tucked a new colored thread into several of the already warped ones to its left, and then she and Juliana continued repeating the process of passing the warping yarn back and forth between them. The threads are never cut.

Next Rosa placed two shed poles, or *mumura k'aspi*, into the crossed openings in order to hold them in place. She then proceeded to make the

Figure 2.8. Warping with the four-stake horizontal ground loom. Tandaña, 1985.

Figure 2.9. Warping with the four-stake horizontal ground loom. Kiko, Q'ero, 1980.

heddles using the same method described for the body and backstrap looms. However, because the four-stake horizontal ground loom allows for wider weavings than the body and backstrap looms, a heddle stick (*illawa k'aspi*) is inserted into the heddles and securely tied to it, which allows for greater heddle control.

Another new step that is needed for weaving with the four-stake horizontal ground loom is the making of the *chukrukata*, a process in which the warps are attached to a second horizontal pole so that they are never cut, creating four selvages. For this step, Rosa placed a second awa k'aspi on top of the first one that was nearest her. She inserted a thick yarn into the shed opening and tied each end to the ends of this new awa k'aspi. Then she took some thick yarn, called *chukrukata q'ayto*, and tied it to the right side of the awa k'aspi and began winding it around a group of several warp threads and the pole at the same time. She repeated this procedure across the entire pole until all the warps had been wrapped with the chukrukata q'ayto. Next,

Figure 2.10. Weaving with the four-stake horizontal
ground loom. Paucartambo, 1979.

beginning at the first loop to the left, she proceeded to tighten the chukru-kata q'ayto with her llama-bone tool (*tullu ruki*) across the entire pole. She removed the first awa k'aspi, which was used in the warping process, and pushed the new awa k'aspi down and in front of the vertical stake that had been pounded into the ground. She untied the threads at both ends of the new awa k'aspi and then inserted them into the first shed opening and wove them. The stick shed was made by inserting a doubled yarn into the opening and tying it into a large loop. This loop was joined to the heddles with a long string that was tied on the top of the heddles.[7] She now had a continuously wound warp that is never cut on her loom.

I have used this loom in many communities outside Q'ero. In Paru-bamba they use a wooden tool called a *pallana* instead of a llama-bone ruki tool to pick up the threads. It should be mentioned that there is no standardization concerning weaving terminology; the terms change from community to community.

⁜ Weaving Techniques ⁜

As mentioned in Chapter 1, the Q'ero still use weaving techniques that are tied to the Incas. Warp-faced weaving and three-color complementary warp weaving, for example, create a two-faced cloth, which was the definitive Inca standard. The Q'ero call their warp-faced plain weave *pampa*. They also weave warp-faced stripes, which can be of various colors: alternating white and red stripes, multicolored stripes, or multicolored natural alpaca-colored stripes (white, brown, gray, black). These are called *chili puka*, *listas*, and *suyu*, respectively (field notes, 1979, 1980; Silverman-Proust 1986b). Warp-faced stripes can also be single-colored: in the *lloq'e paña-manta* technique, which is related to Inca accounting practices (Silverman, in press), the stripes are plied to the left and to the right. The Q'ero use a discontinuous warp weave to produce small carrying cloths called *unkhuña*, which have daily as well as ceremonial functions. Three-color complementary warp weave, called *kinsamanta-iskay uya* by the Q'ero, is their oldest technique; the two-color supplementary warp weave, called *iskaymanta-hoq uya*, is a recent invention (Silverman-Proust 1986a, 1988a, 1988b; Silverman 1994a, 1998, 1999). *Watay* (tie-dyeing) may also have been used, as in the poncho shown by Rowe and Cohen (2002:40, Fig. 4.21), but unfortunately there is no contextual information for this photograph. We know, however, that the Pitumarka highlands shared several weaving techniques and motifs with the Q'ero during the early twentieth century, including kinsamanta-iskay uya as well as watay.

The Q'ero use the twill-weave technique to weave long skirt borders. However, its motif repertory, usually diamonds or triangles, is different from the designs that decorate the daily-wear llikllas and ceremonial ponchos.

⁂ Daily-Wear Costumes ⁂

Like all traditional communities located in the Department of Cuzco, the Q'ero are identified by their distinctive dress type: as a seventeenth-century Spanish chronicler recorded, "Viraqocha, the Creator, made out of mud in Tiahuanaco, all of the nations which were in this land, selecting for each one the clothes which they had to wear" (Cobo [1653] 1956:151). The women's shawl (lliklla) is decorated with two motifs that are woven only in Q'ero: *inti* and *ch'unchu*. The women's hat, worn during festivals, is circular in shape, conical at the top, and divided into four parts by silver and gold threads that also border the rim. Hanging next to the ears are red threads decorated with white (*piñi*) beads. The men's sleeveless tunic (uncu) is woven with a black, thickly spun, warp plain weave called *bayeta* with a red stripe running down both sides. The women's head covering, called *llaqolla*, was still used in 1979.[8]

In all other respects, the dress types worn by the Q'ero are similar to those worn throughout the Department of Cuzco (Cohen 1957; Gisbert et al. 1987; O. Núñez del Prado 1970; Rowe 1977; Schevill et al. 1991; Rowe and Cohen 2002), except for weaving technique, motifs, and ceremonial hats. The typical Q'ero woman's costume consists of a store-bought red sweater, a red bayeta woven jacket (*aymilla*), and a black bayeta woven skirt (*aksu*). A brown-and-white checkerboard-patterned belt is tied around the waist. Store-bought sandals made with automobile tires cover her feet. The trim sewn on the edge of the aymilla and the aksu are woven in Q'ero.

The men's costume consists of a red sweater, knee-high pants woven with black bayeta wool, store-bought sandals made from automobile tires, and the red aymilla jacket, over which they wear the uncu. Like the women, they wear the brown-and-white checkerboard belt (*ch'umpi*). Their daily-wear hat is a needle-knitted cap with ear flaps called *ch'ullu*, which is worn over the European-style hat they wear outside Q'ero. As late as 1966, the Q'ero were set apart from other Quechua-speaking peasants by their

Figure 2.11. Typical men's daily-wear dress in Q'ero. Tandaña, 1985.

Figure 2.12. Woman's dress in Uchu Llucllu. Pitumarka, 1982.

Figure 2.13. Three generations of Q'ero women. The girls wear qheswa pallay llikllas, and their mother wears Q'ero pallay. K'allakancha, 1985.

shoulder-length hair (Núñez del Prado Bejar 2005:83), which hacienda owner Don Ángel Yabar ordered them to cut off.

Small children wear miniature adult-type clothes up until the age of four, both small boys and girls wearing skirts and usually going barefoot.

Textile types woven in Q'ero include the uncu, lliklla, poncho, *ch'uspa* (small ceremonial bag), unkhuña, *wayako* (bag), and *challina* (scarf), as well as hat straps (*watana*) and skirt borders (*golon*). Both Núñez del Prado (1955) and Cohen (1957) collected saddle bags and horse blankets. Knitted items include the *ch'ullu* cap and small bags called *llama sarsillu*. Braided items include slings and assorted ropes, described later in this chapter.

⁜ Q'ero and Qheswa Cloth ⁜

Andean cloth has been extensively studied in an effort to elicit the meaning of its motifs and of the spatial organization of its design panels (Arnold 2000; Crickmay 1997; Cereceda 1978, 1987; Schevill et al. 1991; Zorn 1986). But if we are to uncover the text recorded in both Q'ero and qheswa cloth, we need to know what sorts of differences they exhibit in terms of iconographic content. Here I describe the spatial organization of two textile types that are fairly common in both Q'ero and qheswa cloth—the women's lliklla and the men's ceremonial poncho—in order to compare their iconographic content.

Sample Size

The Q'ero and qheswa textiles I studied came from my own fieldwork from 1979 to 1991, from private Peruvian collections, and from several museum collections. During fieldwork from 1979 to 1991 I documented Q'ero textiles that were woven throughout the entire Q'ero cultural area. Documentation included buying and photographing textiles. In each case, the weaver's name, place of birth, and place of birth of her parents was noted. I also recorded, either on note cards or on tape, all data regarding motif names, looms, weaving technique, and colors.

In addition, I studied two private Peruvian collections of Q'ero textiles held by former Q'ero hacienda owners Manuel Orihuela and Otto de Barry. They allowed me to photograph their entire collections (40 and 30 pieces, respectively), record all relevant data on note cards, and interview them regarding their knowledge concerning Q'ero textiles. Unfortunately, Otto de Barry died before I could interview him, but his son, Eduardo de

Barry, was very helpful in bringing together diverse people and textiles for my study. Another important textile collection I studied is in the possession of Josefina Olivera, the owner of two tourist textile stores in Cuzco.

Finally, I also studied three important collections housed at the American Museum of Natural History. Gathered under the auspices of museum director Junius B. Bird, these textiles were collected in the mid-1950s by Oscar Núñez del Prado, the first anthropologist to visit Q'ero (30 textiles); John Cohen, artist and film maker (18 textiles); and Pedro Beltrán, owner of the Lima newspaper *La Prensa*. All these pieces were collected in the Q'ero cultural area, but no village provenance is given.[9] By studying these textiles along with my own collection, gathered from 1979 to the present, I have been able to see the evolution of iconographic content in Q'ero textiles for the last sixty years.

My qheswa textile sample size is also based on the textiles that I studied and purchased during my fieldwork in the Cuzco area, beginning in 1979 and continuing to the present. I documented with photographs and note cards textiles from Chinchero, Calca, Pisac, Markapata, Kauri, Huancarani, and Pitumarka. I also studied the large collection, more than one thousand pieces, housed in Josefina Olivera's Cuzco stores. Thus I was able to study large numbers of textiles from these communities and compare their iconographic content.[10]

Spatial Organization of the Design Panels

In Q'ero cloth the plain-weave panels are always woven with natural-colored alpaca wool in black, blue, or red. Vicuña wool was used in the oldest textiles, and sheep wool is never used in Q'ero for these fabrics. Outside Q'ero the textile tradition has changed much more rapidly. A case in point is Chinchero, where textile types and iconographic content began to change in the 1920s (Silverman, ed. 1991b). Sheep wool, aniline dyes, and then synthetic fibers were gradually introduced. Today traditional Chinchero costume is worn by only a small percentage of the oldest people and by textile merchants who sell to tourists in Chinchero or Cuzco. Everyone else wears store-bought skirts, sweaters, and pants.

In general, qheswa cloth uses alpaca wools and natural dyes in the oldest textiles, gradually incorporating sheep wool and anilines as modern materials were introduced into the area.

Both Q'ero and qheswa cloth are warped in a continuous figure-eight manner in which the warp threads are never cut (the chukrukata technique, described above), which creates a four-selvage fabric. Both the lliklla and the poncho are woven as two separate rectangular pieces that are joined at the center with embroidery stitches, a technique known as *chukuyni*. Each half is called *qallu*, "tongue." Cusihuamán (1976a:39) defines *chukuy* as "to put something on the head"; González Holguín ([1608] 1989:118) defines it as "to sew points, rings, or to spin," as in *chhactani chhucuni*. The term also refers to the idea of sewing something closed, as in *mattictam chuctani* (González Holguín [1608] 1989:118).

The Q'ero Lliklla

The Q'ero lliklla reproduced in Figure C10 measures 70 by 60 centimeters and is composed of six design panels that are arranged symmetrically around a vertical axis. Q'ero weavers have identified these design panels: (1) *Awapan*, a border trim. (2) *Puka pampa*, a red warp-faced plain-weave panel. (3) *Chili puka*, an alternating warp-faced white- and red-striped panel. (4) Secondary motif: in the oldest textiles it can be *ñawpa silu* (ancient sky), *ñawpa churo* (ancient interior), or *ñawpa inti* (ancient sun). Today this panel is always woven with *k'iraqey puntas* (mountain points). (5) Principal motif, composed of variations of inti (sun), such as hatun inti (the zenith), iskay inti (rising and setting suns), and tawa inti qocha (four sun lake), or the different ch'unchu motifs. (6) *Yana pampa*, a black warp-faced plain-weave panel.[11]

The Quechua terminology used to identify these motifs is interesting. *Awapan* is derived from the verb *awapay* (Cusihuamán 1976a:30), which means "to put a seam or border on cloth." *Puka pampa*, which literally means "red uncultivated land," is derived from *puka*, "red," and *pampa*, "field or unworked land" (Cusihuamán 1976a:105, 100; González Holguín [1608] 1989:292). González Holguín (1989:275) defines *pampa* as "plaza, smooth plain, pastureland, savannah, or field, or space." With regard to *chili puka*, Cusihuamán (1976a:37) identifies *chili* as "bone marrow, or the substance or essence of anything." Elsewhere, I have shown how *chili* means semen and all fertilizing liquids such as rain and rivers (Silverman 1994c), and also means *qhari*, man (Silverman 2001a). *Ñawpa silu* means "ancient sky," derived from *ñawpa*, "old or ancient," and *silu*, from the Spanish for "sky" (*cielo*) (Cusihuamán 1976a:96). Last, *yana pampa* means "black uncultivated land," derived from *yana*, "black," and *pampa*, "unworked land."

The Chinchero Lliklla

The Chinchero lliklla shown in Figure C11 was purchased in Ayllu Pongo in 1979 from Inesa Callanaupa Sayri, who was about seventy years old at the time.[12] It is woven with alpaca wool and uses natural dyed colors of red, blue, and gold, plus natural white. The warp-faced plain-weave panel is natural black alpaca wool. The motifs are from the ñawpa period, being woven with the three-color complementary warp-weaving technique (Silverman ed. 1991b), and are transitional between Q'ero and qheswa pallay.

There are five design panels woven in this lliklla, arranged in a symmetrical manner in relation to a vertical axis. The Chincherinos call this *pisqa pallay*, "five-motif panels." Chinchero textiles also exist with *kinsa pallay*, "three-motif panels," but pisqa pallay is the most valuable. These five-motif panels were identified as (1) *tipana*: one yellow, one green, and one red stripe; (2) *lista*, multicolored stripes composed of one blue, one red, one green, and one yellow; (3) *kuti*, the first primary design panel, a geometric motif in the form of an "S," which represents an agricultural tool; (4) *kesway*, the second primary design panel, a zigzag motif that has many variations; and (5) *waka ñawi*, the third principal motif panel, a diamond with circles in the middle. There are many variations of the diamond motif woven in Chinchero.

Lista is Spanish for "list"; *tipana* means "a place for joining, to stay in an adequate place." In Quechua *waka ñawi* means "the eyes of a cow," but this motif really refers to the agricultural fields and the hole made in the earth in order to plant, as explained to me by the men.

The Pisac Lliklla

The lliklla presented here (Figure C12) was collected in the Pisac market in 1982. It was woven in the community of Amaru and is made with sheep wool and with the two-color supplementary warp technique that the Q'ero call *iskaymanta*.

This lliklla is composed of four design panels that are organized in a symmetrical manner in relation to a vertical axis. They have been identified as (1) puka pampa, a red warp-faced plain-weave panel; (2) lista, warp-faced multicolored stripes; (3) the primary motif panel, decorated with *t'ika qocha* (flower lake), a diamond motif; and (4) the second principal motif panel, woven with *saya qocha*, which means "straight lake" (Cusihuamán 1976a:134).

I now turn to the ceremonial poncho and the identification of the design panels that decorate it.

The Q'ero Ceremonial Poncho

The poncho pictured in Figure C13 measures 158 by 76.4 centimeters and is woven with alpaca wool. It is decorated with four design panels arranged in a symmetrical manner around a vertical axis. The design panels include (1) chili puka, alternating warp-faced white and red stripes; (2) lista, warp-faced multicolored stripes in different widths; (3) k'iraqey puntas, the secondary mountain point motif; and (4) the principal design panel, woven with *ch'unchu inti pupu* (ch'unchu sun navel), the present-day Q'ero ch'unchu motif.

The Markapata Poncho

When I arrived in Chinchero in 1979, adult males wore plain-weave natural gray or light brown alpaca ponchos, not *pallay* (motif) ponchos. The Chinchero plain-weave poncho is very similar to the daily-wear poncho worn by Santiago Salas in Figure 1.20. It is the typical daily-wear garment of Q'ero and throughout the Department of Cuzco.

The Pisac Poncho

The poncho shown in Figure C14 was collected in Pisac during the Sunday market. It was woven in the community of Pampa Corral using the iskaymanta technique and sheep wool. It is composed of four design panels arranged in a symmetrical manner around a vertical axis: (1) tipana, alternating warp-faced white, red, and black stripes; (2) lista, warp-faced multicolored stripes; (3) primary motif panel woven with tawa t'ika qocha (four flower lake) and *isqon ñawi* (nine eyes); and (4) a second primary motif panel woven with t'ika qocha (flower lake), which includes various graphic elements identified as *ñawi* (eye), *organo* (organ), and *sonqocha* (little heart).

Based on the data presented here, we note that there are differences in the principal and secondary motifs used to weave Q'ero and qheswa cloth. First, Q'ero pallay uses inti or ch'unchu as its primary motif and k'iraqey puntas as a secondary motif that borders both sides of inti or ch'unchu. In the case of qheswa pallay, in contrast, the primary motif is a variation of the inti design called t'ika (flower), such as t'ika qocha, tawa t'ika qocha, and

Table 2.1. Principal and Secondary Motifs Used to Weave Q'ero and Qheswa Cloth

Q'e ro Pallay	*Qheswa Pallay*
Kinsamanta	Iskaymanta
Two-faced cloth (iskay uya)	Single-faced cloth (hoq uya)
Primary motifs: inti, ch'unchu, lista	Primary motifs: variations of t'ika (t'ika qocha, tawa t'ika qocha, saya qocha, etc.)
Secondary motifs: k'iraqey puntas (oldest textiles: ñawpa churo, ñawpa silu, ñawpa inti)	Secondary motifs: lista
Graphic elements: light-and dark-colored lines radiating in or out	Graphic elements: organo, ñawi

saya qocha, and there is a secondary lista motif that borders both sides of the primary design panel (see table 2.1).

It should also be noted that the ceremonial poncho is decorated with more primary design panels than the women's lliklla. Next I describe the braiding, knitting, and embellishment techniques used in Q'ero in cloth production.

❈ Braiding, Knitting, and Embellishments ❈

The Q'ero braid ropes and slings, and they knit small caps and llama bags (*llama sarsillu*). Embellishments include fringes, tassels, pom-poms, and beadwork. According to Q'ero men, only the most intelligent can knit the llama sarsillu (Santiago Salas Pauccar, Tandaña, 1985, taped).

As it is beyond the scope of this book to describe all the knitting, braiding, and embellishment techniques used in Q'ero and throughout Cuzco, I discuss only the motifs found in slings and knitted items. As we will see, the motifs used in these items use qheswa pallay instead of Q'ero pallay.

Braiding

At least two kinds of braided slings, called *warak'a*, are made in Q'ero; they are used for dancing and pasturing the herds. Numerous variations of the diamond and zigzag motifs decorate them. Here I describe two of these motifs: *ñawi* and *p'aki*.

Figure 2.14. Making a rope. K'allakancha, 1985.

Figure 2.15. A braided rope made in Q'ero. K'allakancha, 1985.

Ñawi, which means "eye" in Quechua, or "a hole in the ground into which a seed is planted," is composed of a series of repeating diamonds. Woven in natural-colored alpaca yarns, four diamonds are placed one inside the other in decreasing size using light brown and white, black and white, and brown and black. *P'aki*, which is a repeating diamond design that refers to fields that are worked in sections, is woven with natural-colored llama wools in white, brown, gray, and black.

Only Q'ero men braid slings, and they thought it very funny that I would want to learn to make one.

Knitting

Q'ero men also knit the small *ch'ullu* ear-flapped cap, as well as tiny ch'uspas (bags), or llama sarsillu, used for the lead herd animals. Like the warak'a, they are decorated with variations of the diamond and zigzag motif. Unlike the slings, however, they are made with store-bought synthetic yarns in loud, bright colors.

Figure 2.16. Knitting a ch'ullu
cap. Kiko, Q'ero, 1980.

One of the more common motifs
used to decorate the ch'ullu cap in Q'ero
is the diamond motif called saya qocha
(straight lake), composed of a large diamond that is divided into nine smaller
ones. It is also outlined with a series of
squares, called *organo*. This is exactly like
the qheswa pallay t'ika motif with organo
woven as a secondary element. A second
common motif woven in the ch'ullu is *qocha
organo* (lake furrow), which is formed by a
number of diamonds placed one inside the
other in decreasing size. Additional motifs
include multicolored stripes aligned horizontally, multicolored zigzag lines, and
vertically aligned diamonds, all found in
different qheswa pallay.

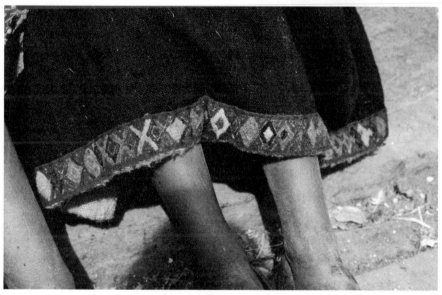

Figure 2.17. A skirt border. Paucartambo, 1979.

The ch'ullu cap is knitted only by the men, who use thin bicycle spokes as knitting needles. The oldest Q'ero ch'ullus are woven with natural-colored alpaca wools in dark brown and are decorated with big diamonds outlined in red or pink. Another rare motif only found in the oldest ch'ullus in Q'ero is the quartered diamond. This is also woven in natural-colored alpaca wool. Today the ch'ullus being knitted in Q'ero in such communities as K'allakancha incorporate the qheswa pallay diamond motif made with synthetic yarns and bright colors.

The ch'ullu, the llama sarsillu, and the warak'a are often additionally embellished with pom-poms, which are also worn by young girls on their braids.

Embroidery is also used in the chukuyni area of the lliklla and poncho. Stitches include *q'enqo* (zigzag, meandering), *ch'aski"* (star, Venus), and horizontal lines.

3

The Structure of Space

From the time of the ancient cultures of Nazca, Huari, Tiahuanaco, and Inca, and continuing to the present-day Quechua and Aymara, the quartered diamond motif has been an important decorative design in textiles, ceramics, wooden drinking cups and gourds (Flores et al. 1998; Phipps 2004, 2005; de la Jara 1965; Kauffmann-Doig 1969; J. Rowe 1999; A. Rowe, ed. 1986:168). Here I focus on the text represented by the quartered diamond motif that is woven in Q'ero and qheswa cloth as it refers to spatial ideas. What types of spatial concepts are recorded with this motif? Who are the people who can read them?

The quartered diamond motif is one of the principal graphic elements the Q'ero use to record cosmological concepts in their cloth. The elements that form this motif—a diamond, radiating lines, a vertical line, and a cross—refer to both spatial and temporal concepts. For example, beginning with the basic graphic unit, which is the diamond placed inside a rectangular frame with lines radiating in opposite directions (in/out), each added element creates a new motif and a new level of meaning. First, the vertical line forms the halved diamond called *hatun inti* (large sun), which both Q'ero and Kauri informants read as the midday sun, seasonal time, and a dual social organization. Next, the addition of a cross forms the quartered *tawa inti qocha* motif (four sun lake), which they read as referring to daily time, seasonal time, and the four-part division of terrestrial space.

⁜ The Quartered Diamond Motif ⁜

Type I: Q'ero Pallay

The Q'ero weave two quartered diamonds: *tawa inti qocha*, woven with kinsamanta, and *tawa t'ika qocha*, woven with iskaymanta. Tawa inti qocha is composed of a large diamond circumscribed inside a rectangular frame and divided into two, four, and eight parts by the addition of a vertical line, light and dark radiating lines, and an X.

Then tawa inti qocha is halved by a color change that creates a vertical dividing line called *sonqocha*, "little heart." The right half, which I call Part A, is woven with long pink lines that begin at the edge of the rectangular frame and radiate in toward the diamond without touching it. The left half, Part B, is woven with long black lines that begin at the edge of the diamond and radiate out toward the rectangular frame without touching it. Part A symbolizes half of *inti lloqsimushan*, sunrise, and Part B signifies half of *inti chinkapushan*, sunset. Parts A and B together represent hatun inti, the sun at zenith.

Each half of the overall motif (Parts A and B) is also divided into four smaller diamonds that are formed with the addition of an X and exhibit the same opposition in color (light/dark). Part a (the right half) is composed of two incomplete diamonds and one complete one. The two partial diamonds, located in the upper and lower parts of the overall motif, are made with short black lines that radiate toward the center, where they touch each other. The single smaller diamond, situated in the center of the larger diamond, is also separated into two parts based on a change of color. One half is formed with short black lines that direct toward the rectangular frame, and the other half is composed of pink lines that radiate toward the center.

As we see from the color change and the direction of the radiating lines, part b is the exact opposite of part a. Part b is also formed with one complete diamond and two partial ones. The two partial diamonds are located in the upper and lower parts of the overall design and are formed with short red lines that radiate out. The complete diamond, situated in the center of the overall motif, is also made of short lines that direct out, red on one half and cranberry on the other half.

The secondary motif that borders both sides of tawa inti qocha is k'iraqey puntas (tooth points), which is composed of a series of repeating

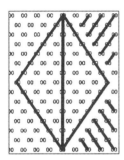

Figure 3.1. Tawa inti qocha, Part A, right half, which represents half of inti lloqsimushan, the rising sun.

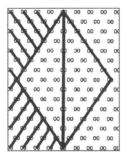

Figure 3.2. Tawa inti qocha, Part B, left half, which represents half of inti chinkapushan, the setting sun.

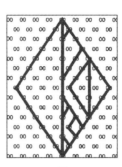

Figure 3.3. Tawa inti qocha, Part A.

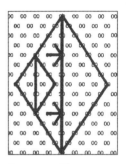

Figure 3.4. Tawa inti qocha, Part B.

isosceles triangles. Both Spanish and Quechua terms—*puntas, puntada, orqo,* and *orqo puntas*—are used to identify this motif. *Puntas* means "points" or "peaks" in Spanish, and *puntada* is Spanish for "stitch" (with a needle and thread). Thus *k'iraqey puntas* means "tooth-like points," derived from the Quechua *kiru,* "tooth." While the female Q'ero weavers use these terms to identify this motif, the Q'ero men call it *orqo puntas,* which means "mountain points," or *orqo,* "mountain." *Orqo* also means "male."

Tawa inti qocha appears once or twice on both halves of the Q'ero lliklla (shawl) and twice on both halves of the ceremonial poncho. When woven on the wayako (bag), it is a repeating motif located in the central design panel. Apparently, it is never woven on the ceremonial ch'uspa (coca bag) or the ch'umpi (belt).

Interestingly, tawa inti qocha is one of the few graphic designs produced by both Q'ero men and women. The women weave it on the lliklla, the men's ceremonial poncho, and the wayako, while the men knit it in the ch'ullu cap and the small bags tied around the neck of the lead pack animal (llama sarsillu).

Temporal-Spatial Distribution

The quartered diamond motif has a long temporal-spatial distribution. During pre-Inca times it was woven in Huari tapestry tunics (Stone-Miller 1992) and decorated Tiahuanco ceramics (Kauffmann-Doig 1969). During the Inca period at least three different subtypes were woven in the imperial uncu (Silverman-Proust 1988b; Silverman 1994a), and it was also painted on the Inca ceremonial cup *(k'ero)*. Rowe (1999:628) reproduces various examples of this motif as a series of quartered diamonds woven around the waist of an Inca uncu.

De la Jara (1967:241, 247; Silverman 1994: 46, F3.6) reproduces three quartered diamond motifs woven in the Inca uncu which are circumscribed inside a quartered square. Differences between them are based on an opposition in the use of color as well as differences in the size of the centrally located diamond. For example, two varieties of the quartered diamond *tocapu* (motifs) are represented. The first one (fifth row, bottom left) is a four-part red diamond with four smaller diamonds each outlined in black, white, and yellow. The entire beige diamond is placed inside an alternating beige and blue quartered rectangle.

The quartered diamond motif is also found in the Inca k'ero. Flores et al. (1998:19) depict a fifteenth-century k'ero in which both the upper and lower parts are painted with a large diamond divided into four smaller ones, two in dark brown and the other two in light orange. Gisbert (1999:27) reproduces Bolivian funerary towers painted with the quartered diamond motif in red and white.

Type II: The Quartered Diamond in Qheswa Pallay

The quartered diamond motif also exists in a modified version outside Q'ero in almost all the communities located in the Department of Cuzco, such as Pisac, Markapata, Kauri, Huancarani, Paucartambo and Lauramarka (Gisbert 1987; Rowe, ed. 1986; Silverman 1995b; Silverman-Proust 1986a, 1988a). The Q'ero call this version qheswa pallay, which I described in Chapter 1 as being woven with the two-color supplementary warp weave called iskaymanta.

I do not know when this motif started to make an appearance in Q'ero. Cohen (1957), O. Núñez del Prado (1970), and Beltrán do not describe it or have examples of it in the textile collections they made in Q'ero in the mid-1950s. During my initial survey in Q'ero in 1979-1980, the only place I saw qheswa pallay was K'allakancha, where young unmarried boys and girls wore it. I also saw qheswa pallay being used in the llikllas worn by the Q'ero Qolla dancers during Corpus Christi at Hatun Q'ero in 1980. There the tawa t'ika qocha motif decorated a small Lauramarka lliklla that these dancers wore on their backs. My impression is that qheswa pallay was introduced by the wool buyers who come from Ocongate and Puno

Figure 3.5. Qheswa pallay. Ocongate lliklla, 1979.

each year. Or perhaps the Q'ero women copied it from a qheswa pallay poncho that was purchased in Ocongate or Paucartambo or was viewed at the yearly festival of Coyllur Rit'i.

There are at least three subtypes of the qheswa pallay quartered diamond motif woven outside Q'ero in the Department of Cuzco, and an innumerable number knitted and braided in hats, slings, and small purses. Here I describe the three major subtypes that are woven in daily-wear lliklla and the ceremonial poncho as well as describing Type III woven in Chinchero, which is transitional between Q'ero and qheswa pallay.

Type IIa

Type IIa is a quartered diamond motif characterized by a flower situated in each of the four smaller diamonds. This flower, called *t'ika* (flower), *waqra t'ika* (horn flower), or *t'ika qocha* (flower lake), defines the subtype. The vertical sonqocha stripe halves the diamond. Finally, the entire motif is outlined by a series of alternating red and white keyboard-like elements called *organo* (a musical instrument, an organ), arranged in a repeating manner.

Figure 3.6. T'ika pallay woven in a Pisac poncho.

In the Uchu Llucllu (Pitumarka highlands) lliklla the motif occurs on the principal design panel on only half the garment. It is bordered on both sides with a three-color striped lista motif woven in red, yellow, and purple on the left edge and green, yellow, and blue on the right edge.

In a poncho collected in Calca and woven in the village of Pampa Corral, Type IIa occurs in the primary motif panel once on each half of the poncho. It is woven in a nonrepeating fashion and is also bordered by a series of six lista stripes woven with various widths in dark green, light red, purple, pink, and green.

Type IIb

Type IIb is almost exactly like Type IIa except for the replacement of the centrally located t'ika (flower) element with a cross, called *cruz*, in each of the four smaller diamonds. In a poncho from Amaru, Pisac, pictured in Figure 3.7, a *ley cruz* (law cross) is bordered by an alternating red and white keyboard-like organo motif.

Type IIb occurs once in the centrally located design panel on both halves of this poncho. It is bordered by a series of lista stripes woven in red, gray-green, yellow, and pink.

Figure 3.7. Ley cruz woven in an Amaru, Pisac, poncho.

Type IIc

Type IIc is exactly like Types IIa and b except for the addition of a flower (*rosa*, Spanish for "rose") located in the center of each of the four smaller diamonds. In 1980 and 1982 I collected many examples of this motif woven in Markapata textiles. In the lliklla illustrated in Figure 3.8, the rosa motif is composed of a series of small triangles that form the central diamond. In some examples the motif is outlined with white seed beads called *piñis*, while in other examples only a white embroidered thread outlines the motif.

Rosas are woven on both halves of the lliklla in a repeating manner. Bordering them are multicolored lista stripes, which are called *sara wachu* (corn furrow). Sara wachu is a seven-stripe motif woven in white, pink, yellow, and green.

Type III

Two other versions of the quartered diamond motif are woven in Chinchero but with the three-color complementary warp-weave technique (Silverman 1991b:5, 6, 7, 9). The first Type IIIa, called *waqaq ñawin loraypu*, is a diamond that is quartered by the occurrence of two circles placed on the top and bottom of the diamond, and two smaller diamonds placed at each

Figure 3.8. Rosas woven in an Ocongate lliklla.

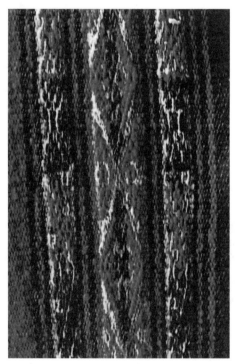

Figure 3.9. The quartered diamond motif woven in a Chinchero lliklla.

side. *Waqaq* comes from the Spanish *vaca*, "cow," and *ñawin* means "his/her eye" in Quechua. *Loraypu* refers to the diamond motif, but I could find no Quechua definition of this term (E. Franquemont et al. 1992:76; C. Franquemont 1986:331).

The second Type IIIa quartered diamond motif woven in Chinchero is called *tanka loraypu*, a subtype of waqaq ñawin loraypu. It is composed of a quartered diamond with a reversed S in the center of each of the four smaller diamonds. *Tanka* means "forked" in Quechua (Cusihuamán 1976a:143). The S is called *kuti* and refers to an agricultural tool used for hoeing (C. Franquemont 1986; Silverman, ed. 1991b).

❖ The Ceque System of Cuzco ❖

We have seen how the quartered diamond motif is fabricated in pre-Inca, Inca, and contemporary cloth, ceramics, and drinking cups. The same structure found in the quartered diamond Types I, II, and III motif is also found in the Inca *ceque* system of Cuzco.

In his pioneering book *The Ceque System of Cuzco*, R. T. Zuidema (1964) demonstrates how the Incas mapped time onto social space using the ceque system of sight lines, in which imaginary lines begin at Cuzco's Temple of the Sun and radiate out to the intercardinal directions. First, a horizontal line separated Cuzco into two moieties: Hanan Cuzco (Upper Cuzco) and Hurin Cuzco (Lower Cuzco). Next a vertical line divided Cuzco into four parts called *suyu*: Antisuyu, located northeast of Cusco; Chinchasuyu, in the northwest; Cuntisuyu, in the southwest; and Collasuyu, in the southeast. Finally, forty-one imaginary lines radiated out of the center of Cuzco, nine lines each in the Antisuyu, Chinchasuyu, and Collasuyu, and seven lines in each half of the Cuntisuyu.

Zuidema (1983), Aveni (1981), and Sherbondy (1982) compare the ceque system, a quartered circle with radiating lines that begin at the center and direct outward, to a giant quipu spread out on the ground. The ceque system can also be compared to the Q'ero quartered diamond motifs because the form is the same. The Q'ero represent the quartered ceque circle as a quartered diamond in their cloth and the radiating ceque lines as long and short lines that radiate in opposite directions.

Just as the Cuzco ceque system is the graphic metaphorical representation of Inca cosmology, so is the Q'ero tawa inti qocha motif the graphic metaphorical representation of Q'ero cosmology. As we will see, the Q'ero

Figure 3.10. The mountain peaks bordering Tandaña. 1985.

use the tawa inti qocha motif to store ideas about space in three ways: as a sign for their village, as a sign for their dual social organization, and as a sign for the quadripartition of terrestrial space.

K'iraqey Puntas:
The Q'ero Village of Tandaña

The Q'ero Totorani village of Tandaña (Lower Q'ero) is located approximately two days' walk from Paucartambo, a distance of about 85 kilometers.

Like all highland Q'ero villages, Tandaña is situated in a long, narrow valley surrounded by mountain peaks. To the east is a range of black, gravel-covered mountains the Q'ero call Yana Orqo (Black Mountain). To the southeast is the snowcapped Apu Wamanllipa, their major mountain deity. Also located to the east is the Apu Wayra Rumi (Sacred Windy Stone Mountain). To the northwest is the grass-covered Qheswawarani Mountain (Silverman 2001a).

I have described the four major mountains that border the Tandaña Valley, but the Q'ero can easily recite a much longer list. For example, in 1985 a young boy who lived in Chuwa Chuwa told me the names of more than forty mountains located there (field notes, 1985).

The importance of mountains in the Andean world has been widely documented in the anthropological literature (Aliaga 1985; Bastien 1978; Mariscotti 1978; Martínez 1983; Reinhard 1991; Rozas 1989). For example, Joe Bastien (1978) views the mountains as metaphors for the way in which the Bolivian Kallawayan structure their ayllu (lineages). Johann Reinhard (1991) discusses the importance of mountain peaks in the circulation of water. Washington Rozas (1989:53), Gabriel Martínez (1983), and Francisco Aliaga (1985) describe the religious function of sacred mountains.

With such an abundant literature on mountain peaks, it would seem reasonable to believe that Andeans record ideas about the mountains in their cloth, and I maintain that they do this with the secondary k'iraqey puntas motif. I base my argument on four kinds of evidence: (1) the Quechua terms used to identify this motif by Q'ero and Kauri informants, (2) how

Figure 3.11. The secondary k'iraqey puntas motif borders ñawpa inka
Type Ia and inti lloqsimushan and inti chinkapushan in a llikIla.

the Q'ero read this motif to mean mountain peaks, (3) the similarity in form
between the drawings the Q'ero men made of the mountain peaks and the
motif, and (4) the use of the isosceles triangles in colonial Spanish and contemporary maps to represent mountain peaks.

My first evidence to support the idea that *k'iraqey puntas* is read as
"mountain peaks" concerns the Quechua terms used to identify this motif.
Cohen (1957:47) and Oscar Núñez del Prado (1983a:14), who collected
their data in 1955, call this motif *kereken* and *k'eraqe*, respectively. But during my fieldwork in 1980, 1985, and 1986 I found that different terms were
used. For example, both Q'ero and non-Q'ero women identified k'iraqey
puntas woven in cloth as *k'iraqey, k'iraqey puntas, puntas,* or, more rarely,
puntada. The Q'ero and Qheswa men called it *k'iraqey puntas* in cloth but

orqo, "mountain," or *orqo puntas*, "mountain points," when identifying my black and white drawing of this motif or their own drawings of the mountains. Whatever the term, the important point is that all the words used to identify this motif either mean "mountain" in Quechua or are used in a metaphorical sense to mean "mountain points."

I showed a photograph of a Q'ero lliklla with the *ñawpa inka* motif, bordered by k'iraqey puntas, to a Kauri star watcher (astronomer), Francisco Lara. After discussing the meaning of ñawpa inka with him, I asked him to identify and explain the meaning of k'iraqey puntas:

> **Q:** ¿Ima sutin kay pallayta?
> [What is the name of this motif?]
>
> **A:** Chay pallaychata…orqochata.
> [This small motif…small mountain.]
>
> **Q:** ¿Orqochachu?
> [Small mountain?]
>
> **A:** Ari, orqocha pallayta.
> [Yes, a small mountain motif.]
>
> **Q:** ¿Imarayku awanku kay orqo pallaychata?
> [Why do they weave this small mountain motif?]
>
> **A:** Tianchis orqopi.
> [We live in the mountain.]

(Taped, 1985)

My second evidence to support the idea that k'iraqey puntas represent mountain peaks is the similarity in form between the motif and the drawings the men made of the mountains. For example, Santiago Salas Pauccar, of Tandaña, drew a picture of the upper moiety of Tandaña in which two sides of the drawing depict mountain peaks. The set on the lower right-hand side is composed of elongated triangles, the same form as k'iraqey puntas. He called both sets of peaks *puntas*, "points," or *orqo puntas*, "mountain points." Benito Salas Pauccar, also of Tandaña, depicted the mountains located at the pilgrimage site of Coyllur Rit'i as elongated triangles (Figure 3.12). Similarly, in drawings made by men from Chinchero, Kauri, and Huancarani, all the mountain peaks are repeated isosceles triangles. Thus both k'iraqey puntas and the informants' drawings of the mountains are made with isosceles triangles.[1]

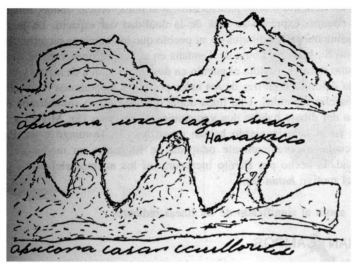

Figure 3.12. Benito Salas's drawing of the mountains
in Coyllur Rit'i as isosceles triangles. 1986.

My last evidence concerns the use of isosceles triangles as symbols for mountain peaks in maps. According to Benjamin Orlove (1991:33 n. 8), isosceles triangles were used to depict mountain peaks in "European maps from the 16th to the 18th century, as well as 18th century maps of Cusco." He also found that contemporary Aymara communities located near Lake Titicaca draw the mountains on their maps as "peaks on the horizon" with isosceles triangles (Orlove 1991:27).

The terminology used to identify this motif, informants' drawings of the mountains and their "readings" of the text recorded with k'iraqey puntas, and graphic elements used in early maps and by present-day Aymara all suggest that the rectangle represents the highland Q'ero village, and the isosceles triangles that border both sides of the rectangle signify the mountain peaks.

I now turn to the spatial meaning of the vertical line and the radiating lines found in hatun inti and tawa inti qocha.

Sonqocha: A Dual Social Organization

The second graphic element found in the quartered diamond motif which records spatial ideas is the vertical line. Q'ero and Qheswa weavers call this line *sonqo*, "heart," or *sonqocha*, "little heart." For example, in 1985 I heard the term used by Rosa Pauccar to identify the vertical line woven in her *wayako*. Beginning at the left edge of this bag, Rosa named the motif panels: "*Washka qocha* [qheswa pallay motif], *sonqo* [vertical stripe that halves washka qocha], *tipana* [brown plain-weave panel], *listan* [white thin stripe], *hatun pampa* [large white plain-weave panel], *lista* [thin black stripe], *hatun yana pampa* [large black plain-weave panel]" (field notes, 1985, Chuwa Chuwa). In fact, *sonqo* and *sonqocha* were the most common terms used to identify the vertical stripe.

But when I showed the men my black and white drawing of hatun inti, as well as the motif, and asked them to identify the vertical line, they called it *mayu*, "river," and *ñan*, "road." Lorenzo Quispe, for example, one of my principal informants from Chuwa Chuwa, called it *mayu*:

> **Q:** ¿Imas chay?
> [What is it?]
>
> **A:** Este lado [*indicating the right half*] pertenece a Q'ero Totorani, y este lado pertenece a Q'ero Grande.
> [This side (the right half) belongs to Q'ero Totorani, and this half belongs to Hatun Q'ero.]
>
> **Q:** ¿Y esta linea que quedan en el centro?
> (And this line that stays in the center?)
>
> **A:** El rayo es como colendero.
> [The line is like a *colendero*.]²
>
> **Q:** ¿Como colendero?
> [Like a *colendero*?]
>
> **A:** En Quechua sutin "mayu."
> [In Quechua it is called "river."]

(Taped, 1985)

For Lorenzo Quispe, the vertical line in hatun inti symbolized a dual social organization: Q'ero Grande, situated in hanan (upper) Q'ero, and Q'ero Totorani, situated in hurin (lower) Q'ero. Josiana Samanta, also from Chuwa Chuwa, stated that the vertical line woven in hatun inti symbolized the Ppausi Mayu (Pausi River), which is one of the boundaries between Q'ero Totorani and Hatun Q'ero. Additional evidence that the Pausi River is a boundary between the two Q'ero moieties is found in archival data from the Cuzco Ministry of Agriculture. On May 20, 1982, the communities of Hatun Q'ero and Q'ero Totorani met in order to establish their boundaries. Among the various topographical features they mentioned as boundary markers are the Pampa Ppausi and Amaru Ppausi: "Beginning at the lagoon called Pampa Ccasa, and continuing in a straight line to the lower river, arriving at the site called Millpuyoq Pampa, in order to stop at Pampan Ppausi, continuing then to the Chuwa Chuwa rivulet, the lower river of the Amaru Ppausi, Pictayoq sector..." (Archivos del Ministerio de Agricultura, Cuzco, 1957).

Francisco Lara looked at my black and white drawing of hatun inti and called this line ñan, "road":

Q: ¿Ima sutin kay chawpita?
[What is the name for the center?]

A: Chawpi suntinqa ñan.
[The center is called road.]

Q: ¿Imarayku kashan hoq ñan?
[Why is there a road?]

A: ¿Imaraykutaq? Purinanchipaq. Runakuna ñannikupaq llaqatanchis purinanchispaq.
[Why? For walking. All of the people of our village have a road in order to walk.]

(Taped, 1985)

In addition to using the terms ñan, *mayu*, and *sonqocha* for the vertical line, two women from K'allakancha called it *iskay t'aqapi*, which means "separated into two parts."

All these terms for the vertical line express the idea of the duality of space. This idea is also found in the drawings that the men made of their village. In 1986, for instance, Benito Salas Pauccar drew a picture of Tandaña in which the vertical line, representing the Tandaña River, divides Tandaña into upper and lower moieties (Figure 3.13). The drawing is bordered on three sides by mountain peaks, depicted as repeating isosceles triangles. A double black line symbolizes the Tandaña River. On the right half of the drawing are two house clusters (those of Miguel Salas and Lorenzo Pauccar), and on the left half is another group of two sets of house clusters (those of Domingo Pauccar and Paulino Sera). The sporadically occupied schoolhouse is located in the middle of the village. Thus Benito's drawing of Tandaña incorporates the same graphic elements as those found in the hatun inti motif.

I now turn to the meaning of the radiating lines.

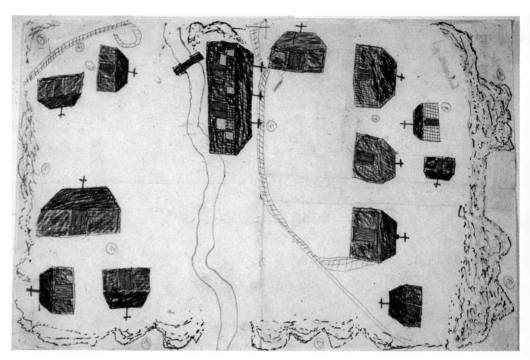

Figure 3.13. Benito Salas drew Tandaña bordered with triangles that represent the mountain peaks. A doubled vertical line represents the Tandaña River, which halves village space. 1985.

Chakrakuna: The Fields

The most common name given to the lines that radiate in opposite directions in the inti motifs was *chakran*, meaning "his/her/its field." In 1985, for example, Austina Flores, of K'allakancha, identified the radiating lines found in a tawa inti qocha motif woven in her lliklla as chakran. When pressed for further information about these lines, she said, "Chakraypuni. Lliuw sutin chakran" (taped, 1985). [Surely, it is the field. All (of them) are called "his/her/its field."]

Another name used by Q'ero and non-Q'ero informants was *loran* or *lorayan*, which means "the roots and stems of a plant" (see Chapter 7). Several informants also called the radiating lines *intiq chakran*, "the sun's field."

Non-Q'ero informants called these lines *wachu wayq'o*. For example, Berna Gutiérrez, of Paucartambo, used this term when identifying the graphic elements that formed the Q'ero hatun inti motif (taped, 1985).

I showed Francisco Lara a photograph of the Q'ero hatun inti motif and my black and white drawing of that motif and asked a simple question: *¿Imas chay?* (What is it?):

A: Kay…muyu. Munaycha. K'aspi chakrakuna kaskallantaq.
[This round…it is a little beautiful. They are only stick-like fields.]

Q: ¿Chakrachu kashan kay muyu?
[Does this round thing have a field?]

A: Allpa pampapi kashan…chakrakuna.
[It is an earth ground…the fields.]

Q: ¿Imarayku ruwanku kay muyu chakrata?
[Why do they make this round field?]

A: Kay muyu chakrata awanku runakuna kausanankupaq.
[These people are weaving this round field for living.]

(Taped, 1985)[3]

These radiating chakran lines are also found in the three diamonds placed one inside the other in decreasing size. Q'ero weavers call them *pata*, which means "high part" (Cusihuamán 1976a:102). Rosa Chura Flores read these chakran lines in the three smaller diamonds as follows: "Chakran. Mayu. Kinsa patapi kashan" (taped, 1985). [His/her/its field. River. It is in three high parts.][4]

Interestingly, Ramón Salas Pauccar drew a picture of Tandaña which incorporates the same graphic elements as those found in Hatun Inti. Ramón's drawing (Figure C17) depicts the vertical mayu/ñan line, radiating chakran lines that exhibit an opposition in color (right side: green, violet; left side: black), and the k'iraqey puntas mountain peaks that border both sides of Tandaña. Thus the same graphic elements that compose the Q'ero hatun inti motif are also found in the drawings made by Q'ero men of village space.

Cruz: The Quadripartition of Space

The addition of an X changes the dualistic hatun inti motif into the quartered tawa inti qocha design. The weavers call this X *cruz*, "cross." They call the four smaller diamonds *pupu*, "navel," or *tawa pupu*, "four navels." For example, looking at tawa inti qocha woven in a llikilla, Francisca Sera, of K'allakancha, said of the four smaller diamonds, "Tawa pupu kashan" (taped, 1985). [There are four navels.] Similarly, Austina Flores, also of K'allakancha, said, "Tawa qocha kashan. Nishan pupu. Nishan chawpi" (taped, 1985). [There are four lakes. It is called navel. It is called the center.] Other weavers named the four smaller diamonds using a variation of the term *pupu*. For instance, Luisa Sera, of Q'achupata, a hamlet near Tandaña, used the word *pupuchan*, "his/her little navel" (taped, 1986).

Austina Flores Waman identified all the graphic elements that compose tawa inti qocha in this way:

Q: ¿Ima sutin kay pallayta?
[What is the name of this motif?]

A: Inti.
[The sun.]

Q: Inti sutin. ¿Y ima sutin kaypi, kay yanapi?
(It is called the sun. And what is this called, this black?]

A: Intipuni. Chakraypuni.
[Surely it is the sun. Surely it is the field.]

Q: ¿Chakranchu sutin?
[Is it called his/her/its field?]

A: Ah, ha. Chakran.
[Yes, it is his/her/its field.]

Q: ¿Ima sutin kaypi, chawpichu intiqpa?
[What is this called in the center of the sun?]

A: Pupu.
[Navel.]

(Taped, 1985)

In this way Austina called the diamond *inti* (sun), the radiating lines *chakran* (his/her/its field), and the four smaller diamonds *pupu* (navel).

But when I showed tawa inti qocha and my black and white drawing of it to the men, I got more detailed answers concerning its meaning. For example, I showed a color photograph of the motif and my black and white drawing of it to Francisco Lara, from Kauri, who read it in the following way:

Q: Hawari. Kashanmi hoq hatun pallay kaypi. Número 10. Chunka pallay.
[Look. Here is one large motif. Number 10. Number 10.]

A: Chunka pallay.
[Number ten.]

Q: ¿Imataq kay?
[What is it?]

A: Ah (*surprise*). Munaycha, Señora. Kaychaqa kay llaqtanchis hina
munay. Mundo hina.
[Oh (*surprise*). This is beautiful, Señora. This small site, it is like
our beautiful village. It is like our world.]

Q: ¿El mundo hinachu?
[Is it the world?]

A: Ari, chawpinta ñan rishan. Kay larutaqmi inti lloqsimuy laru
(*upper right-hand corner*). Kay larutaqmi inti haykuy laru. Kay larutaqmi ñawpa q'epi quedan qhepa: este, oeste, norte, sur.
[Yes. In the center is a road for walking. This side is the sunrise
side. That side is the sunset side. That side is the ancient sack (*q'epi*,
"sack" or "bundle") that holds the future: east, west, north, south.]

Q: ¿Y imarayku kashan tawa partes?
[And why are there four parts?]

A: [No answer]

Q: ¿Y imarayku kashan hoq, iskay, kinsa, tawan partes?
[And why are there one, two, three, four parts?]

A: ¿Imaraykutaq qaynapuni tapunki? Taytanchis kamaran tawan
partes. Tapunki estudiaspas. Ñoqanchis sutinchis este, oeste, norte,
sur. Kauri kashan tawan suyu.
[Why did you ask like that before? Our god created four parts.
Ask when you study. We call them east, west, north, and south.
Kauri has four parts.]

(Taped, 1985)

For Francisco Lara, the quartered diamond motif is read as "our world"
and "our village." The vertical line, called *ñan*, halves village space. Then the
X quarters space. Last, Francisco identified the four cardinal directions as
east, west, north and south.

We have seen how both Q'ero and Kauri informants have read the
graphic elements that compose hatun inti and tawa inti qocha as referring
to spatial concepts. First, isosceles triangles represent the mountain peaks
that border the highland Q'ero valley. Second, the vertical line halves village

space. Third, the radiating lines found in the three smaller diamonds represent the fields. Finally, the X quarters space. I now apply these data to the way in which space is organized in Tandaña.

The Organization of Space in Tandaña

Tandaña is located in the high puna, at an elevation of about 4,800 meters. It is situated in a highland valley that is surrounded by mountain peaks on all four sides. Village space is organized by the structural arrangement of houses, rivers, and footpaths. The duality of space is characterized by the arrangement of house clusters in relation to rivers and footpaths. Tandaña has groups of houses on both sides of the Tandaña River. In Hanan Tandaña (Upper Tandaña) there are two house groups; the first set has two buildings used as living quarters and another two for storage. The second set has two buildings that function as living quarters and one for storage. In Hurin Tandaña (Lower Tandaña), located on the other half of the Tandaña River, there are two more sets of house clusters. Each set has two occupied houses and one storage building.[5]

Located in the middle of Tandaña is the Tandaña River (Tandaña Mayu), which halves village space. The school is situated in Hanan Tandaña, next to the river, on a small hill. The Tandaña River begins northwest of the Qheswawarani Mountains, flows through Tandaña, and continues past the hamlet of Qulluyllu. Here it turns to the east and continues its journey to Q'ero Totorani, reaching Hatun Q'ero, farther east. From Hatun Q'ero it turns sharply northward and descends to the Madre de Dios River, eventually joining the Amazon.

Whereas the Tandaña River halves village space, footpaths quarter village space. One footpath runs from the Q'asa Apacheta (Clear/Freezing Pass) northwest of Tandaña, and continues in a southeasterly direction to the hamlet of Lloqllapampa, the ceremonial center of Q'ero Totorani, finally arriving at Hatun Q'ero. This footpath is crossed by a second path that begins at the Q'ero village of Markachea, located northeast of Tandaña, continues to the hamlet of Qulluyllu, and finally reaches Ocongate in the southwest. Both paths meet at the Chawpi Chaka (Center Bridge).

In this way, terrestrial space is halved by the Tandaña River and then quartered by the axes made by the two footpaths, which run in opposite directions and meet at the center of the village. A similar organization of village space has been described for both the Quechua and Aymara by Nathan Wachtel (1990), Gilles Rivière (1982), Teresa Bouysse-Cassagne

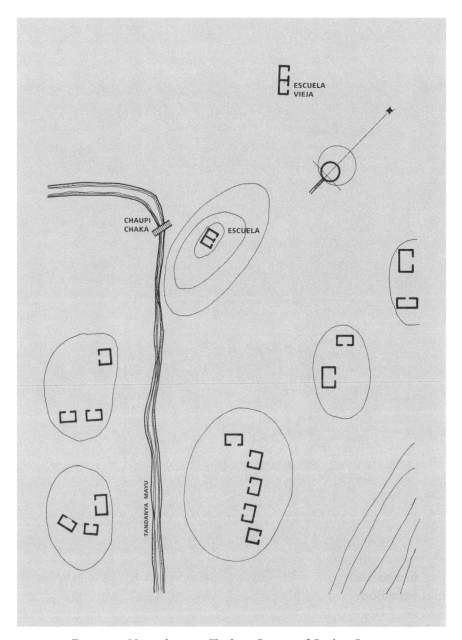

Figure 3.14. House clusters in Tandaña. Courtesy of Catalina Garnica.

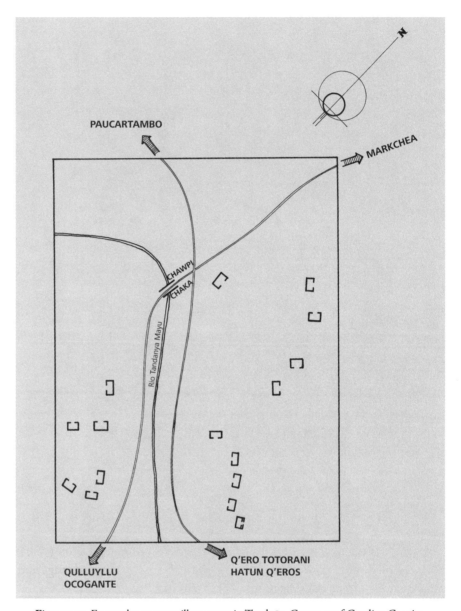

Figure 3.15. Footpaths quarter village space in Tandaña. Courtesy of Catalina Garnica.

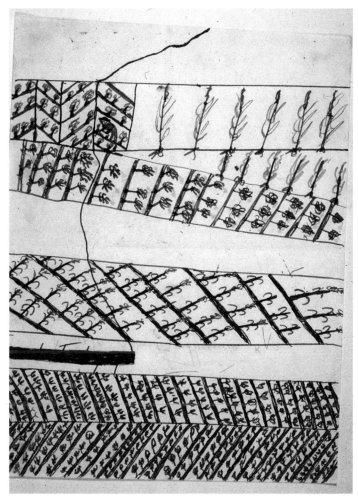

Figure 3.16. José Quispe's drawing of different
kinds of furrows in K'allakancha. 1985.

(1978), Tristan Platt (1978), Olivia Harris (1978), and Gary Urton (1981).
For example, Urton (1981:71) describes how rivers, footpaths, and irrigation
canals halve and quarter village space in Misminay.

Space also displays a three-part division in terms of the three ecological zones exploited by the Q'ero. The highest zone is the *puna*, at an elevation of 3,500-4,500 meters. Permanent residential sites such as Tandaña,
Qochamoqo, Chuwa Chuwa, Kiko, and Hapu are located here because of
their proximity to the *ichhu* vegetation necessary for the alpaca herds. *Ruk'i*

potatoes, used to make the dehydrated *chuño* and *moraya* (Núñez del Prado 1983:15), are also cultivated here.

The middle zone, *qheswa*, is located at 1,800-3,500 meters. At least 88 kinds of potatoes, 8 kinds of *oca* (*Oxalis tuberosa*), 8 kinds of *ulluco* (*Ullucus tuberosus*), and 3 kinds of *anu* (*Tropaeolum tuberosum*) are grown here. The lowest zone is the *monte*, or *yunga*, situated at 1,800 meters. Corn is cultivated in this zone.

In both the puna and qheswa zones the landscape is divided into small agricultural plots that are furrowed. These furrows, as we have seen, are represented by radiating lines in the inti motifs. Called *wachu* by the Q'ero and *organo* or *wachu wayq'o* by the Qheswa, the furrows take different forms depending on soil moisture, the slope of the land, temperature, and the like. For example, Benito Salas drew a picture of Tandaña in which he illustrated three different kinds of furrows (Figure C18). First, he drew a series of vertically aligned furrows located in Hanan Tandaña. Then he drew the Tandaña River, which divided Tandaña into upper and lower moieties. Next he drew a series of zigzag-shaped furrows located in Hurin Tandaña. Last, at the bottom, he drew a partial circle separated by spoke-like lines that he called *chakra pununaypaq* (for a sleeping field; taped, 1985).[6] In another drawing made by a K'allakancha informant, two types of furrows are shown: zigzag-shaped furrows, called *maway wachu*, and vertical furrows, called *kinray wachu* (Figure 3.16).[7]

I also collected the names of furrows used for potato cultivation in the community of Huancarani. According to Marcelino Samanta, there are six basic furrow shapes: (1) *pasaq wachu*: vertically aligned furrows, used in dry soil; (2) *q'enqo wachu*: zigzag-shaped furrows, used in damp soil; (3) *kinray wachu*: horizontal furrows, used where the soil is neither too dry nor too wet; (4) *siskanan wachu*: alternating diagonal and V-shaped furrows, used in dry soil; (5) *senqoyoq wachu*: horizontal furrows with a V-shaped canal in the middle of the field for water drainage; and (6) *kunka wachu*: checkerboard-shaped furrows with a vertical canal cut at one side to allow for gradual drainage (taped, 1984).

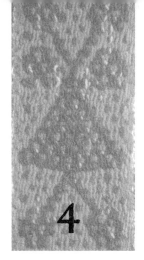

4

The Woven Shadow of Time

In this chapter I turn to the four inti motifs woven in Q'ero—inti lloqsi-mushan, hatun inti, inti chinkapushan, and tawa inti qocha—and how they store ideas about daily time. Basing my argument on the hatun inti motif, I demonstrate how it displays the same form as the observational devices used by the Incas to reckon daily time. Next, using the Q'ero people's own interpretations of the motifs, as well as their drawings, I show how the text stores ideas about sunlight and shadow.

⁑ The Q'ero Inti Motifs ⁑

Inti Lloqsimushan

Inti lloqsimushan has three diamonds placed one inside the other in decreasing size and then circumscribed inside a rectangular frame. This motif is formed with long pink lines that begin at the edge of the rectangle and radiate toward the largest diamond without touching it. This first diamond is composed of short brown-gray lines that are slightly curved. They direct toward the center of the diamond but do not touch it. A row of curving beige lines separates this series of long lines from the first diamond. The second diamond is composed of short, curving, pink lines that are joined to form a small, four-part, centrally located diamond. Several white dots are placed in the center of the smallest diamond.

Inti lloqsimushan is woven with the kinsamanta weaving technique in a discontinuous manner, being separated from the next motif by a horizontal dividing line.

Inti Chinkapushan

Inti chinkapushan is the exact opposite of inti lloqsimushan. It is also formed by three diamonds placed one inside the other in decreasing size and then set inside a rectangular frame. But unlike inti lloqsimushan, which is formed with light-colored lines that radiate in, inti chinkapushan is formed with dark-colored lines that radiate out.

The largest diamond consists of long brown-gray lines that outline it and then radiate toward the edge of the rectangular frame but do not touch it. Short, curving, beige lines separate the first diamond from the second. The second diamond is composed of short, curving, pink lines that begin at the edge of the diamond and radiate toward the rectangle. Placed in the center is a small, beige diamond with four brown-gray dots in the middle.

Hatun Inti

Hatun inti is half inti lloqsimushan (on the right side) and half inti chinkapushan (on the left). Part A (the right half) is woven with red, cranberry, and beige. Long red and short cranberry lines begin at the edge of the rectangle and radiate in toward the diamond. Part B (the left half), in contrast, is composed of black, pink, and beige. Both long black and short pink lines begin at the edge of the diamond and radiate toward the rectangular frame. Hatun inti is divided into three diamonds that are placed one inside the other in decreasing size. These diamonds are exactly like the overall motif; Part A, on the right, consists of short red and cranberry lines that radiate in toward the diamond, while Part B is formed with short black and pink lines that direct toward the rectangular frame.

Tawa Inti Qocha

Tawa inti qocha, described in the previous chapter, is very similar to hatun inti except for the addition of a quartered diamond, which is then halved. Both the opposition in color (light/dark) and in the direction of the radiating lines (in/out) are exactly the same as for hatun inti, inti lloqsimushan, and inti chinkapushan.

All four Q'ero inti motifs are bordered by the secondary k'iraqey puntas motif. In older textiles, dating to at least three generations ago, other secondary motifs are used such as ñawpa churo, ñawpa inti, and ñawpa silu, which I described in Chapter 2.

It should be noted that I have not found these four motifs in any kind of materials from the Inca or colonial period. I have, however, found two of these motifs, inti lloqsimushan and inti chinkapushan, woven with the ch'unchu motif outside Q'ero. In the lliklla reproduced in Chapter 7 (Figure 7.3), which is dated to the early 1900s, inti lloqsimushan and inti chinkapushan border both sides of the ñawpa inka Type Ia motif. This lliklla is believed to have been woven in the Huancarani highlands.[1]

As we have seen, all four inti motifs use some of the same graphic elements, such as the diamond circumscribed inside the rectangular frame, isosceles triangles that border both sides, a vertical line, and differences in the color and direction of the radiating lines. Only the last motif, tawa inti qocha, displays a four-part division of the diamond with the addition of an X.

❦ The Temporal Text Woven in Q'ero Cloth ❦

I interviewed Q'ero men and women regarding the names of the inti motifs in 1980, 1985, and 1986, for a total of twenty-two months. When speaking about these motifs in a general way, they call all of them inti, "the sun," just as they call the four types of the anthropomorphic-geometric figures ch'unchu. But when identifying each variation of inti individually, they use specific names based on the motif's graphic elements, which I shall discuss later in this chapter. The diamond set inside a rectangular frame with light-colored lines radiating in is always called inti lloqsimushan, the rising sun. The diamond set inside a rectangular frame with dark-colored lines radiating out is called inti chinkapushan, the setting sun. The large halved diamond placed inside a rectangular frame with light-colored lines on the right half and dark-colored lines on the left half is called hatun inti, the sun at zenith. Finally, the quartered diamond with light-colored lines on the right half and dark-colored lines on the left half is called tawa inti qocha, the sun at midnight.[2]

But my definitions of these inti motifs as rising sun, setting sun, sun at zenith, and sun at anti-zenith (midnight) do not really express what these motif names reveal in terms of the Quechua language. For example, inti lloqsimushan means more than the "rising sun." Inti is "sun" in Quechua, but lloqsimushan is derived from the Quechua verb lloqsiy, which means "to rise"; the suffix *mu*, which means that the object is away from the speaker and is moving toward him; and the present continuous *shan*, which means it, she, or he is moving. Thus the term *inti lloqsimushan* means "the sun is rising away from the speaker and is moving toward him." In a similar way, *inti chinkapushan* means more than "sunset." *Chinkay* is the verb "to set," but with the addition of the suffix *pu* it denotes the idea that the sun is near the speaker and is moving away from him, hence *inti chinkapushan* can be defined as "the sun is near the speaker and is moving away from him and setting." *Hatun inti* is literally defined as "the large or powerful sun," from the term *hatun*, which means "large" or "powerful." And last, *tawa inti qocha* is literally translated as "four sun lake."[3]

In the case of inti lloqsimushan and inti chinkapushan, there is the idea of movement to or away from the speaker. We come back to this idea later when we talk about the observational devices used by the Incas to reckon daily time and how they are similar to the Q'ero inti motifs. For now, let us see what the men and women from Kauri and Huancarani have to say about the Q'ero inti motifs.

⁜ Reading the Q'ero Inti Motifs ⁜

What do the people who live close to Q'ero have to say about the inti motifs? Do they read them in the same way as the Q'ero or do they read them differently? To explore the answers to these questions, I carried out fieldwork in Kauri and Huancarani.

In 1982 I went to Kauri and undertook an apprenticeship with the weavers so I could learn to weave their entire motif repertory. I went back to Kauri for one-month periods in 1984, 1985, and 1986. I always wove with the same weavers, establishing social ties with them over the years. Then, in 1989, I took one of my students from the University of Cuzco, Filomena Juárez, to Kauri in order for her to undertake a weaving apprenticeship with the same women who had taught me. Later, in 1990, Filomena carried out 53 tape-recorded interviews in Quechua with Kauri men and women concerning the meaning of two Q'ero inti motifs, inti lloqsimushan and inti chinkapushan.

Filomena showed the natives color photographs of these two Q'ero inti motifs and asked the simple question: "What is it?" (*¿Imas chay?*) She heard two answers to this question. Eighteen informants said that these were Q'ero motifs: "Kaypas kashan pallayllaraqmi Q'erollamantataqmi" (taped, 1990). [This is also the same motif, and it is also only from Q'ero.] She heard from two people that the motifs were called *inti*: "Kayqa Q'ero lado pallaymi. Iskay uyayoqmi kashan. Kaypiqa manana pipas chaymanta awankuchu. Manan pipas reqsinkuchu chay pallaytaqa. Q'eropiqa sutin-pasqaku inti pallay nispa. Ashka q'aytumanta allwisqa kashan. Kayqa ancha valeqmi" (taped, 1990). [This motif is from the Q'ero side. It has two faces (two-faced cloth). After that, here, no one can weave like this. No one knows this motif. But in Q'ero they say that it was called *inti pallay*. It was warped from several threads. In this way it is valuable.][4]

I also studied the textile tradition of Huancarani. I began visiting Huancarani in 1985 and returned for two more visits, in 1989 and 1990, always weaving with the women and establishing social ties with several people living in the surrounding area. Huancarani is important for its active Sunday market, when many people come down from their highland villages to barter food. It was during market time that I could conduct preliminary interviews concerning Q'ero textile motifs.

Then, in 1990, I sent two of my Cuzco students to Huancarani to interview the weavers and the men about the Q'ero inti motifs, again asking the simple question, *¿Imas chay?* The two students, Santusa Fernández and Jorge Calanche, carried out 93 tape-recorded interviews in Quechua, showing colored photographs of inti lloqsimushan and inti chinkapushan to the informants; during the same period, the students undertook a weaving apprenticeship with these same people. Thirty-four informants responded correctly to this question, in two ways. First, they said that these motifs were from Q'ero: "Q'ero lado pallaymi." [It's a motif from the Q'ero side.] Second, they said that these were ancient motifs: "Kayqa ñawpa pallay-raqmi" (taped, 1990). [This was an ancient motif.] No one from Huancarani could name these motifs as inti, the sun.

The interviews with Kauri and Huancarani informants revealed that most could correctly identify them as being Q'ero motifs that were ancient designs. The Q'ero, in contrast, related each motif to a specific period of daily time.

❋ Inca Observational Methods ❋

We have seen how the four Q'ero Inti motifs described above are composed of a diamond set into a rectangular frame. Additional graphic elements include the vertical line, differences in color, and direction of the radiating

Figure 4.1. The intiwatana at Pisac..

lines, as well as the X. What can these motifs tell us about how the Q'ero perceive time? Urton (1981:21) notes that the sun is used to reckon time during the day in Misminay and throughout the Andes, and Zuidema (1976:215) states that "shadow or the lack of shadow cast by the sun" was the method used by the Incas to reckon time. What kinds of methods and observational structures do the contemporary Quechua use to reckon daily time?

The Incas built towers, poles, and columns to carry out solar observations. The most well known structure of this type is called the *intiwatana*, or sun clock. George Squier, writing in 1877, described the intiwatana found at Pisac as comprising "a large stone, of geometric form, with a short vertical column in the center. The entire structure was surrounded with a wall" (1877:285). Guamán Poma ([1615] 1980:52-53) explained how the intiwatana was used to reckon daily time: "the sun's rays moved like a sundial with six months moving on the right, while the other six months moved on the left." The contemporary dictionary of Padre Jorge Lira (1982:284) defines the intiwatana as "an observatory or adoratory situated in elevated parts, generally where the sun arrived at three moments: sunrise, zenith, and sunset.... We can judge these *Intiwatana* to be sundials.... The hours were announced on them by the shadow cast by the sun's rays." And recent ethno-archaeological studies at Machu Picchu (Dearborn et al. 1987:350; see also Kauffmann-Doig 2005) have found that the Torreón (tower) at Machu Picchu was, in fact, a solar observatory, an intiwatana "capable of determining the June solstice, as well as the zenith passage date."

Although the *intiwatana* is probably the best-known example of an Inca observational device, other devices are also delineated in the ethnohistoric literature. Zuidema (1982b), for example, describes three different kinds of structures used by the Incas to carry out solar observations: *ushnu*, *sunturhuasi*, and *gnomon*. The ushnu is described as a pile, column, or stone column. There were, in fact, two ushnus, one in Upper Cuzco and the other in Lower Cuzco. Cristóbal de Molina (el Cuzqueño) (1943:37) described the ushnu in 1575: "and in the plaza, in the middle of it [at the side], there was a golden ushnu [*vsno*], which was like a column." The ushnu was used to observe the dates of the August and April sunsets, which mark the beginning and end of the agricultural season (Zuidema 1982b:427).

The sunturhuasi was described by the chronicler Garcilaso as "a building as high as a tower which functioned like the gnomon in order to observe the sun's passage at zenith" (Zuidema 1982b:420). According to Zuidema, the sunturhuasi was situated next to the ushnu at the Huacaypata-Cuspiata Plaza in Hanan Cuzco.

The gnomon was a vertically aligned pole placed in the center of a very large circle. Zuidema (1982b:420) states that the gnomon was used to observe the shadow cast by the sun as well as "the rising and setting sun on the horizon."

The intiwatana, gnomon, ushnu, and sunturwasi all display the same geometry, that is, a vertically aligned pole around which sunlight and shadow move. But before relating these structures to the hatun inti motif, I want to discuss how time is reckoned in Q'ero.

⁜ The Q'ero Conception of Daily Time ⁜

Benito Salas Pauccar described the sun's twenty-four-hour trajectory through the Tandaña sky:

> Kay Wayna Cápac lloqsimushan puntata riki, inti. Chay inti taytanchis riki. Q'oto lloqsimun las tres manañata Inti Wayna Cápacmanta. Kay Inti Wayna Cápac lloqsimushan kay pacha p'unchay luzta purishan riki. Wayna Cápac kay pachata riki puntata chinkapushan. Anchaymanta haykun hoq laduta mayunayaspa kashan qocha. Hinaspa kay uku pachataman pampa ukumansi tutaqa puripushan intiqa. Otro chaymantaq illarimushapaqa uku pachata ñoqapaqa patanta phawaymushan kay pachata intiqa riki. (Taped, 1985)
>
> [Of course, Wayna Cápac, the sun, is rising from the mountain peaks. Of course, he is our Father, the sun. The Pleiades rise at 3 a.m. from Wayna Cápac. Of course, Wayna Cápac, the sun, is rising and is traveling in our world, bringing sunlight. Of course in our world, Wayna Cápac is setting into the mountain peaks. In this way, it goes to one side of the circular lake. After that, the sun is traveling on the floor of the interior world during the night. After that, in my way of looking at it, the sun is rising again in the interior world and then, of course, the sun is flying toward our world.]

THE WOVEN [81] SHADOW OF TIME

Based on Benito's description of the sun's journey, we can see that the Q'ero look at the sun in relation to mountain peaks in order to tell daily time. Sarah Lund Skar (personal communication, 1988) notes that the Peruvian Mataqpuquios "use the face of the mountain across their valley as their clock. This clock on the mountain has the rough shape of a diamond… Zenith is the one point of their clock which is the reference point for all other gradations of light and shadow during the day." In Calcha, Bolivia, Mary Ann Medlin (personal communication, 1984) states that the people watch the shadow cast on the sides of mountains in order to tell time.

The Incas also observed the shadow cast on the sides of a mountain in order to reckon time. According to Guamán Poma ([1615] 1980:168), for example, "in order to plant food, at what month, at what day, and at what hour, and at what point where the sun moved, they looked at the high mountains during the clarity of the morning and they looked at the rays which the sun made in a window of this sundial and they planted and gathered the food for the year in the kingdom."

Prudencio Hakawaya, a Kauri star watcher, explained how the Quechua observed the shadow cast by the sun's rays during ancient times: "Ñawpa tiempupi qhawarankuchu llanthu imay horas chay p'unchay… derechapi llanthu kay. Chay derechapi llanthuchapi willaychaku doce kashan, tardistan kashan" (taped, 1985). [During ancient times, they looked at the shadow cast by the sun's rays in order to know what time it was during the day…this shadow came from the right. This little shadow came from the right and told us when it was noon, when it was sunset.][5]

Both shadow casting and horizon astronomy were used by the Incas to tell time. We can understand how the mountain peaks and sunlight and shadow are expressed in the hatun inti motifs by seeing what the Q'ero have to say about the graphic elements that compose hatun inti.

⁜ The Text: K'iraquey Puntas, Light- and ⁜ Dark-Colored Lines, and the Vertical Line

Inti in Relation to the Mountain Peaks

We have seen how the isosceles triangles woven in Q'ero cloth represent the mountain peaks that surround the highland Q'ero villages. These mountain peaks are directly related to sunrise and sunset. In Benito Salas Pauccar's description of the sun's trajectory in the Tandaña sky, he stated that the sun exited and entered certain mountain peaks during its daily voyage: "Wayna Cápac kay pachata riki puntata chinkapushan" (Taped, 1985). [Of course, in this world Wayna Cápac is setting into a mountain peak.] Benito also drew a picture of the rising and setting suns which clearly shows their relation to the mountain peaks. First, he wrote, "Nindi chikapushan [chinkapushan] por arriba" [The sun sets in the higher moiety], and then he wrote, "Urimanta ninti llusimucsan [lloqsimushan] puntada" [The sun is rising from the mountain peaks in the lower moiety].[6] Then Benito explained how the rising and setting suns were correlated with certain mountain peaks. According to him, the sun rises from the Apu Yana Orqo in Tandaña, travels the sky during the day, and then sets into the Qheswawarani mountain peaks at dusk. In a similar way, Benito Nina, from Kauri, explained how certain mountain peaks were connected to the rising and setting suns there. Benito said that the sun rose from the Apu Ausangate in the east and set into the Apu Akanaku in the west (taped, 1985).

Based on these explanations, we note that the mountain peaks function as doorways to two worlds, the present world, called *kay pacha*, and the interior world, called *uku pacha*. This idea is recorded in Q'ero cloth with the use of the k'iraqey puntas motif, which borders both sides of inti.

Light-Colored Lines In versus Dark-Colored Lines Out

In Benito Salas's drawing of the rising and setting suns in Tandaña, he used distinct colors to represent these two periods of daily time. He drew sunrise with a colorless circle and sunset with a dark purple circle. During a conversation I had with him concerning the use of color to signify these two periods, Benito stated that when the sun first appears in the morning sky, it is red: "Kay Wayna Cápac lloqsimun hoq puntamanta, tutamanta las cuatro y mediata. Hina lloqsimun puka pukacha riki" (taped, 1986). [Wayna Cápac rises from the mountain peak at about 4:30 a.m. Of course it rises a red color, a little red.] Similarly, Juliana Samanta, from the hamlet of Chawpi Wasi, near Tandaña, drew me a picture of the rising sun, which she described as "Inti lloqsimushan orqomanta." [The sun is rising from the mountain.] Her rising sun is a large circle with two smaller circles placed one inside the other. The first circle was drawn with pink, the second with yellow, and the smallest with pink. She called the pink circles

Figure 4.3. The setting sun and rising sun, drawn by Sabino Ccuyro Cusihuamán. Ayllu Pongo, Chinchero. 1990.

Figure 4.2. The rising sun, drawn by Juliana Samanta. Chawpi Wasi, Totorani, 1985.

sonran, "shadow."[7] In this way Juliana showed how sunlight is composed of varying amounts of sunlight and shadow. I also collected drawings of rising and setting suns from Chinchero men. For example, Sabino Ccuyro Cusihuamán, who is thirty-six years old and lives in Pongobamba, drew a yellow rising sun and a dark orange setting sun. In this way Sabino also correlated light-colored lines with sunrise and dark-colored lines with sunset.

Juvenal Casaverde Rojas (1976:167) describes a similar relation between the use of light colors to symbolize sunrise and dark colors to symbolize sunset in the community of Kuyo Grande, Pisac: "Before rising, the sun is *llukusqa*, covered with the dark mantle of the night. From this it slowly rises until it remains totally visible and emits an incandescent red light, when it then turns yellow." Similarly, Juan Ossio (1973:387) states that in the community of Andamarca, Ayacucho, red is used to symbolize the east and sunrise, while black signifies the west and sunset.

The Q'ero represent these differences between a light-colored sunrise and a dark-colored sunset in their cloth by using light colors to signify dawn and dark colors to signify dusk. In order to comprehend the symbolic

Figure 4.4. The Q'ero rising sun is always woven with light colors, and the setting sun is always woven with dark colors.

meanings of color in Q'ero, we must also understand the relation between weaving technique, color, and motif significance.[8]

As we saw in Chapter 2, all the Q'ero inti motifs are woven with the kinsamanta weaving technique, in which two contrasting colors plus white are used to produce these designs. Kinsamanta creates a double-faced cloth in which the motif woven on the face of the fabric is produced on the opposite face of the fabric but in reverse. In other words, if inti lloqsimushan is woven on the face of the fabric, inti chinkapushan automatically appears on the opposite face.

Although there is a significant correlation between weaving technique, color, and motif signification, it is color that controls the meaning of the motifs. For example, in the ceremonial poncho pictured in Figure 4.4, inti lloqsimushan is woven with red as the dominant color and cranberry and white as the secondary colors, whereas inti chinkapushan is woven with cranberry as the dominant color and red and white as the secondary colors. The reverse of a red inti lloqsimushan is a cranberry inti chinkapushan and vice versa.

When a Q'ero weaver uses the kinsamanta weaving technique to produce these inti motifs, she must plan what the motif will look like on both

Table 4.1. Colors Used to Weave Sunrise and Sunset

Motif	Front Face	Reverse Face
Inti lloqsimushan	Sunrise, pink in	Sunset, gray out
Inti chinkapushan	Sunset, gray out	Sunrise, pink in
Inti lloqsimushan	Sunrise, red in	Sunset, purple out
Inti chinkapushan	Sunset, purple out	Sunrise, red in

faces of the fabric. She must then arrange her colors according to whether she is weaving a rising sun or a setting sun. In Table 4.1, we note that sunrise is never woven with dark colors, just as sunset is never woven with light colors.[9]

The Vertical Sonqocha Line: Half Sunlight and Half Shadow

To better understand how the Q'ero perceive sunlight and shadow, we can also look at the Quechua terminology used to express these two concepts. For example, the Quechua suffixes *mu* and *pu* are used in the words for sunrise and sunset, that is, inti lloqsi*mu*shan and inti chinka*pu*shan, respectively. We have already mentioned how the suffix *mu* means that the sunlight is coming toward Q'ero, that is, rising, while the suffix *pu* means that the sun is moving away from Q'ero, that is, setting (R. T. Zuidema, personal communication 1987; Cusihuamán 1976b:213–215). The suffix *pu* also suggests the idea that the sun is no longer benefiting the Q'ero because it is moving away from them (Taylor 1981:88), while *mu* suggests that the sun is benefiting them because it is moving toward them.

We can analyze the words *hatun inti* in the same way. First, *hatun* means "high" or "large" in Quechua and Aymara (Cusihuamán 1976a:53; Bertonio 1984:435). From a structural viewpoint, the high or large sun refers to inti at zenith, because it is the highest and brightest in the sky at noon. Second, hatun inti is composed of a vertical line, called *sonqocha*, "little heart," which indicates that there is a relation between sonqocha and a vertical location, the zenith, in the sky. Austina Flores Waman and Basilia Cruz, two weavers from K'allakancha, also called this vertical line *iskay t'aqapi*, while Benito Nina, from Kauri, called it *t'aqapi*, which means "separated into two" or "separated" (Cusihuamán 1976a:149). Thus the sonqocha line divides the day into equal parts of sunlight and shadow.

Table 4.2. Sunlight: Motifs and Their Meanings

Motif		Meaning
	Inti lloqsimushan	Amount of light to be used for the entire day
B A	Hatun inti	**Part A:** Sunlight left to be used **Part B:** Sunlight used in the morning
	Inti chinkapushan	All shadow has been used

Based on the data presented here, it is apparent that the very structure of hatun inti can be related to the various observational devices used by the Incas—the intiwatana, sunturhuasi, gnomon, and ushnu—to reckon daily time. Hatun inti can be viewed as the graphic representation of these Inca "sundials," in which the quantity and placement of the shadow distributed by the sun's rays indicated the time of day. Thus we can perceive Part A (the right half) of hatun inti as symbolizing the quantity of sunlight left for the day, while Part B (the left half) signifies the amount of sunlight already used. The vertical sonqocha line functions to separate light from shadow, dawn from dusk, and day from night.

To illustrate this idea, we can view the Q'ero inti motifs as a reservoir of energy, sunlight, or daily time. Each of these three inti motifs, inti lloqsimushan, hatun inti, and inti chinkapushan, signifies a different amount of sunlight, as shown in Table 4.2.

To understand how the Q'ero symbolize sunlight with light-colored lines radiating in toward the diamond, and shadow with dark-colored lines

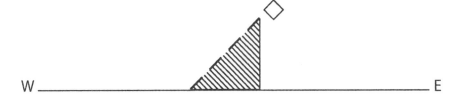

Figure 4.5. "El sol de la mañana," the morning sun.
The morning sun casts its shadow in the west.

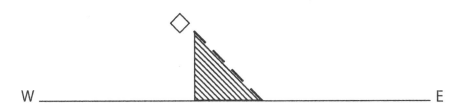

Figure 4.6. "El sol de la tarde," the afternoon sun.
The afternoon sun casts its shadow in the east.

radiating out toward the rectangular frame, we can look at the relation of these lines to the vertical sonqocha line: the morning sun casts its shadow in the west, and the afternoon sun casts its shadow in the east.

In effect, the sonqocha line and the light-and dark-colored radiating lines correspond to the sunlight, time, and energy spent during the day, suggesting, then, that the light-colored lines radiating inward signify the amount of sunlight available for the entire day, and that the dark-colored lines radiating outward symbolize the amount of shadow spent. Each motif can thus be compared to the amount of both sunlight and shadow available for the entire day.

We now understand how light-colored lines radiating in symbolize sunrise and dark-colored lines radiating out symbolize sunset, but we still need to comprehend where the sun goes during the night in order to rise again the next morning. We can understand the cyclical movement of the sun by seeing how the Q'ero interpret the relation between inti and the qocha.

Table 4.3. Sunlight and Shadow Compared

Motif		Sunlight	Shadow
	Inti lloqsimushan	Sunlight to be used for the entire day	No shadow in east or west
	Hatun inti	**Part A:** Light to be used during morning **Part B:** Sunlight left to be used	Shadow in west No shadow in east
	Inti chinkapushan	All sunlight has been used	All shadow has been used

⁜ Inti and Qocha ⁜

In Benito's description of the sun's twenty-four-hour trajectory in the Tandaña sky, he stated that inti traveled through a lake (qocha) situated in the interior world (uku pacha) in order to rise again the next morning. I asked Francisco Lara to explain the relation between the sun, the moon, and the interior lake:

Q: ¿Ima significan qochawan, intiwan, killawan?
   [What is the meaning of the lake with the sun and with the moon?]

A: Intiwan, qochawan, killawan. Killawan killaqa qocha chiri kasqa. Dios kamaraqan chayrayku intiqa alimentakun qochawan. Qochaman hayku inti. Chay mar chinkapunku inti.

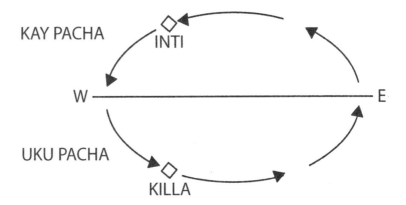

KAY PACHA

INTI

W ———————————————— E

UKU PACHA

KILLA

Figure 4.7. The cyclical movement of the sun and the moon.

[The sun with the lake and with the moon. With the moon, this moon cooled the lake. In this way, God made it that the sun nourishes itself with the lake. Inti enters from the lake. The sun sets into that lake.]

Q: ¿Y ima sutin kay qocha?
[And what is that lake called?]

A: Kay qocha sutin mar…sutin Oceano Atalantico. Kay qochatapi kashan allpa.
[This lake is called the sea…it is called the Atlantic Ocean. There is earth in that sea.]

(Taped, 1985).

In a similar way Benino Quispe, of K'allakancha, stated that the lake functioned to cool off the sun during the night:

Inti k'anchamushawanchis mana hina hinachu intiqa qochapuni. Kayta… qhawaranchis intiqa k'anchay tutamanta qochaylla unulla phawaymushan q'omer. Q'omer qocha phawaymushan inti. Lliuw, lliuw, lliuw qochalla mana intipuni hinachu q'ellutarachu k'anchamunqa. Inti qocha anchay vale.

(Taped, 1986)

[The sun's rays surely are not burning the lake. During the night, the sun's rays are flying completely into the lake, which is composed of green water. The sun is flying into the green water. Surely, all, all, all of the sun's yellow rays will not burn the lake. For that reason, inti and the qocha have value.][10]

I collected several drawings of the Q'ero and Kauri world made by male informants in which they always drew the qocha as a primary component. Benito Salas, of Tandaña, drew a three-part division of the world in which the qocha is composed of a huge, bodiless head from which small people are sprouting (Figure C24). He also included the kay pacha, placed in the center of his drawing, and the hanan pacha, situated at the top and composed of various stars (1985). A male informant from Kauri also drew his world as being formed with three parts: the left side is the hanan pacha, with various stars; the middle is the kay pacha, in which the triangles depict the mountain peaks; and the right side is formed with the qocha, made of blue water (1986) (Figure C25).

Francisco and Benino's descriptions of the relation between the sun, the moon, and the lake revealed several new ideas. First, the lake is composed of green water and earth. Second, both the sun and the moon travel through the qocha, but they function in different ways. The sun heats the qocha whereas the moon cools it off. Last, inti receives its energy by drinking the lake's water in order to rise again the next morning.

There is also a cyclical movement between the sun and the moon. When inti enters this world (kay pacha) through the doorways of the sacred mountains located in the east, the moon is leaving the kay pacha and entering the interior world of the uku pacha through the doorways of the sacred mountains located in the west. So while the sun is journeying through the sky during the day, giving off sunlight, the moon is traveling through the interior world in order to cool off its waters. Then inti enters the uku pacha and drinks its waters in order to rise again the next morning, while the moon travels through the sky in the kay pacha in order to bring moonlight to the night sky.

This cyclical movement of the sun and the moon between the kay pacha and the uku pacha is stored in Q'ero cloth with the four inti motifs: sunrise, inti lloqsimushan; zenith, hatun inti; sunset, inti chinkapushan; and midnight, tawa inti qocha. Urton (1981:68) describes a similar twenty-four-hour trajectory for the sun in the village of Misminay: "The sun rises from the east and moves through the sky from east to west. After entering the sea...it makes a twisting motion to the right (north) and begins its journey back to the east beneath the Vilcanota River. It takes all night for the sun to move from the *mar* (sea) to *Inti seqamuna* (sunrise)."

These three periods of daily time—sunrise, noon, and sunset— were worshiped by the Incas during the festival of Inti Raymi. Cristóbal de Molina ([1575] 1916:26) stated that the sun was worshiped at the site of Huancarani when it rose, at Korikancha at noon, and on Mount Aepiran when it set. Huancarani is located to the east of Cuzco, Mount Aepiran is situated to the west, and Korikancha is at the center of Cuzco. Thus inti was worshiped at three specific sites that correspond to the three stages of the sun's daily journey through the sky from sunrise to noon to sunset.

Ancient and contemporary Quechua dictionaries name these three periods of daily time:

Sunrise. *Pacarimun cecamun* [or] *ceccarcumun* [or] *pacarirccumun* (González Holguín [1608] 1989:671)

Sunrise. *Yndilluscimunc* [or] *yndiceccamunc* (Santo Tomás [1560] 1951:283)

East. *Intikk wach'inan* (Lira 1982:283)

Sunset. *Intiyaucun chincay cupun* [or] *yaucutamun chincaycutamun* (González Holguín [1608] 1989:671)

Sunset. *Yndiyaucuni, gui,* [or] *indicapani qui* (Santo Tomás [1560] 1951:301)

West. *Intikk muchuynin* (Lira 1982:283-284)

Zenith. *Intikk sayanan* (Lira 1982:283-284)

Zenith. *Yndip llucsimuc* [or] *yndipeccamunc* (Santo Tomás [1560] 1951:301)

Zenith, sun arrives to midday. *Inti ttiksumun ttiksuycumun* (González Holguín [1608] 1989:671)

Ethnolinguistic research conducted in the Department of Cuzco reveals the following terminology used to denote sunrise, noon, and sunset. I also collected one term used to depict midnight (anti-zenith):

Sunrise. *Inti lloqsimushan* (Q'ero; Silverman-Proust 1986a, 1987a)

Sunrise. *Inti seqay* (Cuzco; Cusihuamán 1976a:60)

East. *Inti seqamuna* (Misminay; Urton 1981)

Zenith. *Hatun inti* (Q'ero; Silverman-Proust 1986a, 1987a)

Zenith. *Doce inti* [or] *kushkan p'unchay* (Kauri; Silverman-Proust 1986a)

Zenith. *Chawpi p'unchay* (Cusihuamán 1976a:108)

Midnight (anti-zenith). *Kushka tuta* (Kauri; Silverman-Proust 1986a)

Sunset. *Inti chinkapushan* (Q'ero; Silverman-Proust 1986a, 1987a)

Sunset. *Inti haykuy* [or] *inti chinkaypun* (Kauri; Silverman-Proust 1986a)

Sunset. *Inti haykuy* (Cuzco; Cusihuamán 1976a:60)

West. *Mar, oceano* (Misminay; Urton 1981)[11]

The terminology I collected refers to textile motifs as well as the drawings made by informants from Q'ero, Kauri, Huancarani, and Chinchero.

Several problems arise when one attempts to correlate contemporary terminology for the three periods of daily time with the vocabulary used in ancient Quechua dictionaries. First, during the sixteenth century there was no standardization with reference to the words used to designate sunrise, zenith, and sunset. Second, since Santo Tomás used the verb *lloqsiy*, which means "to rise," to refer to both zenith and sunrise, there is some confusion as to the exact meaning of this verb. In addition, in the little data collected referring to temporal concepts among the contemporary Quechua of the Department of Cuzco, there is also a lack of standardization used to denote these three periods of daily time. But what is important to note is the fact that the contemporary Quechua, like their Inca ancestors, name these three periods of daily time based on their observations of sunlight and shadow cast by the sun and that these periods are graphically represented in Q'ero cloth with four inti motifs.

Para Tiempo and Osari Tiempo

Seasonal Time

The graphic elements comprising the Q'ero quartered diamond motif denote important ideas about seasonal time. Four graphic elements are fundamental for understanding how the Q'ero perceive the seasons: isosceles triangles, long and short radiating lines, the vertical line, and the cross. Not only do these graphic elements denote ideas about hot and cold, dry and wet, but they also refer to ideas about germination, life, and death.

⁜ Terminology ⁜

The tawa inti qocha motif, like all the other Q'ero diamond motifs, is called by the general term *inti*, the sun. But when the Q'ero identify the graphic elements that form this motif, they call it tawa inti qocha. For example, one day I was weaving tawa inti qocha with Rosa Chura, of Tandaña, and she identified the graphic elements that compose this motif in the following way. First, she called the overall diamond *inti*. Then she called the three diamonds placed one inside the other in decreasing size *pupu*, "navel," or *pata*, "zone." Next she called the light-colored lines radiating in, as well as the dark-colored lines radiating out, *chakra*, "field." Then she named the vertical line, *sonqocha*, "little heart." Last, she called the X that quarters the diamond, *qocha*, "lake." When I asked her how many suns there were, she replied, "Tawa inti kashan" (taped, 1986). [There are four suns.] Rosa then named the entire motif: "Tawa kashan inti. Ñanchata" (taped, 1986). [There are four suns. And a little road.][1]

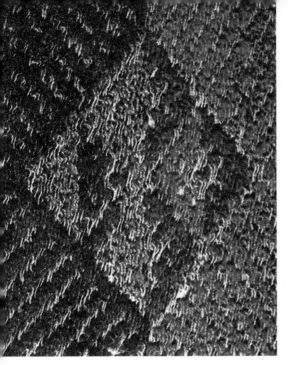

Figure 5.1. The quartered diamond as woven in the Q'ero lliklla.

Why do Q'ero informants read this motif as depicting four suns and a lake? What do these graphic elements have to do with seasonal time? Before demonstrating how the graphic elements of tawa inti qocha denote ideas about seasonal time, I discuss how seasonal time was reckoned by the Incas.

⚜ Seasonal Time among the Incas ⚜

In Chapter 4 we saw how the Incas used observational devices such as pillars, towers, and vertically aligned poles to calculate daily time. According to the chroniclers, the Incas used similar observational devices to figure seasonal time (Guamán Poma [1615] 1980; Garcilaso [1609] 1960:34-35; Cobo [1653] 1956:251; Sarmiento de Gamboa [1572] 1942:93; Acosta [1590] 1979:283; Polo de Ondegardo [1585] 1916:16-17). The observation of the June and December solstices was important for helping the Incas coordinate their agricultural and pasturing duties with a state calendar (Zuidema 1983; Aveni 1981).

Acosta ([1590] 1979:283) described twelve pillars, called *succanga*, which were raised in the mountains around Cuzco to calculate the rising and setting suns for each month. Polo de Ondegardo ([1585] 1916:16-17) stated that the pillar called *chiroa sucanca* was used to observe the June solstice, and the one called *pucuy sucanca* was used to observe the December solstice. In a similar way, Garcilaso ([1609] 1960:34-35) described how the Incas constructed eight towers "on either side of the city of Cuzco, four of which faced the rising and four the setting sun. Each one of these groups of constructions comprised two small towers, about three stades in height, surrounded by two other, much higher towers. All these towers were separated regularly about 18-20 feet one from the other. The tall ones...seemed to indicate the place between which the sun rose and set at the time of the solstice." Sarmiento de Gamboa (1572] 1942:93), in contrast, described four poles that were situated in the high mountains of Cuzco. A small hole was made at the top of each pole, and when the sun passed through it, the people knew that it was time to plow or time to plant.

Urton (1981:6-7) discusses the contradictory descriptions given by the Spanish chroniclers concerning the structures used by the Incas to tell seasonal time. None of the accounts agree on the number of observational devices used or the types of structures made, some describing towers and others pillars or poles. Nevertheless, we can note two important points: first, it is certain that the Incas built observational devices to reckon seasonal time, and second, whatever the device used, they all exhibit the same form, that is, a vertically aligned structure against which sunlight and shadow were measured. Let us now examine how the Q'ero read the four graphic elements of tawa inti qocha as they refer to seasonal time.

✢ Seasonal Time: How the Q'ero ✢ Read the Graphic Elements

K'iraqey Puntas

The first graphic element woven in tawa inti qocha which denotes ideas about seasonal time is the secondary k'iraqey puntas motif. We have already seen how k'iraqey puntas represents the mountain peaks that function as doorways for the sun to move between the kay pacha (present world) and the uku pacha (interior world). These mountain peaks are also important in determining seasonal time.

In Chapter 4 we saw how the Tandaña sun rises and sets from certain mountain peaks during the year. Benito Salas Pauccar described how the sun rose in Tandaña from the Yana Orqo Mountains and then set into the Qheswawarani Mountains. Each day, the Tandaña sun rises a little farther to the north and sets a little farther to the south, until the solstice, when it reverses its daily journey.

Anthony Aveni (1981:62-63) describes how the change in the position of the rising and setting sun along the horizon allowed the Incas to establish an annual calendar. The Incas used the horizon as a calibration device in which specific mountain peaks and valleys functioned as time markers. According to Aveni (1981:62-63), the points on the horizon at which the sun rises and sets "do not change at a uniform rate throughout the year. In the low altitudes, such as those inhabited by the civilizations of Mexico (20 degrees N) and Peru (15 degrees S), the range of horizon covered annually by sunrise and sunset points is smaller, and consequently, the daily change is less. Around the time of the solstices, they change their position very little, while during the equinoxes their contact point with the horizon shifts noticeably from day to day."

This difference in the daily change in the sun's horizon point is clearly pictured in a drawing made by Benito Salas Pauccar of two rising and two setting suns (Figure C26). First, Benito drew a sun rising from the mountain peaks in the southeast, and then he drew it setting in the mountain peaks in the northwest. Then he sketched a second sun rising from the mountain peaks in the northeast and drew it setting into the mountains in the southwest.

I asked Benito, "¿Sapa killa, inti lloqsimushan kikin orqo puntapi, o cambianchu?" [Is the sun rising from the same mountain peak every month or does it change?] He replied, "Cambian. Para tiempo, lloqsimun kaymanta. Abrilmanta lloqsimun kaymanta" (taped, 1985). [It changes. During the rainy season, it rises from here. From April, it rises from there.] Benito called the first set of rising and setting suns *para tiempo*, "rainy season," and the second set *osari tiempo*, "cold season" (taped, 1986).

Similar descriptions of the sun's changing rising and setting positions on the horizon are found in the Andean literature. For instance, Grebe Vicuña (personal communication, 1988) has collected both Mapuche and Isluga drawings that clearly depict a series of rising and setting suns along different points on the horizon.

Differences in Line Length: Chakran, Loran, and Suñkha

The long and short radiating lines of the inti motifs also refer to seasonal time. In addition to Benito Salas Pauccar, several other male Q'ero informants described the two seasons, para tiempo, the rainy season, and osari or osaq tiempo, the cold season. Para tiempo occurs from September to April, during which time the sun, the moon, and the stars are rarely seen in Q'ero. Martín Salas Cápac told me, "Setiembremanta pacha para haykun hasta mayo" (taped, 1986). [The rains come from September to May.] And Benito Salas Pauccar said, "Para tiempo mana estrellatapis rikunkichu" (taped, 1986). [During the rainy season you never see the stars.][2] Osari tiempo, in contrast, is a shorter period that lasts from May to August and is characterized by cold, sunny days with almost no cloud cover: "Maynin p'unchay intitapis rikunku...osari tiempupiqa a veceslla phuyuramun rakuchalla osari tiempupiqa" (taped, 1986) [They see the sun during the day...sometimes during osari tiempo there is a little cloud cover.][3]

The Q'ero name the sun according to inti's visibility in the Tandaña sky. For instance, during osari tiempo the sun is always seen and so it is called *hatun inti*: "Osari Tiempo hatun inti hamushan" (Martín Cápac, taped, 1986). [During osari tiempo, a large sun is appearing.] During para tiempo, in contrast, the sun is rarely seen and is said to be small and weak, so there is no name for it during this season: "Mana kanchu sutin Intipaq para tiempo" (Agustino Machaca, taped, 1986). [There is no name for inti during para tiempo.]

It is not the size of the sun that allows us to understand how the Q'ero perceive seasonal time, but the length of the sun's beard in relation to growing plants, which is depicted in the inti motifs as radiating lines. Several different Quechua terms that refer to ideas about sexual arousal, regeneration, and growth were used by both Q'ero and Kauri informants to identify these radiating lines.

First, when the Q'ero talk about the ideas concerning seasonal time which are recorded in their inti motifs, they call both sets of radiating lines (long/short, light color/dark color) *chakran*, which is Quechua for "field," "his/her/its field," or "agricultural field." For example, a K'allakancha weaver, Austina Waman, called the radiating lines in both inti lloqsimushan and inti chinkapushan "*chakran*" (taped, 1985). *Chakran* was the term used by all the Q'ero weavers for these radiating lines. A second Quechua word used for these lines was *lorayan* or *loran* (stems, roots). For instance, Basilia Cruz, also from K'allakancha, called the lines woven in inti lloqsimushan and inti chinkapushan "loran...loranchan...inti loran kashan" (taped, 1985). [Stems and roots...little stems and little roots...the sun has stems and roots.]

A Kauri star watcher, Benito Nina Warkasaya, called the long lines woven in the Q'ero inti motifs *intiq suñkha*, "the sun's beard," and said that the short lines had no name: "Mana sutin kanchu" (taped, 1986). [There is no name.] An important idea about seasonal time is represented with this term. *Suñkha* refers to facial hairs: "a beard, the entire facial hairs or those which develop on the beard" (Lira 1982:275). *Suñkha* also refers to reproduction, "the act of passing the beard in front of a person." "To pass the beard in front of the woman before the sexual act. It is a custom which indicates passion of the lover and which is sometimes done with a kiss" (Lira 1982:275).

Hair used as a symbol for sexual arousal has been widely described in the South American anthropological literature. For example, Peter Roe (1982:222) states that "hair is usually a symbol for unbridled libidinous

Figure 5.2. The sun grows a beard during the December solstice (Guamán Poma [1615] 1980:180).

Figure 5.3. The sun is beardless during the June solstice (Guamán Poma [1615] 1980:172).

energy, either generally or specifically in South American culture." In addition, Stephen Hugh-Jones (1976:109) describes Barasana women as becoming sexually aroused on seeing hair: "They also menstruate, a condition in which their vaginas become 'open,' as a result of seeing their hair."

In light of this reading of all the radiating lines as *chakran*, "his/her/its field," and *loran*, "stems and roots," we can see that these lines represent the agricultural fields with plants in various stages of growth. Only the long radiating lines represent the plants that are growing tall in the fields, because the term used to identify these long lines, *suñkha*, refers to both sexual arousal and regenerative forces, whereas there is no name for the short lines, because they represent vacant fields that have already been harvested.

Support for my argument that the long radiating lines in the Q'ero *inti* motifs refer to the sun's beard, the height of growing plants, sexual arousal, and regenerative forces can be found in one of the drawings of Guamán Poma de Ayala ([1615] 1980:232), who clearly shows *inti* with a long beard during the Inca festival of Cápac Raymi. Cápac Raymi took place during December, the time of the summer solstice in the Southern Hemisphere and also the middle of the rainy season. R. T. Zuidema (personal communication, 1987) relates the beard worn by *inti* during Cápac Raymi to the height of the plants growing in the fields, because during para tiempo the maturing plants stand tall in the fields. This image can be contrasted with Guamán Poma's ([1615] 1980:172) depiction of the sun during Inti Raymi, in which *inti* does not wear a beard. This is because during mid-June, the time of the winter solstice, the fields are barren because they have been harvested.

An analysis of the relation between seasonal time and the sun's beard or lack of beard, the height of growing plants, and both the long and short radiating lines in the Q'ero inti motifs indicates that the long lines represent the growing plants during the rainy season while the short lines signify the recently harvested and now barren fields during the cold season.

The next graphic element that the Q'ero read as referring to seasonal time is the vertical line.

Mayu: The Milky Way

The Q'ero call the vertical line Mayu, meaning "river" in Quechua, and it is the name for the Milky Way (Aveni 1981; Urton 1981:103; Zuidema 1982a).

The Q'ero view the Mayu as halving the night sky. For instance, Benito Salas Pauccar's drawing of the sky in Tandaña exhibits a long, horizontally penciled line that runs from the mountain peaks bordering the right half of his drawing all the way over to the mountain peaks bordering the left half. Benito called this line Mayu, the celestial river. He then proceeded to draw various constellations (and killa, the moon) on both sides of the Mayu and named them: Para Tiempo, Osari Tiempo, Mayu, Pasión Cruz, Sepultura, Q'oto, Killa, Llama Kancha, Oveja Kancha, Llama Ñawi, and La Mar, Qocha (taped, 1986). I then asked Benito why there was a mayu, and he replied: "Mayu, ah. Esta Pasión Cruz. Kashan Llama Ñawi,[4] kashan Oveja Kancha, Llama Kancha, Mayu kashan" (taped, 1986). [Ah, the River. There is the Cross of the Passion. There is the Eye(s) of the Llama, there is the Sheep Corral, the Llama Corral, there is the River.] In this way Benito showed how the vertical line woven in Q'ero cloth represents the Milky Way, the celestial river, which can be used to locate certain constellations in the sky.

Next I discuss the various stars in Benito's drawing as they refer to seasonal time.

The Cross of the Passion

An important group of stars drawn by Benito was a large purple cross that he called Pasión Cruz, the Cross of the Passion. Benito placed it above the Mayu, on the right half of the drawing very close to the mountain peaks. He drew it as a large cross composed of eight stars: three stars formed the top of the cross, two formed the bottom, and one was at the center with a star at each end. Benito Nina, from Kauri, also drew Pasión Cruz with eight stars.

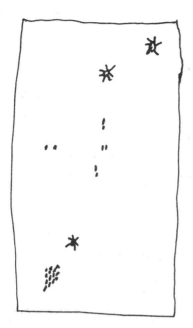

Figure 5.4. Benito Nina's drawing of stars in the night sky. From top to bottom: Llama Ñawi, Pasión Cruz, Ch'aska, and Q'oto. 1986.

Urton (1981:134) reproduced a drawing of the Pasión Cruz star by an informant from Lucre which is composed of "two intersecting line of stars with small dots along one side of it." The Pasión Cruz drawn by Benito Salas may be what Urton calls Hatun Cruz (1981:43), which is related to the arrival and disappearance of the June solstice.

Sepultura

Sepultura is another group of stars that forms a cross in the sky. Benito Salas Pauccar drew it below the Milky Way.

Like Pasión Cruz, Sepultura is formed with eight stars, but their size and arrangement are different. Sepultura is composed of a pair of intersecting lines with three stars in triangular form making up the top, and two stars at the bottom of this first line. Then it is intersected with a horizontal line with a star in its center and one at both ends, as in Pasión Cruz. Pasión Cruz is drawn with bigger dots for the stars, however, and the cross is much larger.

Sepultura is Spanish for "interment, tomb, or grave." Benito said that Sepultura marked the disappearance of the solstices: "Sepultura. Wañunaykupas raymi kan. Wañunaykupaq significan" (taped, 1986). [Sepultura. In order that the solstices will die. It means in order (for it) to die.] Sepultura may be Urton's (1981:108) *chakana*, the Belt of Orion.

Q'oto

Benito also drew the Pleiades, which he called *Q'oto*. *Q'oto* means "frozen and cold" in Quechua (Lira 1982:154; Cusihuamán 1976a:76). He drew this group of stars as a large circular object filled with different-colored (green, purple, yellow) stars. He did not say how many stars compose Q'oto.

Figure 5.5. "Kcoto chasca," drawn by Francisco Lara. Kauri, 1985.

Figure 5.6. "Q'oto," drawn by Prudencio Hakawaya. Kauri, 1985.

I also collected drawings of Q'oto by two Kauri star watchers, Francisco Lara and Prudencio Hakawaya. Francisco drew what he called "Kcoto Chasca" as a large pointed star with many stars inside it, and Prudencio drew "Q'oto" as a cluster of seven stars in an oval form (1986).[5]

The Pleiades are important to the Q'ero for predicting the weather for the next year and determining when to plant in each of the three zones they exploit. The Q'ero observe the Pleiades on two separate dates in order to make weather predictions. For example, Luis Damaso, who lives in K'allakancha, explained that the Q'ero look at the Pleiades on August 1 to predict the weather for the month of August of the next year. Then, on August 2, they read the Pleiades to judge the weather for the month of September of the next year, and on August 3 to predict the weather for the month of October, and so on until all twelve months are read. The Q'ero repeat the process in mid-August, reading for the month of August on August 13, the month of September on August 14, the month of October on August 15, and so on until the entire year has been read.

Using a different method, the Q'ero also watch the Pleiades on June 24. According to Luis Damaso (taped, 1986), on this day the Q'ero divide the Pleiades into three parts. When the top section is clear and bright, planting will begin in August. When the middle section is clear, planting will begin in November, and when the bottom section is bright, planting will begin in December. Urton (1981:118) describes a similar prediction method for Misminay: "rear part, October and November, head of the group, late July through September."

The importance of the Pleiades in Inca and Quechua astronomy and calendrics has been described in the literature (Aveni 1981; Zuidema 1982a; Urton 1981). Aveni (1981:297), for instance, states that the Pleiades' appearance and disappearance are "used to set up the local agricultural calendar." Both my Q'ero data and that collected by Urton in Misminay show that in the Cuzco area the appearance of the Pleiades is related to the success or failure of the coming harvest.

Oveja Kancha and Llama Kancha

Oveja kancha means "sheep corral" in Quechua, and *llama kancha* means "llama corral." Benito drew both corrals as rectangular clusters of stars. First, using purple and green dots, he drew Llama Kancha as a vertically aligned rectangle. Then he drew Oveja Kancha to the right of Llama Kancha, aligned in a horizontal manner and also formed with purple and green stars. But the stars that compose Oveja Kancha are closer together and there are more of them than in Llama Kancha. Both corrals are in the middle of the night sky at the upper part of the Milky Way.[6]

Urton (1981:100) describes a constellation in the Misminay sky called "Llama Cancha," a "group of 56 stars." Lizarraga (1988:8) depicts the planet Jupiter accompanied by a group of three llamas. Is there a relation between Llama Kancha and the planet Jupiter?

Llama Ñawi

Llama Ñawi, "Llama Eye," is the name Benito Salas Pauccar gave the two small dots he drew right next to Pasión Cruz, bordering the celestial river. Benito Nina drew Llama Ñawi as two stars with a small dot in the center of each one.

This star has been identified by Zuidema (1982a) and Urton (1981) as representing Alpha Centauri and Beta Centauri. According to Zuidema (1982a:104), Alpha Centauri and Beta Centauri, along with the Pleiades and the Southern Cross, were used by the Incas "for constructing a sidereal lunar calendar of 328 nights."[7]

Killa

Killa is the Quechua name for the moon. I gathered very little information about the moon in Q'ero because I was told that killa and inti are the same but function in different ways (see Chapter 4). The Q'ero believe that the sun heats the sky whereas the moon cools the sky, and that both bring light.

Table 5.1. Relation of the Moon and the Sun in Q'ero Motifs

Shadow/Light	Misminay Moon	Q'ero Sun
All light	Pura	Inti lloqsimushan
Half shadow	Cuscan	Hatun inti
All shadow	Wanu	Inti chinkapushan

Interestingly, Urton (1981:83-85) illustrates different phases of the moon as described in Misminay which can be related to the Q'ero inti motifs: *pura*, full moon; *cuscan* or *chawpi*, half moon; and *wanu*, no moon. We can compare the different amounts of sunlight and shadow found in the Q'ero inti motifs—inti lloqsimushan, hatun inti, and inti chinkapushan—with the different amounts of moonlight and shadow found in Urton's moons (see table 5.1). Urton also found that the moon was used in Misminay "in deciding when best to plant potatoes" (1981:85).

La Mar, Qocha

Benito drew an oval object at the left edge of his drawing which he called *la mar, qocha*. This object represents the lake found in the uku pacha. As we saw in Chapter 4, the sun rises from and sets into the interior lake in order to rise again the next day. I return to the qocha and lakes in general, in Chapter 9 when I discuss the organizational principles that structure the Inca and Andean world.

The Cross

The last graphic element woven in tawa inti qocha which denotes ideas about seasonal time is the cross. The Q'ero use two different terms to identify this element. First, they call it *cruz*, Spanish for "cross." For example, Prudencio Hakawaya described tawa inti qocha with four terms, including a cross: "Inti cruzwan. Estrellapi chawpi. Mayu. Ñan" (taped, 1985). [The sun with a cross. Stars are in the center. River. Road.][8] In a similar way, Benito Nina Wakasaya, also from Kauri, called the cross woven in tawa inti qocha: "Inti cruzwan. Intiman cruz kashan" (taped, 1985). [The sun with a cross. From the sun there is a cross.] Second, they call the cross *iskay raymi*, "two solstices." Cilio Quispe Waman, of K'allakancha, for example, said: "Iskay raymi kashan" (taped, 1985). [There are two solstices.] Luis Damaso, also from K'allakancha, looked at a colored photograph of

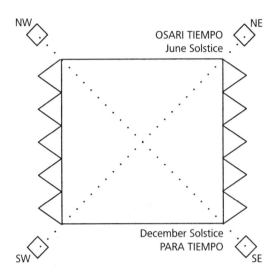

Figure 5.7. Iskay Raymi, the June and December solstices.

tawa inti qocha and said, "Raymi iskaylla kan" (taped, 1985). [There are only two solstices.] Both Sabino Quispe and Martin Pauccar Salas, from K'allakancha and Tandaña, respectively, called the cross found in tawa inti qocha *iskay raymi*, "two solstices" (taped, 1985, 1986).

This cross is also represented in Benito's drawing of celestial space: his two rising and setting suns form an imaginary cross. Benito's drawing is in agreement with Benito Nina Warkasaya, who expressly said that the cross came from the sun. Earlier in this chapter I discussed these rising and setting suns in relation to the mountain peaks. But here I want to discuss the imaginary cross they form in the Tandaña sky.

As we recall, Benito Salas first drew a rising sun in the southeast and showed how it set in the northwest. Then he drew a second rising sun in the northeast and showed how it set in the southwest. He called these sets of suns *para tiempo*, "rainy season," and *osaq tiempo*, "dry season" (taped, 1986).

The solstices refer to seasonal time. For example, Luis Damaso said: "Juniopi hasta Juliopi nishu ruphay. Enero hasta febrero, nishu para" (taped, 1985). [From June to July, it is too hot. From January to February, there is too much rain.] Informants also stated that para tiempo represents the December solstice, which falls on the 24th, and osari tiempo represents the June solstice, which also falls on the 24th. These dates mark the midpoints of the rainy and dry seasons.[9]

The imaginary axes made by the rising and setting suns for the December and June solstices quarter the Tandaña sky. In Misminay, however, Urton (1981:68) found that celestial space was quartered by the axes made by the rising and setting of the Milky Way during the year: "the overall twenty-four-hour pattern of the Milky Way as it crosses the zenith is two intersecting, intercardinal axes.... In this way, the celestial sphere is divided into quarters (*suyus*)."

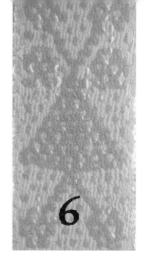

6

Lista

A Color Classification for Goods

In 1955, when Oscar Núñez del Prado conducted the first anthropological expedition to Q'ero, he was surprised to come upon Lázaro Quispe using a quipu to keep track of the hacienda owner's herds. It had long been thought that this Inca tool had disappeared from the Andes.

Demetrio Túpac Yupanqui, writing in the Lima newspaper *La Prensa*, described the quipu: "The quipu is knotted in ones, tens, and hundreds. There is no sign for numbers over one hundred. They calculate with these three numbers. The ones are attached to fine threads, while the tens are composed of thicker or doubled threads that are connected to the hundreds" (1955b:2). Oscar Núñez del Prado (1990:173-174) discussed how the quipu he saw in 1955 was related to the multicolored stripes of the Q'ero Wayako: "after the number of ears of corn placed into a bag were counted, colored threads marked the place where the kernels reached." Thirty years later Marcia and Robert Ascher (1981:69) reproduced a bag, similar to the wayakos being woven in Q'ero today.

The wayako shown by Ascher and Ascher is formed with a single piece of fabric, sewn together on both sides, with a doubled string attached to an upper corner. A series of stripes is

Figure 6.1. The Q'ero wayako is similar to the quipu maker's bag used in the mid-1950s in Q'ero.

woven throughout. Unfortunately, as this bag was reproduced in black in white, we do not know what colors were used for the stripes.

Nevertheless, it can be compared with the contemporary wayako, which is also woven of a single piece of fabric and sewn up both sides, leaving the top open. Unlike the 1955 quipu bag, however, which is decorated with stripes running throughout, the contemporary wayako has four decorative panels: alternating white and red stripes called *chili puka*, multicolored stripes called *listas*, the secondary kiraqey puntas motif, and a centrally located panel that is woven with either a ch'unchu motif type or different types of inti.

❀ Lista Woven in the Q'ero Wayako ❀

The lista motif panel is woven on both sides of the wayako, between panels 1 and 3. It never occurs next to the principal motif panel in Q'ero cloth woven with kinsamanta, the three-color complementary warp-faced technique.

Figure 6.2. Listas woven in the Q'ero wayako.

Lista has two main characteristics: the use of multicolored stripes and variations in stripe width. For example, in the wayako reproduced in Figure 6.2 there are the following colors and stripe widths: 3 red threads, 1 orange thread, 3 pink, 3 red, 1 orange, 1 red, 1 orange, 3 red, 2 pink, 2 black, 2 pink, 2 black, 2 pink, 2 black, and 2 red (Silverman-Proust 1988d:38; 1983; 1984: 281–308). The lista panel woven on the other half of this wayako is exactly like the first half except that it is a mirror image of the first. Red, orange, pink, and black are used to weave lista in this bag, but the Q'ero also use cranberry and various hues of red and purple.

In Q'ero, lista is woven only in the men's ceremonial poncho and the wayako. The latter is used by both men and women. Lista is never woven in the lliklla or in the ceremonial coca bag (ch'uspa).

⁜ Warping and Weaving of Lista in Q'ero ⁜

Lista is warped on a four-stake horizontal ground loom using the techniques and weaving tools described in Chapter 2. I wove *lista* many times while learning how to weave in Q'ero and throughout the Department of Cuzco. For example, one day in 1985 I was learning how to weave the contemporary Q'ero ch'unchu motif called ch'unchu inti pupu with Felipa Pauccar in Chuwa Chuwa. We decided to weave in her house, as her son, Cristóbal, was sick. In fact, Felipa told me she did most of her weaving inside her house because Cristóbal had a bad heart and was too weak to be outside for any length of time.

We set up a four-stake horizontal ground loom on the floor of her house. First, Felipa pounded a vertical stake (*takarpu*) into the earth floor. Then, with a measuring cord (*tupu*), she aligned a second stake horizontally to the first one and also pounded it into the ground. Next she gave Cristóbal two more takarpus, which he aligned with the first two and pounded into the ground. The next step consisted of attaching a horizontally aligned pole (*awa k'aspi*) to the two takarpus, tying them together with a braided rope (*warak'a*) called *awa watana*. In this way Felipa and Cristóbal constructed a rectangular weaving loom.

Once the loom had been formed, they began the warping process. First, Felipa took a ball of yarn and tied it to the awa k'aspi to her left. Then they began passing it back and forth over and under the two awa k'aspis, forming a large figure eight in which the warp threads make a cross in the middle.

In order to warp for lista, Felipa first chose all the colored yarns she would use for this motif by placing one color with another and then deciding if it was beautiful (*munaycha*) or ugly (*millay*). She finally settled on red, black, and purple as her lista colors.

Then she began warping. First, she took a red ball of yarn, tucked one end of it into the threads that had previously been warped on the awa k'aspi bar, and, placing it over the awa k'aspi, passed it over to Cristóbal, who put it under and then over his bar and passed it back to Felipa. Felipa tucked this red ball of yarn into the previously warped threads, without breaking them from the ball of yarn, and then picked up a black ball of yarn. She tucked a black thread into the previously warped threads to her left, placed it over the awa k'aspi, and then passed it back to Cristóbal, who put it under and then over the awa k'aspi and then passed it back to Felipa. They continued to warp like this for black, then purple, and then the principal motif, followed by lista, until the entire belt was warped. Last, they formed the stick shed, the heddles, and the chukrukata, the process used to create the uncut selvages, just as I described in Chapter 2. Only when Felipa finished the chukrukata did she break the loose warping threads. Finally, Felipa began weaving several rows of plain weave before beginning the main motif panel (Silverman-Proust 1988d).

❧ Lista Woven in the Department of Cuzco ❧

The multicolored lista stripe panel is also woven outside Q'ero throughout the Department of Cuzco in such communities as Kauri, Paucartambo, Calca, Pisac, Markapata, Lauramarka, and Huancarani (Gisbert et al. 1987; Rowe 1977; Silverman, ed. 1991b; Zorn 1979). There it is woven in the lliklla, poncho, carrying cloths (qhepina, unkhuña), and belts. For example, multicolored lista stripes that are also characterized by width differences are woven in Markapata. In the Markapata lliklla, seven lista stripes are woven in white, red, blue, yellow, and purple. But only the yellow stripe, located in the middle of this panel, is wider than the other stripes. In the lliklla I collected near Ocongate in 1980, lista resembles the Markapata lliklla in terms of colors used as well as stripe width. This lliklla is also composed of seven lista stripes. All are of the same width, except for the yellow stripe, which is the widest and located in the middle of the panel.

In ponchos collected throughout the Pisac-Calca highlands, the lista panel displays slight variations in both width and color. For instance, in the poncho reproduced in Figure 6.3, which was woven in the Pisac highlands, lista is woven with red, pink, and green stripes. The red stripe is wider than the others. Multicolored lista stripes also decorate ponchos, llikllas, unkus, qhepinas, and unkhuñas woven throughout Bolivia (Cochabamba, Lleque, Yanahuaya, Tarabuco) (Gisbert et al. 1987; Meisch 1988; Silverman, ed. 1991a).[1]

A comparison of lista woven in Q'ero and non-Q'ero textiles reveals two important points. First, only in Q'ero textiles is lista woven with the colors red, pink, cranberry, orange, dark purple, black, and gray, while outside Q'ero it is woven with bright colors such as yellow, blue, and green. Second, only the lista stripes woven in Q'ero display significant differences in stripe width. Outside Q'ero, only the centrally located stripe is wider than the other lista stripes.

It is also interesting to note that the term *lista* is one of the few Spanish words used to identify Q'ero motifs. *Lista* means "slip of paper, shred of linen, a list or strip of cloth. Selvage, the edge of cloth" (Velásquez 1974:431).

Figure 6.3. Listas woven in the Pisac poncho.

Figure 6.4. The Inca chromatic quipu (Radicati 1990:50B). Courtesy of CONCYTEC.

And *listado* means "striped" (Zorn 1986:304). Thus *lista* refers to either stripes woven in cloth or a slip of paper. Are the lista stripes woven in Q'ero related to a piece of paper? Do these stripes list something?

In her pioneering work Verónica Cereceda (1978:1033) asked if the stripes woven in the Isluga *talega* (wayako) were not related to the language knotted in the Inca quipu. Whereas Cereceda relates quipu to language, I connect quipu to writing because the striped lista motif functions as a sign.

Here I demonstrate how the lista motif that is woven in Q'ero cloth in particular, and in contemporary Quechua and Aymara cloth in general, records information much as the Inca quipu does, because the Q'ero lista motif probably evolved from both the Inca quipu and the quipu bag. I base my argument on several kinds of evidence: (1) the similarity in form and function between a Q'ero talega or wayako collected in 1955, which contained a quipu, and the contemporary Q'ero wayako and *pukllay p'acha* (a braided rope used for dancing); (2) the similarity in function between the Q'ero lista motif and the Inca quipu; and (3) the connection between the lista motif and a color classification for corn.

In order to explore the answers to these questions, I began asking Q'ero men if they had any quipus. Everyone interviewed said that there were no quipus now in Q'ero but that there had been quipus many years ago. For example, I asked Benito Salas Pauccar if he had any quipus, and he said, "Quipu mana kanchu kunan" (taped, 1986). [There are no quipus now.] But he went into his storehouse and came out with something that he said was a present-day quipu: "Kan pukllay p'acha.... Ñawpa Inka tusunanpaq. Kan quipu" (taped, 1986). [This is a pukllay p'acha.... The ancient Incas used it for dancing. It is a quipu.][2]

The Q'ero pukllay p'acha is composed of a wide braided belt called a *warak'a tusuypaq* (a rope for dancing) decorated with gray and pink repeating isosceles triangles as well as repeating diamonds (ñawi). Benito said these were ancient Inca motifs ("Ñawpa Inka pallay" [taped, 1986]). Hanging from the braided belt are a series of twenty braided cords called *karana*. These cords display differences in braiding technique, color, and cord width. The first fourteen karanas are made with natural brown and dyed orange llama wool. The fifteenth karana is braided with dyed purple and black llama wool. These are all braided in the same widths and use the same braiding technique. The last five karanas, in contrast, are braided with natural brown and dyed pink llama wool. They are half the width of the first fifteen cords and are braided using a different technique.

Running horizontally through the karanas are doubled threads. A doubled purple thread and seven dyed pink threads run through all the cords. Spaced at intervals and tied onto the pukllay p'acha are five inch-long threads that form thick tassels. Benito called these *patilla* or *castilla*. They are arranged in the following manner: the left half of the first row is red, and the right half is cranberry and red. The second row is all pink. The third row is made up of two rows of dark blue, one above the other. The fourth row is all red. Benito called them *castilla chukcha puka patilla* (red hair-like fringe), *castilla chukcha panti patilla* (pink hair-like fringe), and *castilla chukcha azul patilla* (blue hair-like fringe [taped, 1986]).

Miguel Salas Espinosa looked at these pukllay p'acha and told me that the karana threads were a type of quipu. Miguel also stated that his grandfather had made this pukllay p'acha: "Mana kanchu quipukamayoq kunan Q'eropi. Abuelaymi atin leyeta pero ñoqa mana atinichu. Mana pipas atinchu leyeta kay quipu kunan. Sasapuni" (taped, 1986). [There are no qipukamayoqs (quipu makers) in Q'ero now. My grandfather could read the quipu, but I can't read it. No one can read it now. It is very difficult (to read.)]

Figure 6.5. The Q'ero pukllay p'acha. Tandaña, 1985.

The Q'ero lista motif and the pukllay p'acha display some of the same characteristics. Both use different-colored threads and different thread widths. These two traits are also found in the Inca quipu. These connections between the Q'ero lista motif, the pukllay p'acha, and the Inca quipu are corroborated by Laura Laurencich Minelli and Paulina Numhauser (2004:184), who describe numerous kinds of quipus not mentioned before the publication of the chronicle Exsul Immeritus Blas Valera Populo Suo. One of them is the *pucclacohuarmakipu* (*pukllaqo warma kipu*, "the children's quipu for play"), used by noble Inca children to learn how to read the quipu by singing *tican tican* (his/her/its flower).

⁑ The Inca Quipu ⁑

The Spanish chroniclers are an important source of information concerning the Inca quipu (Acosta [1590] 1979:290-291; Cieza de León [1553] 1985; Cobo [1653] 1956:251-257; Garcilaso [1609] 1960:23; Guamán Poma [1650] 1980:251; Murua [1590] 1962:56-57). Cobo ([1653] 1956:254) described the quipu as being composed of "diverse strings of different colors, and on each string there were several knots." Garcilaso ([1609] 1960:158) stated that "the cords were of different widths and colors, each one of which had a special meaning." Guamán Poma ([1650] 1980:183) described how the quipu functioned: "And in this way, they made quipus of the expenses and quantities and of everything that happened in this kingdom in each year, the philosopher-astrologers, in order to plant and collect the meals and foodstuffs, and for other occasions, and rules and government are noted with their quipus."

Recent research concerning contemporary specimens of quipus or those found in museum collections (Arellano 1999; Arnold and Yapita 2000; Ascher and Ascher 1978, 1981; Burns 1981, 1990, 2002; Dransart 1995; Locke 1923; Mackey et al. 1990; Oscar Núñez del Prado 1990; Pereyra 1997; Pimentel 2005; Quilter and Urton 2002; Radicati di Primeglio 1979, 1990; Salomon 2004; Urton 2003) have broadened our knowledge about the form and function of the quipu. Probably the most complete description of the Inca quipu can be found in the work of Ascher and Ascher, *Code of the Quipu* (1981). The authors demonstrate that both color and knots are fundamental in the construction and meaning of the quipu. They relate color to the "symbolic system of the quipu," and both simple and complex knots to numbers (1981:18).

Figure 6.6. Guamán Poma's drawing of the Inca quipu ([1615] 1980:258).

These same studies also describe how the quipu functioned. Most agree that the quipu was used for recording a census of animals, foodstuffs, and people for the state (Murua [1590] 1962:123; Acosta [1590] 1979:290; Garcilaso [1609] 1960:159; Guamán Poma [1650] 1980:250-51); for calendrical and astronomical purposes (Murua [1590] 1962:124-25); and for recording historical data (Murua [1590] 1962:123; Santa Cruz Pachacuti [1613] 1959).

Based on these descriptions of the Inca quipu, we can correlate the lista motif to the quipu in three main ways: (1) both use multicolored threads, (2) the variations in stripe width can be related to the simple and double quipu knots, with a single lista stripe being related to a simple knot and several threads being correlated to doubled knots, and (3) both the lista motif and the Inca quipu function to record a classification for goods.

I found support in the community of Markapata for my argument that the lista motif evolved from the quipu and recorded a color classification for goods. One day I was learning how to weave the tawa rosas qocha (four rose lake) motif in Markapata with Paulina Quispe. We wove it with the multicolored lista stripe. Later I showed this belt to Ana de Sequieros, who told me that the lista stripes were called *sara wachu* (corn furrow). She then took me to where there were long rows of corn lying on the ground to dry. Ana related each colored stripe in my belt sample to one of the rows of colored corn in the following manner: *q'ellu sara wachu*, yellow corn; *paraqay sara wachu*, white corn; *paychay sara wachu*, red corn; *quilly sara wachu*, black corn; *inti muru sara wachu*, yellow corn with black grains; *pisqo runtun sara wachu*, light yellow corn with black grains (Silverman-Proust 1988a:226-227, Fig. 22). Thus the yellow stripe on her lliklla referred to *q'ellu*-colored corn, the white stripe referred to *paraqay* corn, the red stripe to *paychay* corn, and so on.

Numerous anthropologists have discussed the symbolism of the multicolored stripes woven in both Quechua and Aymara cloth. Bastien (1978) describes certain colors as symbolizing "vertical

Figure 6.7. Ana de Sequieros stands next to her rows of corn drying in Markapata, 1980.

land ownership and even specific crops which grow at each altitude." Cereceda (1978:1030) believes the multicolored stripes woven in the Isluga talega (wayako) signify baby animals. Arnold and Yapita (1998) relate multicolored stripes to "celestial roads," alpaca corrals, male and female, and Aymara social organization. And Hilda Araujo (1998:468) describes how "categories of Ayacucho social organization" are registered with various colored stripes woven in cloth. Here I argue that the multicolored lista stripes woven in the Q'ero wayako record a color classification for the different goods and animals the Q'ero raise and cultivate.

Figure 6.8. Ramón Salas
harvests corn, 1985.

⊹ Lista Stripes: A Color Classification ⊹
for Goods Produced in Q'ero

Corn

In 1986 I went with the Q'ero down to their maize fields, which are located at approximately 1,800 meters above sea level in a valley called Inti Qhawa Valle (Sun See Valley). I left Tandaña with my "mother," Tomasa Pauccar, at about 6 a.m. and arrived at our wall-less shelter at about 3 p.m. It was during the corn harvest that I collected a color classification for corn based on data obtained from both Q'ero men and women.

Corn cultivation is carried out on steep, sloping land. The Q'ero grow two types of corn: *qolla sara* (queen corn) and *hank'a sara* (roasted corn). The first is boiled or roasted; the second is eaten only roasted. Q'ero corn is grown in a variety of single colors or combinations of colors, and usually the kernels are small.

The following classification for Q'ero corn is based only on color: *chumpi sara*, red corn; *oqe sara*, gray corn; *parakay sara*, white corn; *q'ellu sara*, yellow corn; *kuti*, yellow and white kernels; *musa*, white and brown kernels; *panti*, purple and red kernels; *yana*, black kernels; *q'ellu pukayoq*, yellow and red kernels; *nina wacha*, dark yellow with some black kernels; *chumpi wacha*, brown and yellow kernels; *owina sara*, white kernels; *qori chullpi*, gold kernels; *panti chullpi*, pink kernels; and *yana q'ellu*, black and yellow kernels (taped, 1985, 1986).[3] The most common colors for corn are red, gray, white, yellow, black, brown, purple, and gold, as well as combinations of colors such as black and yellow, red and yellow, and brown and yellow.

Potatoes

In Q'ero potatoes are grown in two ecological zones, the puna, located at about 3,500 meters above sea level, and the qheswa, at around 2,500 to 3,500 meters. Potatoes are grown in different-shaped furrows, depending on land gradient, soil type, and moisture (see Chapter 3).

The color classification for potatoes described here was gathered in Q'ero in 1985 and 1986 and is based on data obtained primarily from male

Figure 6.9. Different kinds of corn from Q'ero, 1985.

Figure 6.10. Ramón Salas's drawing of Q'ero corn, 1986.

informants. The colors cited refer not to the skin but to the potato itself, which takes on a hue in its outer part or has the color running through it: *maqtillo papa*, black; *rahku maqtillo*, white; *yana pulli*, black; *compas*, white; *pitykinay*, black; *phoya*, black; *lluntus*, yellow; *q'ellu maqtillo*, yellow; *azul ruk'i*, blue; *papa orlunes*, gray; and *azul kita*, blue. Thus the Q'ero recognize black, white, gray, yellow, and blue as potato colors.[4]

Bodies of Water

The Q'ero also classify various bodies of water according to color. The data collected here are based on my informal interviews with male Q'ero informants in 1985 and 1986. The following colors apply to small lakes and ponds found in the puna: (1) *Yana qocha*: "Wichaypi lomapi kashan. Vale paqocha toman." [The black lake is located in the hills of the high puna. It is valuable for the alpaca.] (2) *Q'omer qocha*: "Vale paqocha, sirvena wichayllapi kashan." [Green lake. It is valuable for the alpaca, it is in the high part.] (3) *Puka qocha*: "Vale animal wichaypi." [Red lake. It is valuable for the animals in the highlands.] (4) *Ch'aki qocha*: "Paqocha saylla qocha. Saylla color kashan. Paqocha vale mikuynaypaq. Mana ichhu kanchu." [Alternating wet and dry lake. A yellow-green lake for the alpaca. It is a yellow green color. It is valuable for the alpaca to eat. There is no ichhu grass.]

(5) *Millayniyoq qocha*: This is a black lake that is important for the cows. (6) *Lawir qocha*: "Q'achu color." [Dark green color.] This lake is important for the horses. (7) *Chuslla kana qocha*: "Yana qocha kashan. Chaypi tian pato." [This is a black lake. There the duck lives.] (8) *Puna qocha*: "Q'achu color. Yana pukawan kashan." [A lake in the puna. A dark green color. It is a black-red lake.] This lake is important for the alpacas.

Soil Types

Soil classification is also based on color. The Q'ero work land in three ecological zones—the puna, qheswa, and monte—but I describe soil types only from the puna and qheswa, based on explanations from Q'ero men: *puka allpa*, red soil that has no value; *yuraq allpa*, white soil that is used for the fireplace; *azul allpa*, blue soil used to build fireplaces; *yana allpa*, black soil used in potato cultivation; *q'ellu allpa*, yellow soil without value; and *oqe allpa*, gray soil used to build fireplaces.

Stephen Webster (1972:100) also studied the soil types in Q'ero and found that yana allpa, when located in the monte, was useless for corn cultivation but the best soil for potatoes. Soils have also been classified as hot/cold and superficial/big. Mario Escobar (1983:7) added *yana allpa*, which was used for the hacienda owner's fields, and *alqa allpa*, which was used for the Q'ero fields and must be fertilized.

Llamas

The following classification for llamas and alpacas is derived principally from a drawing (Figure C27) made by Santiago Salas Pauccar, who named 20 different color combinations of his herd: (1) *yuraq llama*, a completely white animal; (2) *ch'iñiko alqa*, a very small animal with a white neck and brown legs;[5] (3) *chumpi alqa*, a white neck and pinkish brown legs; (4) *yuraq mut'u*, "mut'u kashan ninri," a white animal with mutilated ears;[6] (5) *q'ellu muru-chumpi muru*, brown spots on a dirty (yellow) coat;[7] (6) *cruzta*, gray crossed with black and white;[8] (7) *yana suri*, "yana yuraqwan," a white coat with silky black; (8) *ch'iñiko alqa*, a very small white animal with half its coat and its back legs brown; (9) *q'ellu llama*, "yuraq umayniyoq," a white head with the rest of the animal a dirty yellow; (10) *yana alqa*, "kunkan yuraq, iskay maki yuraq," a black alpaca, a white neck and two white legs; (11) *chumpi chullumpi*, "yuraq wasayoq," entirely brown except for a white back;[9] (12) *yana wallata*, "yana wasayoq," an almost entirely white llama except for a black back; (13) *paraqay muru,* "*yuraq, oqewan,*" gray spots on a white coat; (14) *qheswa maqta, ch'iñiko yuraq chakiniyoq,* a small brown animal except for the two back white legs; (15) *puka paro, chumbiwan yuraq,* the front part is a reddish brown with the back part white-brown; (16) *vicuña,* the yellowish white color of the vicuña; (17) *q'ellu paro, yuraqwan q'elluwan,* white with yellow coat; (18) *yana chullumpi, yuraq wasayoq,* a completely black animal except for a white back; (19) *sumaq p'allchay, yuraq wasayoq,* a white animal with black spots and a white back;[10] (20) *ch'iñiko paro, chumpi yuraqwan,* a small brown and white llama with the color divided diagonally across its side, brown-white; (21) *cruza, makito panti, yuraq makiyoq,* a cross-colored animal with pink and white feet; (22) *ch'iñiko alqawaya, yuraq uyayoq,* a small brown animal with a white face; (23) *qolla pantalon, puka chumbi, hoq chaki yuraq,* a brownish red animal with a white foot; and (24) *q'achu, chumpi yuraq,*[11] the front part is light brown and the back is white (taped, 1986). As we see, the color classification for llamas takes into consideration not only those animals that exhibit a single color but those that have different-colored spots on a solid-colored coat or combinations of colors.

Flores Ochoa (1978) provides a color classification for llamas and alpacas in which he uses 33 different Quechua classificatory terms. Zorn (1986:292) found that in Macusani, Peru, different-colored grains were used to symbolize animals.

A study of the color classification for goods in Q'ero allows us to understand what types of colors of threads the Q'ero use in their *wayako* to represent specific foods and animals. For example, potatoes, bodies of water, and soils are symbolized with single-colored threads such as black, red, and white. But both single colors and combinations of colors are used to symbolize llamas, alpacas, and corn.

C1. Qochamoqo, 1979.

C2. Sheared llama.
Tandaña, 1985.

C3. Spinning in Willoq, 2005.

C4. Rosa Chura prepares the spun yarns for plying. Tandaña, 1985.

C5. Weaving with the backstrap loom. Parubamba, 2001.

C6. Warping with the four-stake horizontal ground loom. Willoq, 2005.

C7. Typical women's dress in Q'ero. Tandaña, 1985.

C8. Woman's dress in Ocongate. Coyllur Rit'i, 1979.

C9. Woman's dress in Chinchero. Ayllu Umasbamba, 1979.

C10. A Q'ero lliklla.

C11. A Chinchero lliklla.

C12. A Pisac lliklla.

C13. A Q'ero ceremonial poncho.

C14. A Pisac ceremonial poncho.

C15. Tawa inti qocha woven in a Q'ero lliklla.

C16. Santiago Salas's drawing of the hanan pacha with brown and black mountain peaks. *Left:* Inti, the sun. *Right:* Killa, the moon. Middle: Ch'aska, star. 1985.

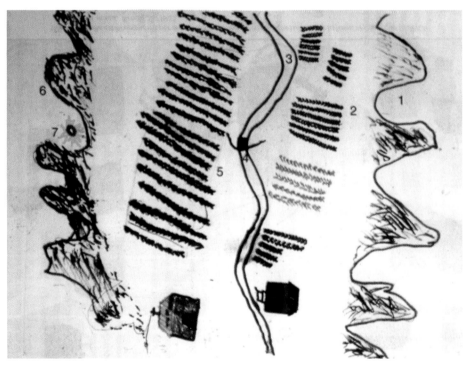

C17. Tandaña, as drawn by Ramón Salas in 1986: (1) Orqo puntas, the mountain peaks. (2) Chakra, fields. (3) Tandaña Mayu, the Tandaña River. (4) Chawpi chaka, the center bridge. (5) Chakra, fields. (6) Puntas orqo, the mountain peaks. (7) Inti haykushan, the setting sun.

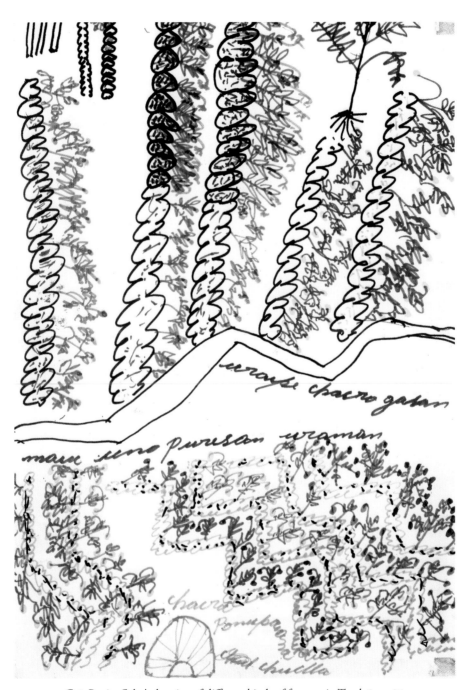

C18. Benito Salas's drawing of different kinds of furrows in Tandaña. 1986.

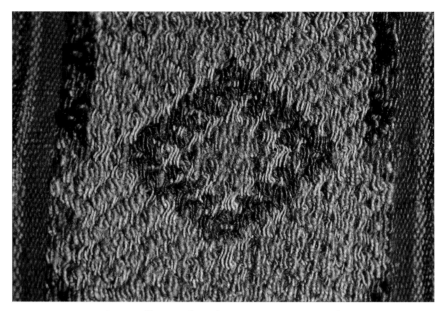

C19. Inti lloqsimushan, the rising sun, is woven with light-colored lines that direct inward. Q'ero lliklla.

C20. Inti chinkapushan, the setting sun, is woven with dark-colored lines that direct outward. Q'ero lliklla.

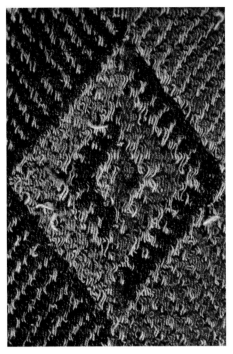

C21. Hatun inti, the sun at noon,
is half of the rising sun and half of
the setting sun. Q'ero lliklla.

C22. Tawa inti qocha, the sun at midnight, contains the four parts
of daily time: sunrise, noon, sunset, and midnight. Q'ero ceremonial poncho.

C23. The relation of the rising and setting sun to the mountain peaks in Tandaña, drawn by Benito Salas Pauccar. 1986.

C25. Benino Quispe's drawing of the world. The uku pacha, formed by a qocha, is at the right; the hanan pacha is at the left; and the kay pacha is in the center. 1986.

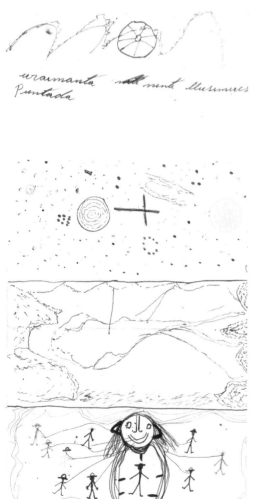

C24. Benito Salas's drawing of the world. The hanan pacha is at the top, the qocha is at the bottom, and the kay pacha is in the center. 1986.

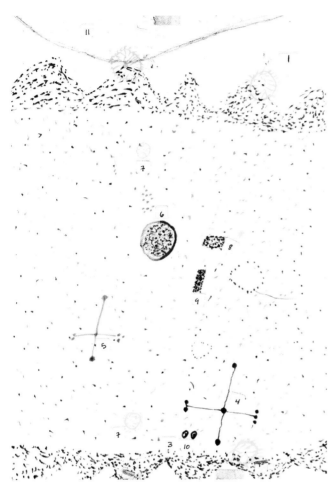

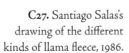

C26. Hanan pacha, drawn by Benito Salas Pauccar. 1985. (1) Para tiempo, rainy season, December solstice. (2) Osari tiempo, cold season, June solstice. (3) Mayu, the river, Milky Way. (4) Pasión Cruz, the Cross of the Passion. (5) Sepultura, Chakana. (6) Q'oto, Pleiades. (7) Killa, Moon. (8) Llama kancha, llama corral. (9) Oveja kancha, sheep corral. (10) Llama ñawi, Alpha Centauri and Beta Centauri, the eyes of the llama. (11) La mar, the sea. 1985.

C27. Santiago Salas's drawing of the different kinds of llama fleece, 1986.

C28. Ch'unchu Type Ia woven in the Q'ero lliklla.

C29. Ch'unchu Type Ib. Qollari.

C30. Ch'unchu Type II.

C31. Ch'unchu Type III.

C32. The last Inca, drawn by a K'allakancha man as a bodiless head with stems and roots growing out of his head. 1985. Courtesy of Parvati Staal.

7

The Graphic Representation
of the Myth of Inkarri

The myth of Inkarri has fascinated Andeanists since it was first presented by Oscar Núñez del Prado (1973) and Morote Best (1983) in 1955. Briefly, the myth tells the story of the first Inca and cultural hero of the Q'ero, Inkarri, who was born from the union of the sun and an uncivilized woman. Inkarri's appearance in the Andes initiated the Inca civilization. Inkarri taught the Q'ero men agricultural techniques, and Qollari, his wife, taught the women the textile arts. They established their capital at Cuzco after attempting to do so at other places, including Q'ero. With the arrival of the Spaniards, however, Inkarri was captured and decapitated. The myth ends by predicting Inkarri's return when his dismembered body reconstitutes itself.

What I have recounted is a summary of the myth as found throughout the Andes (Ortiz 1973; Ossio 1973). But the last part, concerning Inkarri's capture and decapitation by the Spanish, is not discussed in the versions found in Q'ero (Oscar Núñez del Prado 1983; Arguedas and Pineda 1973; Morote Best 1983; Mueller and Mueller 1984). Why do the myths told in Q'ero remain silent about Inkarri's execution and postulated return? Do they record Inkarri's return in some other way?

The myth of Inkarri has been studied as messianism (Ortiz 1973; Ossio 1973), as ideology (Getzels 1983; Gow 1974, 1976; Sallnow 1974; Pease 1973; Randall 1982), and as mythic history (Millones 1988; Gisbert 1980). However, little attention has been paid to the recording of the myth in

colonial and contemporary art. Gisbert (1980:199) describes the capture
and execution of the last Inca as drawn in colonial paintings; the first representation of the Inkarri myth in cloth probably occurred sometime after
the Túpac Amaru revolt in 1781 (Gisbert 1980:199). Wilson (1990) discusses
the meaning of only one type of the ch'unchu motif (the anthropomorphic
motif that represents Inkarri) woven in Cuzco-area textiles but does not
address changes in this design over time and space.

In this chapter I demonstrate that although the Inkarri myths collected in Q'ero do not describe Inkarri's return, the Q'ero not only postulate
his return but graphically portray it in their cloth. The Q'ero identify two
ch'unchu motif types, ñawpa inka and ñawpa ch'unchu (Types Ia and Ib),
which depict Inkarri as their cultural hero and founder. They weave Inkarri's decapitation with the ch'unchu simicha Type II motif, and they show
how Inkarri returns with the ch'unchu motif type that is currently being
woven in Q'ero, called ch'unchu inti pupu (Type III). This last motif is the
only Q'ero motif not woven outside Q'ero today. Both Q'ero and non-Q'ero
informants read these motifs and the graphic elements that compose them
(a bodiless head, radiating lines, a navel) as recording ideas about fertilization, growth, death, and regeneration.

⁑ How the Q'ero Ch'unchu Motif Is Read ⁑

During fieldwork carried out in Q'ero in 1980, 1985, and 1986, I collected
information concerning the ch'unchu motif. At that time I identified three
ch'unchu motif types, which show that this motif evolved from an anthropomorphic design (Types Ia, Ib), to a two-part geometric motif (Type II),
and finally to a three-part geometric motif (Type III) (Silverman-Proust
1983, 1986b, 1987a, 1989, 1990; Silverman, ed. 1993). Why do these motifs
change form through time? What do the people of Q'ero have to say about
their meaning? In order to answer these questions, I asked both Q'ero and
non-Q'ero men and women to identify these motifs, using the simple question ¿Imas chay? (What is it?).

With regard to the data collected in Q'ero, several Q'ero men compared their cloth to a book in which they can read both the inti and ch'unchu motifs (José Quispe, Lorenzo Quispe). In addition, one of my principal male informants from Chuwa Chuwa told me that the Q'ero read the
myth of Manco Cápac and Mama Ocllo, the founders of the Inca empire,
the primordial pair, with ch'unchu. Thus Q'ero cloth is perceived by the

very people who weave it and wear it as a visual record of mytho-historical events, a record of the myth of Inkarri.

The most common term used for all the ch'unchu motif types is *ch'unchu*. But when asked to identify the graphic elements that compose the motifs, the Q'ero use different names. With regard to the ch'unchu Type Ia motif, 55 men and women called it *ñawpa inka* (ancient Inca). The ch'unchu Type Ib was called either *ñawpa ch'unchu* (ancient ch'unchu) or *ñawpa ch'unchu lorayan* (ancient ch'unchu stems and roots). Type II was called either *ch'unchu simicha* (ch'unchu little mouth) or, less frequently, *uma ch'unchu* (head ch'unchu). Type III was called *ch'unchu inti pupu* (ch'unchu sun navel) or *kunan ch'unchu* (contemporary ch'unchu) (Silverman-Proust 1987a; taped, 1985, 1986).[1]

Several graphic elements that compose the ch'unchu figure were also identified by Q'ero informants. With the ch'unchu Type Ia and Ib motifs, triangular objects are woven on both sides of the face. Tomasa Pauccar, of Tandaña, called them *pinchinchu*, which means "to shine, to shine again" (Cusihuamán 1976a:103; Lira 1982:224; taped, 1985). A male informant who also lives in Tandaña called them *urpi*, which means "bird" (taped, 1985).

Another graphic element found only in Type Ia and Ib is a square or triangular object. The triangular one is attached between the legs, while the square one is located in the middle of the legs but unattached. These can also be woven as a series of repeating squares somewhat reminiscent of Lyons' indented vaginas (1979:98). The Q'ero call these *sapota*, "frog." Elsewhere I have identified the triangular object as signifying Inkarri and the squares as representing Qollari (Silverman-Proust 1987a). The last graphic elements identified in Type Ia were two lines radiating diagonally from the shoulders. These are called *vara*, "pole" (taped, 1985, 1986).

With regard to Type II, the triangular faces were called *simicha*, "little mouth," by almost all the 55 people interviewed. Another term used for this motif was *qhoro*, which means "mutilated," and *qhoro ch'unchu*, "mutilated ch'unchu" or "ch'unchu without a head" (Cusihuamán 1976a:126; taped, 1985, 1986). Almost all the Q'ero called the radiating lines *loran* or *lorayan*, "stems and roots of a plant," though several weavers called them *chakran*, "his/hers/its field."

The centrally located geometric design in the ch'unchu Type III motif was called *pupu*, "navel," or *inti pupu*, "sun navel."

Besides naming the graphic elements that compose these three ch'unchu motif types, the Q'ero related them to specific periods of time. For example, when I asked if they could weave ch'unchu Type Ia and Ib ("¿Awankichu kay ñawpa inka pallayta?" [Do you weave the ñawpa Inca motif?]), they replied that it was woven during an older period: "Manan atinichu away kay ñawpa ch'unchu. Qhepa wiñay. Abuelaymikuna awankun hinata. Mamaymi mana atinchu away hinata" (Santusa Waman, K'allakancha, taped, 1985). [I can't weave this ñawpa ch'unchu. It grew from a previous period. Grandmothers wove like this. My mother can't weave like this.] A similar answer was given by Cilio Apasa Samanta, who also lives in K'allakancha: "Ñawpa warmikunata awankun kay pallayta. Inka warmikunata awankun kay pallayta. Ñawpa tiempota" (taped, 1985). [Women from ancient times wove this motif. Inca women wove this motif. It is from an ancient period.] Serephino Apasa Quispe, who lives in Palcabamba, stated that these motifs were not woven by the present generation of Q'ero weavers: "Manan kanchu kay pallayta kunan" (taped, 1985). [There isn't this motif now.]

I also asked many Q'ero weavers if they could weave ch'unchu simicha with the following question: "¿Awankichu kay ch'unchu simicha pallayta?" [Do you weave this ch'unchu simicha motif?] Victoria Pauccar Sera, of Tandaña, said that it was woven by the last generation of Q'ero weavers: "Kunan mana atinichu awayta kay ch'unchu simicha. Mamaymi mana awanchu. Abuelaymi atin awayta kay ch'unchu simicha pallayta" (taped, 1985). [I can't weave this ch'unchu simicha now. My mother can't weave it. My grandmother could weave this ch'unchu simicha motif.]

Finally, Type III is woven by the present generation of Q'ero weavers. For example, Domingo Pauccar Waman, of Tandaña, said, "Kunan awan hinata" (taped, 1985). [She weaves like this now.] Interestingly, Tomasa Pauccar stated that when her five-year-old granddaughter begins learning how to weave, she will learn not ch'unchu inti pupu but a different ch'unchu motif type that has not been woven before in Q'ero (taped, 1986).[2]

Based on these data, we can say that the ch'unchu Types Ia and Ib are the oldest ch'unchu motifs so far documented for Q'ero and were woven at least three or four generations ago. Type II was probably woven before 1935, and Type III was woven sometime during the last two generations. Various investigators have mentioned that during the Velasco administration in the 1970s, the president used the myth of Inkarri as a symbol for his social programs (Flores Ochoa 2005:33), so Type III might have developed during that time.

I also interviewed men and women from the communities of Kauri, Huancarani, Chinchero, Pisac, and Pitumarka. In Kauri 53 men and women were shown color photographs of two ch'unchu motifs (Types Ia and II) and asked, *¿Imas chay?* (What is it?). Eighteen of them stated that these were Q'ero motifs, and 20 informants said that they were called *ch'unchu pallay*. For example, a female informant said, "Kaypas Q'ero pallaymi" (taped, 1990). [This is also a Q'ero motif.] Another informant replied, "Kayqa Q'eromanta" (taped, 1990). [This is from Q'ero.] Many Kauri informants called Type Ia either *ch'unchu* or *ch'unchucha*, that is, ch'unchu or little ch'unchu (taped, 1990).

One Kauri informant looked at ch'unchu inti pupu and said that it was a Q'ero motif in this way: "Kay pallayqa qhepa Q'ero pallaymi. Chanin valeqnin, finucha" (taped, 1990). [This is the last Q'ero motif. Correctly that is valuable, it is very fine.][3] Several Kauri informants also stated that these were ancient Inca motifs. For instance, one person said, "Q'eron! Kayqa inkakunaq awasqan pallaychakunaraqmi" (taped, 1990). [Q'ero! This was a small motif from Inca times.] One woman stated that these were motifs from Lower Cuzco: "Kay pallayqa Urin Qosqomantan" (taped, 1990). [This motif is from Lower Cuzco.][4] Another woman said that she couldn't warp it because it was an old motif: "Manan yachanichu allwinta. Kayqa ñawpa inkakunaraq pallayninraqmi" (taped, 1990). [I don't know how to warp it. This was an Inca motif.]

We also conducted 93 interviews in Huancarani in 1990. Sixty-three informants could identify the motifs as Q'ero. For example, a female informant said: "Q'ero pallaymi kashan. Ch'unchu pallay. Antiguo pallaymi kayqa" (taped, 1990). [It is a Q'ero motif. Ch'unchu motif. It was an ancient motif.] Another informant said: "Ch'unchu pallay. Kay pallayqa ñawpa abuelayqin ruwanankuna" (taped, 1990).[5] [The ch'unchu motif. The ancient ancestors made this motif.] An elderly woman said: "Ch'unchu pallaytaq kashan. Ch'unchu pallay. Ñawpa taytaykuq pallayninmi. Mana kunan tiempuqa ruwanankunachu" (taped, 1990).[6] [And this motif is ch'unchu. Ch'unchu motif. It is the motif from the ancient ancestors. They don't make them now.] Another woman stated: "Kinsa q'aytumanta kay pallayqa. Ñawpa machulaykuq pallayninmi karan. Kunan tiempuqa mana ruwankunachu" (taped, 1990). [This motif is from three threads. It was an ancient ancestor motif. They don't make it now.] Only two Huancarani informants called Type II by a specific name. For example, one of the oldest people interviewed stated: "Uma ch'unchu pallay kayqa. Q'ero lado" (taped, 1990).[7] [The ch'unchu head motif. From the Q'ero side.] Thus we see that non-Q'ero informants related the Q'ero ch'unchu motifs specifically to the Q'ero. They also stated that they were ancient motifs that were no longer woven in their communities.

⚜ Q'ero Ch'unchu Motif Types ⚜

Ñawpa Inka and Ñawpa Ch'unchu: Inkarri Depicted as a Human Being

Ñawpa inka Type Ia is the oldest of the four ch'unchu motifs collected in the Department of Cuzco, being found in Choquecancha, the Pitumarka highlands, and the Calca and Pisac highlands (Silverman 1993). It is an anthropomorphic motif in which Inkarri's head (*uma*) and body (*kurku*) are composed of two inverted triangles that meet at the center of the chest. Facial features include both eyes (*ñawi*) and a mouth (*simi*). Inkarri also sports two, four, or six diagonal lines, which the Q'ero call lorayan or loran and which they identify as referring to the stems and roots of a plant. The shoulders are formed by a short horizontal line that divides the body into an upper and lower torso. The arms are bent at the elbows and are placed with the hands positioned horizontally to the waist. The legs are aligned diagonally to the lower torso with the feet pointing outward. Located between the legs and attached to the body is a small triangle that represents the phallus, while in the case of Qollari, several square-like graphic elements indicate the vagina. The motif panel is completed with a partial geometric design that is located on both sides of Inkarri's head. Q'ero weavers call this *chili*, which is a type of grass important for llamas and alpacas. Chili is composed of a partial diamond with a series of repeating triangles that either outline the diamond or are located inside it.

Ñawpa inka Type Ia is woven in the women's shawl, the men's ceremonial poncho, the ch'uspa, and the wayako. In the ceremonial poncho it is found in three design panels, while in the lliklla it is woven in only two design panels, one on each half of the garment. In the ceremonial ch'uspa it occurs in all three panels, while in the wayako it is found only in the central motif panel.

Figure 7.1. Ñawpa inka, Type Ia. Inkarri.

Like the Q'ero inti motifs, ñawpa inka Type Ia is woven with the kinsamanta technique in at least three different ways. First, it is woven as a single design that occurs in a repeating manner. For example, a lliklla from a private Peruvian collection is woven with blue and dark cranberry as the primary colors and red and white as the secondary colors, or with red and white as the primary colors and blue and dark cranberry as the background colors. Second, ñawpa inka can be divided vertically into two separate colors with blue on one half and a pink ñawpa inka on the other half. Third, it can be woven as two separate motifs that are placed next to each other in the same design panel. These are woven in a discontinuous manner, varying between a series of alternating blue and red ñawpa inkas on one half and a series of alternating cranberry and orange motifs on the other half.

Figure 7.2. Ñawpa inka, Type Ib. Qollari.

The Secondary Motifs

Four different secondary motifs border the primary ñawpa inka motif panel. K'iraqey puntas is the most common secondary motif that is woven with ñawpa inka. In previous chapters I described k'iraqey puntas as representing the mountain peaks that function as doorways to the kay pacha and the uku pacha, as well as horizon markers used to tell daily and seasonal time. Next is ñawpa inti (ancient sun, ancient period), which is also woven with the three-color kinsamanta weaving technique. In the lliklla in Figure 7.3, ñawpa inti is composed of two alternating sun motifs woven with red, green, and yellow: a green sun on a yellow background with lines directing outward and signifying the setting sun, inti chinkapushan; and a yellow sun on a red background with lines that direct inward and symbolize the rising sun, inti lloqsimushan. The third secondary motif is *ñawpa churo* (ancient snail), which represents the ancient interior world, the uku pacha. It is formed with a series of repeating hook-like elements. Last is *ñawpa silu* (ancient sky), which is formed with a series of partial circles that open either to the right or to the left.[8]

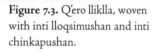

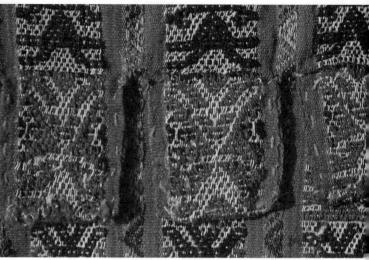

Figure 7.3. Q'ero lliklla, woven with inti lloqsimushan and inti chinkapushan.

Figure 7.4. Ñawpa inka Type Ia woven in the Q'ero ch'uspa.

Ñawpa inka is also woven in the ceremonial ch'uspa. In this case, in contrast to the llikllas and poncho, a secondary plain-weave panel replaces the other secondary motifs described above. The Q'ero call these panels *puka pampa* (red uncultivated land), *yana pampa* (black uncultivated land), and *chumpi pampa* (brown uncultivated land; taped, 1985, 1986). In a ch'uspa that I collected in the Q'ero hamlet of Wañunapampa in 1980, either an inti lloqsimushan or inti chinkapushan motif replaces the chili design at the side of ñawpa inka's face.

Ñawpa Ch'unchu Type Ib

There is another variety of ñawpa inka Type I woven in Q'ero called ñawpa ch'unchu Type Ib. It is exactly like ñawpa inka Type Ia except for a series of very long diagonal lines that occupy three-quarters of the design panel, while the body is reduced in size.

Unfortunately, I have been able to document Type Ib from only a few villages located in the Pitumarka highlands and in private collections of Q'ero textiles from the mid-1950s or earlier. I was also able to take a photograph of Type Ib woven in a llikllas by a woman who lives in the hamlet of Uno Raki, in the Huancarani highlands. Juana Quispe, the owner of the llikllas, told me that only a few very old women still wove ñawpa ch'unchu or ñawpa inka in her village because it had died out (taped, 1985). In addition, I was able to locate several ñawpa ch'unchus woven in the llikllas hung in

Figure 7.5. Ñawpa inka Type Ib woven in a lliklla
from Uno Raki, Huancarani, 1985.

Figure 7.6. Ñawpa inka Type Ia woven
in a Pitumarka highlands lliklla.

the church in Choquecancha, some of which were woven in the same garment with the ñawpa inka Type Ia motif as well as the dual ch'unchu simicha, Type II.

Several ethnographers mention the existence of the ch'unchu motif woven in both Peru and Bolivia, and they are probably referring to the oldest ch'unchu motif, that is, ñawpa inka. For example, Catherine Mangeot (1975:152, 177), mentions ch'unchu in both Pisac and Ollantaytambo textiles, and Arthur Tracht (personal communication, 1984) states that it is woven throughout Bolivia. Based on fieldwork, Percy Paz (personal communication, 1985) says that ch'unchu is woven in the communities of Chaywatiri, Sipaskancha, Tt'io, and Pampa Llaqta, located in the Calca and Pisac highlands. Wilson (1990) notes that ch'unchu (ñawpa inka Type Ia) is woven in the areas already mentioned, as well as Pitumarka and Chilka. Unfortunately, Mangeot, Tracht, and Paz do not supply photographic evidence for these motifs.

Figure 7.7. Ñawpa inka Type Ia woven in a
lliklla in the Huancarani highlands, 1985.

Figure 7.8. Variation of ñawpa inka Type Ia woven in a Pitumarka lliklla, 1985.

Figure 7.9. Ñawpa inka Type Ia woven in a Q'ero lliklla.

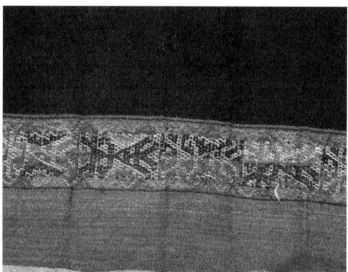

Figure 7.10. Ñawpa inka Type Ib. Qollari woven in a Q'ero lliklla.

Figure 7.11. Ñawpa inka Type Ia. Inkarri woven in a Q'ero lliklla.

The Wayri Ch'unchu Dancers

The first stage in Inkarri's life is his representation as the cultural hero and founder of the Incas. Inkarri is not depicted as a human being in cloth woven by the present generation of Q'ero weavers, although such a depiction was woven at least two generations ago, and even earlier outside Q'ero, but he is portrayed as a human being in another aspect of Q'ero material culture. One day, sitting outside and enjoying the sun in Tandaña with Benito Salas, I asked him who Ch'unchu was ("Pin kay Ch'unchu?"), and he replied that Ch'unchu was "para bailar en Corpus" (taped, 1985). [For dancing during Corpus.[9]] He then proceeded to draw me a picture of Ch'unchu in which the feathered headdress and a pole are the graphic elements that identify Ch'unchu with the Qolla, non-Inca, dancers pictured in Figure 7.12. In fact, the three principal graphic elements that make up both ñawpa inka and ñawpa ch'unchu are long diagonal lines, a staff, and ear ornaments. These traits are also found in the costumes worn by the Q'ero wayri ch'unchu dancers.

The wayri ch'unchus perform during Corpus Christi in Q'ero and at the festival of Coyllur Rit'i (Núñez del Prado 1983a; Getzels 1983; Gow 1976; Rozas 1989; Webster 1972). I saw them dance during Corpus in Hatun Q'ero in 1980 and in Coyllur Rit'i in 1980 and 1985. Their costumes are a blend of Spanish and indigenous elements. The Spanish elements

Figure 7.12. Wayri ch'unchu dancers in Hatun Q'ero for Corpus Christi, 1980.

Figure 7.13. The thirteenth captain of the Antisuyu wearing a feathered headdress with the chonta tree behind him (Guamán Poma [1615] 1980:146).

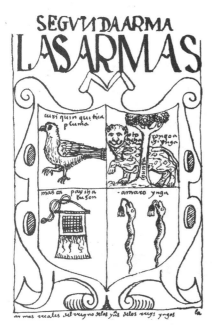

Figure 7.14. Inca coat of arms with the chonta tree (Guamán Poma [1615] 1980:65

include a white long-sleeved shirt worn with long black pants and store-bought black shoes or boots. The indigenous elements include the feather headdress, a ch'ullu (knitted cap with large ear flaps) and a *vara*, or wooden staff.

Both the feathered headdress and the wooden staff were used by the Inca captains from the Antisuyu, the region northeast of Cuzco. Gow (1976:252-253) states that the feathered headdress was made from the feathers of the *guacamayo* bird, and the vara was made from the wood of the *chonta* tree, which was also used to make bows and arrows. The chonta tree was so important that it occupied a prominent place in the Inca coat of arms, pictured alongside an *otorango* (jaguar) in the drawing by Guamán Poma ([1615] 1980:65). Guamán Poma ([1615] 1980:146) also drew the captain from the Antisuyu wearing a feathered headdress and holding a chonta pole in his hand. In fact, the Indians from the Antisuyu, called Ch'unchus, used the chonta bow and arrow and wore the guacamayo feathered headdress.

Comparing the graphic elements of the ñawpa inka and ñawpa ch'unchu motifs with those of the costumes worn by the Q'ero wayri ch'unchu dancers, we note that the feathered headdress of the wayri ch'unchus symbolize the long diagonal lines placed on top of ñawpa inka's head. Next, chonta staffs carried by the dancers represent the poles that radiate out of ñawpa inka's shoulders. Last, the large ch'ullu ear flaps worn by the dancers represent the pinchinchu ear elements in the ñawpa inka motif. Thus a feathered headdress, a staff, and ear ornaments are the graphic elements that characterize Inkarri as a human being in the Q'ero Type Ia and Ib ch'unchu motifs and in the Q'ero wayri ch'unchu dancers' costumes. Gow (1976:252, 269) also describes the wayri ch'unchus as "representatives of the ancestors, particularly the Incas."

Ch'unchu Simicha: Inkarri Represented as a Bodiless Head

The second stage in Inkarri's life is his capture by the Spaniards and his decapitation: "Inkarri was captured by the Spanish king; he was sacrificed and decapitated" (Arguedas and Pineda (1973:231). Inkarri's decapitation is an important theme in both the myths and the chronicles. Guamán Poma ([1615] 1980:362), for example, drew a picture of Inkarri's beheading and included the following description: "Atagualpa Inga was decapitated and sentenced, and Don Francisco Pizarro ordered that they cut off his head."

The custom of decapitating enemies was common practice during Inca times. For example, the fifth captain of the Incas, Auqui Topa Inga, cut off the heads of enemies at war and presented them to the Inca king: "The fifth Captain, Auqui Topa Inga Yupanqui, who was the son of Cápac Yupanqui, was a brave captain, who killed many Indians and captains and nobles; and he cut off the heads of his enemies in order to present them to his father" (Guamán Poma [1615] 1980:130).

After a particularly arduous battle the Inca ruler celebrated his victory by drinking a corn brew called *chicha* from cups made from the heads of his enemies: "The heads of important enemies killed in battle were taken as trophies, and fitted with a metal cup in the crown to be drained through the mouth by a tube. The victor drank *chicha* from the trophy cup to recall the victory" (Rowe 1946: 297-298).

After an enemy had been decapitated, the victim's body and head were separated and taken to two different places. In the case of Inca warriors, the body was usually left on the battlefield. In the case of Inkarri, a myth collected by Ortiz (1973:132) states that Inkarri's head is in Spain but

Figure 7.15. Guamán Poma's drawing of the execution of the last Inca ([1615] 1980:362).

Figure 7.16. The fifth captain, Auqui Topa Inga, presents a bodiless head to the Inca king (Guamán Poma [1615] 1980:130).

THE GRAPHIC REPRESENTATION OF [135] THE MYTH OF INKARRI

his body rests in the village where the myth was collected: "They cut off the head and sent it to Spain. His body remains here."

The Incas believed that bodiless heads could regenerate themselves. Thus, at the demise of a family member, Inca women cut off their hair and covered their hairless heads with black mantles so the deceased could not return. Rowe (1946:297) stated that the Incas were afraid of traveling heads, called *oma puriq*, which "went abroad at night saying 'wis, wis.' The wandering heads were believed to be witches who assumed that shape in the course of their evil activities."

In the Inkarri myth collected by Thomas and Helga Mueller in Q'ero in 1984, and in those collected by Arguedas and Pineda (1973), Núñez del Prado (1973), and Morote Best (1983), no mention is made of Inkarri's decapitation, though it is a prominent theme in Inkarri myths collected throughout the Andes. Nevertheless, Inkarri is symbolized in Q'ero cloth as a bodiless head with the ch'unchu simicha textile motif.

Ch'unchu Simicha Motif Type II

Ch'unchu simicha is a geometric motif composed of two triangles that are joined at the chins. Two eyes and a mouth are depicted in each of the two inverted triangular faces. Each face also wears an eight-line loran/lorayan headdress, or in some cases four or six loran lines radiate out of the top of the heads.

Ch'unchu simicha is woven in the Q'ero lliklla, ceremonial poncho, and ch'uspa with exactly the same weaving technique, color, and formal organization of the design panels as ñawpa Inka and ñawpa ch'unchu. An incomplete chili motif is woven on both sides of the inverted faces. Then the secondary k'iraqey puntas, ñawpa churo, or ñawpa silu motifs are woven on both sides of ch'unchu simicha. In the ceremonial ch'uspa, however, the puka pampa, a red plain-weave panel, occurs. Ch'unchu simicha is also woven in the wayako with k'iraqey puntas as the secondary motif.

Today a few examples of ch'unchu simicha can be found in textiles woven outside Q'ero in the Department of Cuzco. I photographed one in a textile collected in 1939 without provenience information. Because the secondary motif is lista, I believe this textile was not woven in Q'ero but probably comes from the Pisac-Calca highlands. Rowe (1977:87) reproduces a lliklla from Lares with both the anthropomorphic ch'unchu and the two-part ch'unchu simicha in which both the eyes and mouth are shown (Silverman, ed. 1993). It is also found in older Choquecancha textiles (field notes,

Figure 7.17. Q'ero woman wearing a lliklla decorated with ch'unchu Type II. Tandaña, 1985.

Figure 7.18. Ch'unchu Type II woven in a Q'ero lliklla.

Figure 7.19. Ch'unchu Type II woven in a Q'ero lliklla.

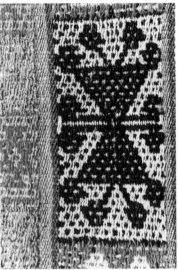

Figure 7.20. Ch'unchu Type II woven in a lliklla collected in Cuzco in 1939. Provenance unknown. Courtesy of the Tropenmuseum of Amsterdam.

Figure 7.21. Ch'unchu Type II woven in a lliklla from the Pitumarka highlands.

Figure 7.22. A Casma ceramic with a motif similar to ch'unchu Type II. Courtesy of Federico Kauffmann-Doig (1969:432).

1998), and I have published this motif woven in llikllas from the Pitumarka highlands (Silverman, ed. 1993:44, 45, 46, 47, 48). A motif very similar to ch'unchu simicha is also found on Casma ceramics. For example, Federico Kauffmann-Doig (1969:432) illustrates such a ceramic decorated with a motif in the form of two triangular, intertwined heads sporting feathered headdresses. Kauffmann-Doig (1969:432) describes this motif as representing "a mythical scene," while Francisco Aliaga (1985:76) says that it symbolizes the "reproduction of humans and animals."

The Graphic Elements of Ch'unchu Simicha

The characteristic graphic elements of ch'unchu simicha are the two inverted heads joined together at the chins, and the diagonal lines radiating out of the top of the two inverted faces. A structural and linguistic analysis of these elements allows us to understand how the Q'ero perceive their symbolic content.

The term *loran* or *lorayan* is used by the Q'ero to describe the diagonal lines placed on the top of the heads of the four ch'unchu motif types. This term may come from the Aymara word *lura*, which means "the border of a textile" (Jacqueline Weller, personal communication 1984). But in order to understand the meaning of this term, I had to turn to the explanations provided by the Q'ero men, and not to those of the weavers, who gave only general ideas regarding its meaning. For example, one day I asked Benito Salas Pauccar to draw me a picture of the agricultural fields located in Tandaña. He drew a field located in the lower part of Tandaña: "Uraypi charka kashan" (taped, 1985). [There is a field in the lower part.] Benito wrote Quechua descriptions of this picture and also gave verbal explanations concerning the different elements that compose it. First, he wrote that potato plants are in the furrows: "Wachupi papa kashan." Next he described these potato plants, and it was this description that defined the term *lorayan* for me: "Loran kan, q'omer loran t'ika pantita" (taped, 1985). [There is a stem, a green stem of a panti flower.] So *loran*, or *lorayan*, refers to the green stems of growing potato plants.

On another occasion I discussed the meaning of *lorayan* with Sebastian Flores, from Chuwa Chuwa, whom I interviewed while sitting in the patio of the mayor's office in Paucartambo. Looking at the ñawpa ch'unchu textile motif woven in one of my textiles, Sebastian called the long diagonal lines radiating out of the top of the head *lorayan*. When I questioned him about its meaning, Sebastian walked over to one of the flowers growing in the garden, touched its stem, and said, "Kay lorayan" [This is *lorayan*.] Thus Sebastian corroborated Benito's use of the term *q'omer loran* as the stem of a growing plant.

The other graphic element is the pair of triangular faces joined at the chins. These are woven bilaterally in relation to a horizontal axis. The spatial organization of the motif creates an opposition between the upper and lower faces (*uya*), which symbolizes the Quechua conception of space. The Incas divided their world into two moieties: hanan pacha, the upper world, and hurin pacha, the lower world. Previous studies by Zuidema (1976), Randall (1982), and others have demonstrated that the hanan pacha is associated with such concepts as above, male, elder brother, and right hand, while the hurin pacha is associated with opposite ideas such as below, younger brother, female, and left hand. Analyzed in this way, the upper face of ch'unchu simicha represents the hanan pacha and everything associated with it, while the second, inverted face symbolizes the hurin pacha and the concepts related to it.

Q'ero weavers called the imaginary horizontal dividing line *pampa*, "ground." Viewed from this perspective, the upper face is above ground, while the second, inverted face is below, or buried in the ground. This opposition is symbolized in the myth of Inkarri in two ways. First, the myth states that Inkarri's head or his entire body is buried: "They say that only Inkarri's head exists. From his head he is growing from the inside. They say that he is growing to his feet" (Arguedas and Pineda 1973:222). Second, the myth states that Inkarri is hiding in the jungle or in the mysterious city of Patiti, which is believed to be located in the jungle: "Finishing his work, he decided to leave again with Qollari, in order to teach the people his knowledge, and newly passing by Q'ero, they hid in the jungle" (Núñez del Prado 1973:279).

Both the interment of Inkarri's head and his refuge in the jungle refer to the Quechua concept of hurin. Analyzed from a vertical ecological perspective, the jungle is located in the lowlands in relation to Q'ero and Cuzco, both of which are in the highlands. But this dual opposition between the two triangular heads that symbolize the Andean spatial organization of the upper and lower worlds does not explain what their correlation is to the diagonal lorayan lines. A woman from Paucartambo hinted at this relation when she gave her interpretation of the four Inkarri motifs. Looking at ñawpa ch'unchu, Salsaro Vilabar identified it as a plant: "It seems to be a plant. The roots appear to be from below, and the upper part is the stem. The plant is growing from the top" (taped, 1986). What does this identification of the diagonal lines viewed as depicting the roots and stems of a plant have to do with Inkarri's return?

The graphic elements that form ch'unchu simicha, that is, two inverted faces joined at the chins, and the diagonal lorayan lines radiating out of the tops of the faces, are related in Q'ero mythology and in their cloth to ideas about interment and germination. These concepts are enlarged on and clarified with the study of the ch'unchu inti pupu motif.

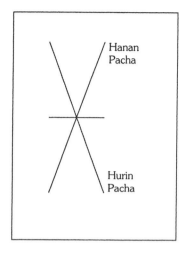

Figure 7.23. Ch'unchu simicha Type II represents the duality of space.

Ch'unchu Inti Pupu: Inkarri's Bodiless Head as a Germinating Seed

Although the myths do not explain how Inkarri's dismembered body will be reunited, they contain the conditions necessary for the restoration of his body and his eventual return. First, Inkarri's dismembered body must be restored if he is to return: "But Inkarri's head is alive and the body of Inkarri, our god, is reconstituting itself from below. When Inkarri's body is complete, he will return" (Arguedas and Pineda 1973:228). Second, the appearance of the sun is necessary for the revival of Inkarri's body: "We shall be in a time of encounter and when this period has ended, different men will appear. Now the sun rises from that side, but when the sun rises from this side, what will be below, will be above" (Mueller and Mueller 1984:134).

In the myths the restoration of Inkarri's body is described with the use of verbs such as *hatariy*, *brotar*, *crecer*, and *levantar*, Spanish and Quechua verbs which mean, respectively, "to awake," "to bud," "to grow," and "to get up": "They say that he is rising now. From now, only his head is growing; already he is rising" (Mueller and Mueller 1984:135-136). "He is growing from his head into the center. They say that he is growing to his feet" (Ortiz 1973:141-142). The verbs "to rise," "to bud," and "to grow" are all synonyms for the idea of germinating and growing plants. Thus the myth tells us that Inkarri's bodiless head, represented by ch'unchu simicha, is related

Figure 7.24. Ch'unchu inti pupu Type III woven in a Q'ero ceremonial poncho.

to growing plants. But while ch'unchu simicha hints at this relation, the ch'unchu inti pupu motif graphically represents the restoration of Inkarri's head and body.

Description of Ch'unchu Inti Pupu

Ch'unchu inti pupu is almost exactly like ch'unchu simicha except for one small difference. Ch'unchu's two inverted faces are replaced in this motif by a single, centrally located sun motif.

Like ch'unchu simicha, ch'unchu inti pupu is woven in three different ways. First, it is woven as a single, nonrepeating motif with alternating colors. Second, it is also woven as two separate, discontinuous motifs, placed next to each other in the same motif panel. These alternate between two different colors, such as blue and red. Third, the tawa inti qocha motif borders both sides of ch'unchu inti pupu instead of chili. Other than these differences, ch'unchu inti pupu is exactly the same as ch'unchu Types I and II in weaving technique, in the formal organization of the primary and secondary design panels, in textile type, and in the use of color.

I first learned to weave ch'unchu inti pupu in 1980 in Hatun Q'ero. I warped it with Juliana Quispe on a four-stake horizontal ground loom and wove it on this same loom. I also wove this motif in Tandaña, Chuwa Chuwa, and K'allakancha, using the four-stake horizontal ground loom.

The Graphic Elements of Ch'unchu Inti Pupu

Ch'unchu inti pupu is identified by two graphic elements: the sun (inti), which is located in ch'unchu's navel (pupu). A structural and linguistic analysis of these terms allows us to comprehend how Inkarri's bodiless head will reconstitute itself.

We have already noted that ñawpa ch'unchu refers to Q'ero ancestors from the recent past. Based on both ancient and contemporary dictionaries, the term *ch'unchu* also means an uncivilized person or a person from the jungle: "Savage, heretic, inhabitant of the jungle" (Cusihuamán 1976a:46). "Jungle, uncivilized, living in the jungle. Not civilized" (Lira 1982:69). "A province or the Andes of War" (González Holguín [1608] 1989:121). Thus ch'unchu refers to the lower world (hurin), the jungle, and the ideas of non-Inca culture, past ancestors, death, and interment.

The Quechua word *pupu* also has three different meanings that are important in understanding the significance of this motif. First, it refers to the navel of either a person or a plant: "Navel" (Cusihuamán 1976a:105). "Navel" (González Holguín [1608] 1989:296). "Navel, central scar in the stomach after taking out the umbilical cord" (Lira 1982:228). Second, it refers to the idea of origin or beginning, as in the case of the word *puquio*, which means "the source or origin of water" (Cusihuamán 1976a:105). The familiar use of *pupu* also means "the middle point of a plant" (Lira 1982:228).

Thus *pupu* is related to the origin of both plants and human beings, just as the Quechua verb *hatariy* and the Spanish verbs *crecer, brotar,* and *levantar* all refer to the germination and growth of human beings and plants. Based on these definitions, we can see that the terms *ch'unchu, pupu,* and *lorayan* have a dualistic symbolic meaning (Table 7.1). On the one hand, these terms refer to the ancestors who are buried in the ground, and on the other hand, they refer to the plants that are growing in the ground.

Table 7.1. Symbolic Relationships of Plants and People

Graphic Element	Plant/Person
Ch'unchu simicha	Seed of a plant Human egg
Lorayan	Stems and roots of a plant Upper and lower body
Pupu	Center of plant Human navel

The term *inti* also has a dualistic meaning. First, *inti* is the general word used for the Inca sun. Second, Inti is the father of Inkarri and of the Incas. Thus *inti* can be viewed as a source of light for humankind or energy for growing plants, as well as the Inca patriarch.

Table 7.2. Graphic Elements of Ch'unchu Inti Pupu

Graphic Element	Time	Space
Inti	Inkarri's father, founder of Incas	Hanan
Ch'unchu	Recent Q'ero ancestors	Hurin
Pupu	Origin	Uku

Inti refers to the father of Inkarri and represents the hanan pacha, the world of above. *Ch'unchu* pertains to the Q'ero ancestors of the recent past and the hurin pacha, the world of below. *Pupu* signifies the beginning of Inca civilization and the center from which they came, the uku pacha.

A structural analysis of the formal organization of the graphic elements that make up ch'unchu inti pupu demonstrates that it can be correlated with the tripartition of space: the motif is divided into three parts in relation to a horizontal axis. The central part of ch'unchu inti pupu represents Inkarri's head as a germinating seed. The upper lorayan lines signify the stems of a growing plant, and the bottom lorayan lines symbolize the roots. In addition, the appearance of the sun in the center of this motif signifies that the seed (head) has been fertilized by the sun (i.e., Inkarri's father) and is now growing.

In the Quechua organization of space, the top lorayan lines symbolize the hanan pacha and the concepts related to it such as male, the stem of a plant, and the present. The centrally located sun symbolizes the uku pacha and such ideas as center, the navel of a person or a plant, the union of male and female, and the future. The bottom lorayan lines represent the hurin pacha and such ideas as below, the roots of a plant, female, and past. Viewed in relation to a person's body, the top lorayan lines signify the formation of Inkarri's upper torso, the central part represents Inkarri's head, and the lower lorayan lines signify the growth of Inkarri's lower torso.

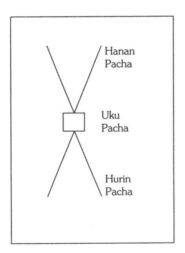

Figure 7.25. Ch'unchu inti pupu depicts the three-part division of space.

❧ Q'ero Drawings of the Last Inca ❧

When asked to draw the last Inca, Q'ero men depict a bodiless head with stems radiating out of the head. For example, Felix Samanta Álvarez, from K'allakancha, drew a picture of a bodiless "Atahaualpa," the last Inca king, or Inkarri, with sprouts growing out of the upper and lower part of the head (Figure C32). Felix described Atahualpa as carrying *su walto de oro y su barrito con su cabeza de challo* (his staff of gold and his small staff with his head of stems; taped, 1986). The sprout-like objects radiating out of the top and lower part of his head are called *challo* (or *tallo*), which is Spanish for "roots or stems of a plant." A second K'allakancha informant drew Inkarri's bodiless head placed on a tree trunk or a pole (Figure 7.26). Numerous tallos, stems, are radiating out of his head.[10]

    Based on these two drawings of the last Inca, coupled with the structural and linguistic analysis of ch'unchu inti pupu's graphic elements, we now understand that the Q'ero perceive Inkarri's bodiless head as a seed that has been planted in the earth and is now sprouting his upper and lower torso.

Figure 7.26. The last Inca, drawn by a K'allakancha man as a bodiless head resting on a tree trunk with sprouts and roots growing out of his head. 1985. Courtesy of Parvati Staal.

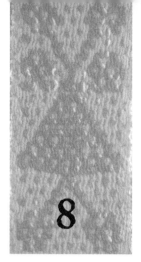

8

The Graphic Lexicon

Throughout this book we have seen how both Q'ero and qheswa cloth record knowledge. The Q'ero inti motifs register spatial and temporal concepts, while the qheswa motifs record only spatial ideas. The lista motif stores a color classification for goods. And four types of the ch'unchu motif record the life of the Q'ero cultural hero and founder, Inkarri.

Here I present a graphic dictionary of Q'ero and qheswa motifs. I deconstruct each motif into its component parts and provide their names. Finally, I show how these motifs are related to writing and to language.

Following Denise Schmandt-Besserat's definition of a symbol viewed as a word sign (1992), Q'ero textile iconography functions as word signs that are endowed with specific meanings. Q'ero pictographic writing is composed of two types of word signs: those that represent an object or subject and those that represent a preposition or adverb.

To understand how Q'ero and qheswa motifs function as word signs, we must deconstruct the motifs into their smallest graphic units, name them, and show their meaning. For example, five graphic elements form the Q'ero quartered diamond motif, tawa inti qocha: (1) isosceles triangles in relation to a rectangular frame, (2) a vertical line, (3) three diamonds placed one inside the other in decreasing size, (4) radiating lines that display an opposition in direction and color, and (5) a cross.

We have previously seen that the basic graphic unit identified by the Q'ero is the diamond circumscribed inside a rectangular frame that is bordered on both sides by isosceles triangles. This word sign signifies the highland Q'ero village surrounded by mountain peaks. The light-colored lines radiating inward represent sunlight and the fields in the upper moiety of Q'ero, and the dark-colored lines radiating outward signify shadow and the fields in the lower moiety. Long lines depict the height of growing plants during the rainy season, and short lines denote the harvested fields, which are bare during the freezing season. The vertical line signifies the center of village space, the sun at zenith, and the Milky Way. The three diamonds placed one inside the other in decreasing size symbolize the three ecological zones exploited by the Q'ero. Finally, the cross that quarters the diamond unites the four periods of daily time and symbolizes the June and December solstices.

The secondary motif functions as a preposition or as an adverb. For example, the isosceles triangles function as doorways used by the sun to travel from this world (kay pacha, present) to the interior world (uku pacha, future), or from the rainy season (para tiempo) to the freezing season (osari tiempo). In a similar way the secondary ñawpa inti, ñawpa silu, and ñawpa churo motifs, found only in older Q'ero textiles, also place the principal motif in a temporal context because they are word signs that mean ancient Inca period, ancient sky, ancient upper world, and ancient interior world.

Whereas the Q'ero inti motifs are word signs that refer to both temporal and spatial ideas, qheswa pallay is made up of word signs that stand only for spatial ideas, because they do not contain the graphic elements necessary for storing ideas about sunlight and shadow. For example, six graphic elements form tawa t'ika qocha: (1) a large diamond, (2) a vertical line, (3) four smaller diamonds, (4) four flower elements inside the four smaller diamonds, (5) alternating red and white squares, and (6) alternating red and white rectangles.

The large diamond is a word sign for village, and the vertical line is a sign for the duality of space. The four smaller diamonds are signs for the quadripartition of space, tawa suyu. The flower elements are signs for the flowering plants (potatoes, beans, etc.). The alternating red and white squares are signs for the hole made for planting or as a source of water, and the alternating red and white rectangles signify the furrows made in the fields.

In the case of the graphic elements that form the four types of ch'unchu motifs, the diagonal lines are signs for the roots and stems of a plant. The two inverted faces organized around a horizontal axis symbolize the separation of Inkarri's head from his body and the interment of his head. The centrally located sun motif in ch'unchu Type III is a sign for the fertilization by the sun of Inkarri's head, which is now growing an upper and lower torso.

In at least two cases, a graphic element may signify a sound. The light-colored lines that begin at the edge of the rectangular frame and radiate in can be read as *mu*, as in inti lloqsimushan, sunrise. The *pu* sound is represented by the dark-colored lines that begin at the edge of the diamond and radiate out, signifying inti chinkapushan, sunset. These suffixes express two kinds of movement: toward me, *mu*, and toward you, *pu*. Thus Q'ero pictographic writing contains at least two graphic elements that denote specific sounds as well as suffixes.

The Chinchero motifs presented here are from the ñawpa (ancient) period and are related to several Q'ero motifs. Motif 52, *pasñacha*, may have evolved from the Q'ero bipart ch'unchu motif, while motifs 49 and 56 could have evolved from the Q'ero quartered-diamond motif (Silverman, ed. 1991b:37-38). However, unlike Q'ero pallay, which registers both temporal and spatial concepts, these Chinchero motifs from the ñawpa period only refer to spatial concepts with regard to their agricultural fields, growing plants, and sources of water, even if they are woven with the three-color complementary warp-weave technique. At the time of my fieldwork, the Chinchero natives had adopted modern ways of telling time (radios, almanacs, and watches) and were selling their textiles to "forget their Inca ancestors" (field notes 1979; Silverman-Proust 1988:238-239), as well as incorporating new motifs from Kachin, Choquecancha, and Cotabambas into their textiles for the tourist market.

It should be mentioned that certain qheswa motifs such as t'ika, organo, ñawi, and q'enqo are woven throughout the Department of Cuzco and have many subtypes. Other common motifs are the multicolored lista stripes and the isosceles triangles. Table 8.1, on pages 150–173, provides an archive of 58 textile motifs with their names and meanings as read by the people who weave and wear them. Motifs 1-18 are from Q'ero, and the rest are found outside Q'ero.

Table 8.1. The Graphic Lexicon

Motif	Space	Time

■ **1. Inti lloqsimushan**

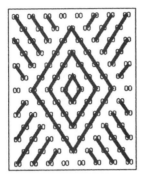

Llaqata
(village) east

Sunrise

■ **1a. Kinsa pata**

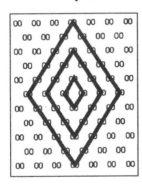

Three zones:
puna, qheswa, monte

Kinsa pupu
(three periods)

■ **1b. K'anchay**

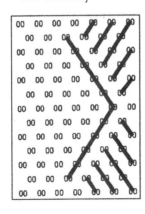

Intiq chakran
(the sun's field)

Sunlight

Motif	Space	Time

■ 2. Inti chinkapushan

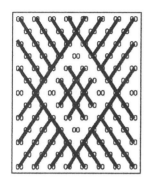

Llaqata (village), west

Sunset

■ 2a. Llanthu

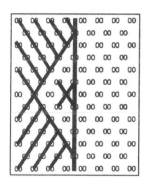

Intiq chakran (the sun's field)

Shadow

■ 3. Hatun inti

Hanan, hurin (upper and lower worlds)

Noon

Motif	Space	Time

■ **3a. Sonqocha**

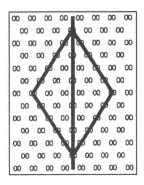

Chawpi (center); Mayu (Milky Way); ñan (road); sonqocha iskay t'aqapi (divided into two parts)

K'anchay, llanthu (sunlight, shadow)

■ **4. Tawa inti qocha**

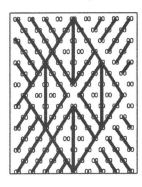

Four sun lake; east, north, west, south

Sunrise, noon, sunset, midnight

■ **4a. Cruz**

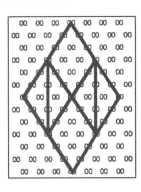

Tawa suyu (four regions)

Iskay raymi (two solstices, December and June)

■ **5. Ichhu inti**

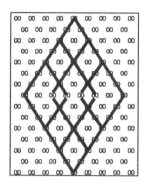

Pasture

■ **5a. Isqon chakran**

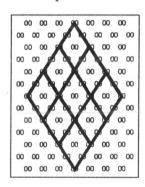

Nine fields

Isqon pupu
(nine periods)

■ **6. Pilli inti**

Pasture

Motif	*Space*	*Time*

■ **6a. Chili**

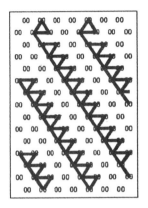

Pasture

■ **7. Tawa t'ika qocha**

Chakra (field),
t'ika (flower)

Planting time

■ **7a. Organo**

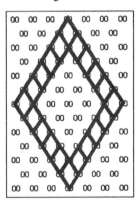

Furrows

Motif	Space	Time

■ 7b. T'ika

Flowering plants

■ 8. Saya qocha

Straight lake

■ 9. Ñawpa inka

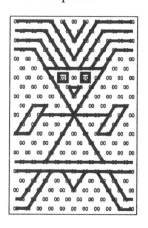

Uku pacha   Inca period; first
(interior world)   Inca ancestor, Inkarri

Motif	Space	Time

■ **10.** Ch'unchu simicha

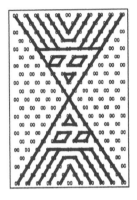

Hanan, hurin
(upper, lower worlds)

Beheading
of Inkarri

■ **11.** Ch'unchu inti pupu

Hanan, uku,
hurin (upper, inte-
rior, lower world)

Near future

■ **11a.** Lorayan/loran

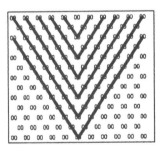

Upper and lower
worlds

Germination, stems
and roots

Motif	Space	Time

11b. Inti pupu

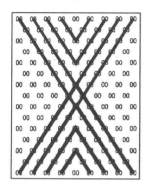

Uku pacha
(interior world)

Fertilization

12. Pampa

Uncultivated land

13. Lloq'e pañamanta

Hanan, Inca
nobility

Motif	Space	Time

■ **14.** Chili puka

Semen and blood,
male and female

■ **15.** Listas

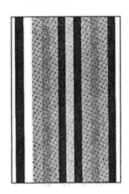

Color classification
for corn, potatoes,
bodies of water,
alpaca and
llama fleece

■ **16.** Suyu

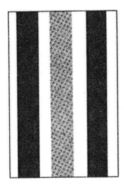

Classification of soils

Motif	*Space*	*Time*

■ 17. K'iraqey puntas

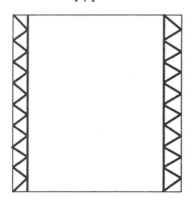

Mountain peaks as boundaries — Horizon markers

■ 18. Ñawpa inti

Ancient space, Inca, hurin (lower world) — Inca past

■ 19. Mayu

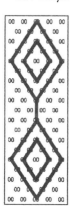

Milky Way — December and June solstices

Motif	Space	Time

■ **20. Ese**

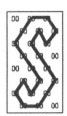

Kuti (hoe)

■ **21. Kinray organo[1]**

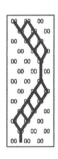

Horizontally aligned
furrows

■ **22. Ñawi organo[2]**

Furrows, hole

23. T'ika pallay

Field, flowering plant

24. Saqas pallay[3]

Sprinkled field,
flowering plant

25. Guitarra (Spanish)
keyboard elements

Field, furrow shaped
like keyboards

■ **26. Guitarra**

Two fields
together in the shape
of keyboards

■ **27. Q'ewe chili**[4]

Plied pasture grass

■ **28. T'ika**

Flowering plant

■ **29. Kiqwa**[5]

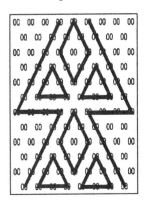

Narrow field

■ **30. Saqas t'ika**

Field, flowering plant

■ **31. Banda**[6]

Furrows in bands.

■ **32. Q'ampo (Spanish)**[7]

Field

■ **33. P'aki**[8]

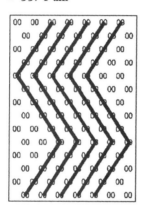

Broken field

■ **34. Rueda (Spanish)**[9]

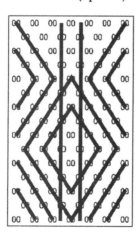

Field, sonqocha, little heart, center

Motif	Space	Time

■ 35. Qocha ley

Field

■ 36. Ley p'aki

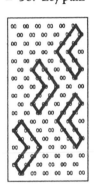

Furrows

■ 37. Organo

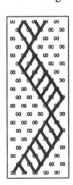

Furrows

Motif	Space	Time

■ **38. Puma**[10]

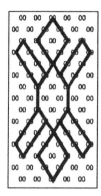

Cat   Ch'unchu past

■ **39. Jara**[11]

Field, furrows

■ **40. Mayu**

Field

Motif	Space	Time

■ **41.** Silu (Spanish)[12]

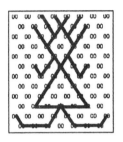

Sky

Ch'unchu
Inca past

■ **42.** Ese[13]

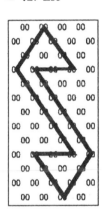

Hoe

■ **43.** Qocha

Field

■ **44.** Organo

Field, furrow

■ **45.** Loraypu[14]

Field, furrow

■ **46.** Waqaq ñawin loraypu

Field, furrow, hole

Motif	Space	Time

■ **47. Ch'unchu loraypu**

Inkarri · Inca past

■ **48. Keswa loraypu**[15]

Hanan, hurin (upper, lower)

■ **49. Tanka loraypu**[16]

Four regions, fields, furrows, hole

Motif	Space	Time

50. Keswa wachu ñawin

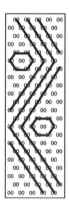

Furrows, hole

51. Ch'aska

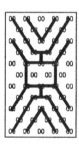

Venus, star

52. Pasñacha[17]

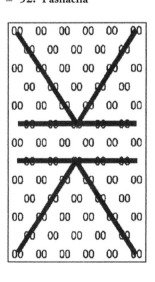

Inkarri   Inca past

■ 53. Hakaku sisan

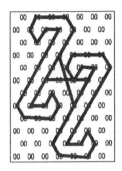

Hoe

■ 54. Shallaypu

Field

■ 55. Aysa kuti[18]

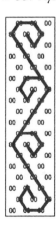

Growing plants

Motif	Space	Time

■ **56. Raki raki**[19]

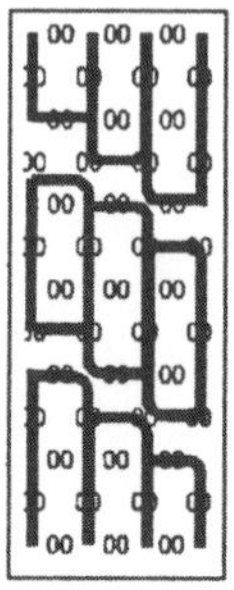

Plant

■ **57. K'enko**

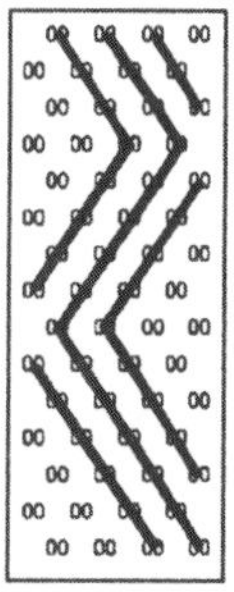

Furrow

■ **58. Ley (Spanish)**[20]

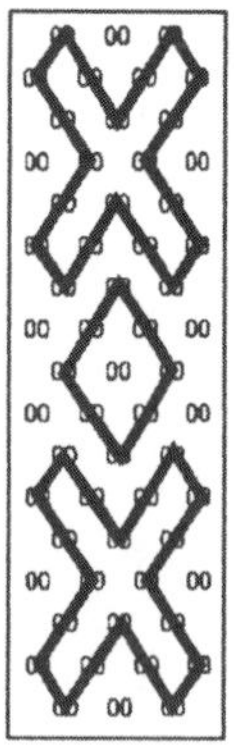

Field

Note: Motifs 1-18 are from Q'ero, and the rest are found in Chinchero, Pisac, Calca, Kauri, and Huancarani.

[1] *Kinray*, a horizontally aligned furrow.

[2] *Ñawi* means "eye," but with reference to agricultural practices it means "hole."

[3] *Saqas* means "sprinkled," with the idea of different colors here and there on a plant or in the earth.

[4] *Q'ewe* means "plied."

[5] *Kiqwa* means "narrow." It may be a synonym for *kikullu*.

[6] *Banda* is Spanish for "band, ribbon, border."

[7] *Q'ampo* is *campo*, Spanish for "field."

[8] *P'aki* means "broken" (Cusihuamán 1976a:106).

[9] *Rueda* is Spanish for "wheel."

[10] *Puma* is Spanish for "cougar."

[11] *Jara* is a proper name.

[12] *Silu* is from the Spanish *cielo*, "sky."

[13] *Ese* is *kuti*, "hoe." It is the Quechua pronunciation for the letter *s*.

[14] Name for a plant.

[15] *Keswa* is *qheswa*, "valley, middle land."

[16] *Tanka* is a V-shaped pole.

[17] *Pasña* means "young girl."

[18] *Aysay* is a verb that means "to till."

[19] *Raki raki* means "to divide," in reference to a plant.

[20] *Ley* is Spanish for "law."

9

The Book of Knowledge
Woven in Q'ero Cloth

In this book I have demonstrated how a Quechua-speaking people called the Q'ero, who live in a remote part of Cuzco, Peru, use textile iconography to register knowledge. Using two different weaving techniques, the Q'ero store two types of knowledge, and two types of logic, in their cloth. The Q'ero read their motifs in gender-specific ways, and these readings relate to Andean cosmological concepts. Because it stores knowledge, the textile iconography of the Q'ero functions as nonalphabetic writing.

⚜ Q'ero versus Qheswa Pallay ⚜

In Chapters 3, 4, and 5 I showed that Q'ero pallay is valuable because it creates a two-faced cloth in which the motif woven on the first face occurs on the second face but in reverse. This is not the case with those motifs woven with qheswa pallay, which creates a one-faced cloth in which the motif appears only on the front of the fabric.

These two types of cloth also show marked differences in their iconographic content. Q'ero pallay, woven with kinsamanta-iskay uya, creates a diamond design called *inti*, "the sun," which is characterized by differences in color and direction of the radiating lines, as well as the secondary k'iraqey puntas motif. These graphic elements store both spatial and temporal concepts at the same time. Qheswa pallay, woven with iskaymanta-hoq uya,

Figure 9.1. Furrows carved out of the fields in Kauri
look remarkably like the organo motif.

creates diamonds with alternating white and red squares or rectangles that
refer only to space. Due to the weaving technique used, a different text
is woven with these two types of cloth. In the case of Q'ero pallay, both
spatial and temporal concepts are registered based on differences in the
radiating lines (light colors in/dark colors out), as well as the secondary
k'iraqey puntas motif that borders both sides of inti. Both the radiating
lines and k'iraqey puntas permit Q'ero pallay to register spatial-temporal
concepts because time is mapped onto social space based on differences in
the quantity of sunlight and shadow. In the case of the diamonds woven
with qheswa pallay, no temporal concepts are recorded because these motifs lack the graphic elements necessary for storing ideas about sunlight and
shadow.

In qheswa pallay, instead of long and short radiating lines, a series of
alternating red and white rectangles outlines the entire qheswa diamond,
which is called *organo*. When pressed for explanations regarding the meaning of this element, weavers call it *guitarra*, "guitar" (field notes, 1982, 1984,
1985, 1986). But the real meaning of *organo* is *wachuchan*, "its/hers/his little
furrow," or *wachu way'qo*, "furrow" (Berna Gutiérrez, taped, 1985). The organo design carved out of the earth in fields in Kauri (Figure 9.1) is remarkably similar to both the organo and ñawi motifs.

Another graphic element that replaces the long and short radiating
lines found only in Q'ero pallay is the set of alternating red and white squares
called *ñawi*. Jorge Machaca, of Huancarani, stated that the ñawi motif

represents the hole that is made in the earth in order to plant a seed (taped, 1985). Interestingly, the chronicler Guamán Poma de Ayala ([1615] 1980:468) drew a field in which the furrows are in the shape of alternating squares that look like both the organo and ñawi motifs (Figure 9.2). A third element is the small geometric shape placed inside each of the four smaller diamonds that compose this motif. This shape can be a flower (rose, *t'ika*) or a cross (*cruz*). The flowers refer to the different kinds of flowering plants, such as potatoes and beans, and the crosses may refer to the festival of the cross, which is celebrated during the first days of May. Finally, whereas Q'ero pallay is bordered by the k'iraqey puntas motif, qheswa pallay is bordered by multicolored lista stripes. K'iraqey puntas represents the mountain peaks that help the people tell daily and seasonal time, while the multicolored stripes are a color classification for the goods they grow.

Figure 9.2. Guamán Poma's drawing of square fields surrounded by triangular mountain peaks ([1615] 1980:468).

Not only do these two weaving techniques create two different motifs that store different kinds of knowledge, but these two techniques are also related to the storage of two different kinds of logic. Q'ero pallay is made with three threads, usually white, black, and cranberry, which represent trinary logic. Qheswa pallay is made with two threads, usually white and red, which represent binary logic. We can understand how binary and trinary logic function in different ways by relating these two types of logic, as expressed in the iskaymanta and kinsamanta weaving techniques, to the ceque system of Cuzco, described in Chapter 3. Here I am concerned with the structure displayed by the ceque system and how it relates to the structure of the Q'ero inti motifs. According to Gutiérrez de Santa Clara ([1556] 1963:214), Cuzco was divided into two moieties: "the most important one was called Anan Cuzco, which means the high district of Cuzco, and the other one was called Hurin Cuzco, which signifies the lower district." Next Cuzco was quartered with four straight lines called *ceque*: "From the Sun Temple radiated four lines at the center, which the Indians called *ceques*, and they made four parts conforming to the four royal roads which left from Cuzco" (Cobo [1653] 1956:129). These four parts were called Anti-suyu (northeast), Chinchasuyu (northwest), Cuntisuyu (southeast), and Collasuyu (southwest). Forty-one ceque lines began at the center of Cuzco, at the Temple of Korikancha, and radiated out to the intercardinal directions. Nine ceques each radiated out in the Antisuyu, Chinchasuyu, and Collasuyu, while the Cuntisuyu was halved, with seven ceques in each half (Zuidema 1977). Last, distributed along the 41 ceques were 328 sacred sites called *huacas*, which were rivers, springs, trees, rock formations, houses, and the like.

We can look at the geometry represented by the ceques and the huacas in order to comprehend how binary and trinary logic function differently. First, the chroniclers describe the ceques as straight lines that begin at Korikancha and radiate out toward the intercardinal directions, usually stopping at the horizon. In terms of mathematical notions, they signify the numbers 0 and 1, which are drawn as a straight line: 0———1. The ceques function to identify the boundaries of a designated area because the numbers 0 and 1 depict its beginning and end (Davies 1988:129). The huacas, in contrast, are multidimensional because they are formed by irregular surfaces such as rocks, mountains, and trees, all of which have shape. In terms of mathematical notions, the huacas represent the numbers 0, 1, and 2, which can be drawn as a triangle with the 2 at the top (Davies 1988:129):

Thus the huacas identify the center of space because the number 2 represents the center.

We can look at the definitions of the Quechua terms *ceque* and *huaca* in order to understand their different functions. Cusihuamán (1976a:135) defines *"seq'e"* as *"marcar, grabar, firmar"* (to mark, to engrave, to sign). Lira (1982:266) defines *"se'ke"* as *"garabato, garrapato, escarbajo, letras o rasgos mal trazados. Familiar. Firma, rasgo rasa, esbozo"* (scrawling letters, to scribble, to scrape, letters or badly traced strokes. Familiar: to sign, to stroke lightly, to outline). González Holguín ([1608] 1989:652) defines *"seqque"* as *"raya, linea termino"* (ray, line, boundary). Lira (1982:324) defines *"waka"* as *"dios familiar o doméstico e idolillo que la representa, penantes"* (familiar god or domestic idol which it represents, suffering).

The Quechua definitions of ceque and huaca agree with the mathematical definitions. The ceques represent binary logic and identify the beginning and end of a specific area, whereas the huacas represent trinary logic and identify the center of a specific space.

In terms of Andean mythology, the huacas are the places of origin for humanity in general and the Inca ancestors in particular. For example, Juan de Betanzos ([1551] 1987:11) stated: "In ancient times...everything was night. They say that a señor that they call Con Tici Viracocha appeared from a lake that is in that land of Peru, they say in the province of Collasuyu, who, they say, had taken out a certain number of people." Guamán Poma ([1615] 1980:45-46) stated that humankind originated from lakes, mountains, and caves: "These Purunruna Indians...did not know how to write or read, they all committed errors, and because they committed errors, it is said that they appeared from caves and grottoes, lakes and mountains and rivers."

Whereas the huacas were places of origin for the Incas, the ceques were sightlines used for astronomical observations. For example, according to Zuidema (1978:470, 1982a:215), the ushnu (stone column) located in the principal plaza of Cuzco was used to observe the sun during the month of August, and another huaca called Susurpuquio was "found on the ceque that indicated the June solstice." Thus we can see how the iskaymanta weaving technique is based on binary logic and creates a spatial text, because binary logic organizes space. We can also see how the kinsamanta technique is based on trinary logic and creates both a spatial and temporal text, because trinary logic identifies the center as the place of creation and joins time and space together.

⚜ Gender, Textiles, and Knowledge ⚜

Throughout this book we have seen that the readings of the motifs by the Q'ero and Qheswa people are gender specific. In her review of studies of gender, Arnold (1997) identifies several themes: the daily life of Andean women, the role of Andean women and development, Andean women as preservers of native languages, and new forms of identity after the Spanish Conquest. In the book *Río de vellón, río de canto* (Arnold and Yapita 1998) she looks at the songs women created for their animals, and in *El Rincón de las Cabezas* (2000) she examines the texts made by men and by women as well as differences in the language they use to read these texts. In a similar way Lindsey Crickmay (1997) and Penny Dransart (2002) have studied gender and knowledge in textiles woven in northern Chile, and Henry Stobart (1998) has investigated the knowledge stored in Bolivian music. Finally, Astvaldur Astvaldsson (2002) has looked at the relation between knowledge and political authority in Bolivia. The data presented in this book show, first, how women and men use different terminology to identify the Q'ero motifs and, second, that men have more detailed answers concerning the meaning of motifs than their wives. For example, we have seen that the women use metaphoric language to name the mountain peaks and that these terms are almost always in Spanish. The men, in contrast, use Quechua to give names for the motifs, and they also give more detailed answers concerning the significance of the motifs.

These data have implications for Andean ideas about gender and knowledge, areas that have not been explored enough in Andean studies. Both Iña Rosing (1990) and Joseph Bastien (1978), for example, have shown that Bolivian ritualists and healers are almost exclusively men and that their ritual language may not be known to the women of their communities. This idea has also been explored by Irene Silverblatt (1987), who demonstrates how the Incas isolated Andean women from sacred knowledge. We need more studies concerning gender, text, and knowledge in contemporary Andean communities to elicit general theories concerning this theme.

❋ Andean Cosmology ❋

This book has also explored Andean cosmology. The most important idea expressed here has been the relational aspect between the self and the natural world. For example, we saw in Chapter 4 how the terminology for the rising and setting sun establishes a relationship with the speaker: for example, the sun is rising from behind that mountain peak and little by little is coming toward the speaker. This idea contrasts with the nonrelational concepts of sunrise and sunset in the West.

In addition, we have seen how different aspects of the natural world—the stars, the mountain peaks, the rivers and lakes, and the Milky Way—are represented as geometric forms because their very forms are made from geometric shapes.

This intimate connection between the Andean people and the natural world is further accentuated in the myth of Inkarri. Through their textile iconography, the Q'ero perceive Inkarri's bodiless head as a seed that has been planted and fertilized by the sun and is sprouting an upper and lower torso, just as a plant seed sprouts roots and stems. Thus Andeans hold animistic beliefs about life.

❧ Textile Iconography, Signs, and Writing ❧

The most important theme expressed by this book is the relation between textile iconography, signs, and writing. We have seen how the Q'ero use two different weaving techniques to create two different texts, one based on trinary logic in which the resulting sign stores both time and space, and the other based on binary logic in which the resulting sign stores only space. The two-faced cloth, created by trinary logic, has far-reaching implications for the study of all iconography in relation to its material support. If internal structure is related to the storage of specific kinds of data, then we must ask, Can Andean motifs be treated the same with regard to meaning if the material support is different (wood, ceramic, stone, metal)? We must begin to elaborate an archive of motifs and classify them by their internal structure.

Finally, if Andean textile iconography, composed of geometric shapes, functions as word signs with names and meaning, then what type of writing is it? Obviously, it is not alphabetic writing, and therefore we must begin to study the prehispanic geometric representation of Quechua. This research has important implications for the study of Quechua and its relation to nonalphabetic writing such as Egyptian hieroglyphics and Mandarin Chinese. The Quechua language was formed with geometric shapes found in nature, and the Incas used these forms to decorate their textiles, ceramics, and metals. Now is the time to classify, seriate, and study them in order to investigate the existence of Inca writing.

Notes

1. Q'ero: A Window on the Inca World

1. Before 1986 Q'ero was not represented on Peruvian military maps.

2. See Glave and Remy 1983 for the impact of colonialism in Ollantaytambo.

3. In 1979-1980 Qochamoqo and Hatun Kiko had 50 houses each and Chuwa Chuwa had 44.

4. See O. Núñez del Prado 1970, 1983b, and 2005 and Ossio 2005 for descriptions of the permanent residences.

5. See O. Núñez del Prado 1983a and Webster 1983 for descriptions of Q'ero social organization.

6. Otto de Barry, owner of the Hacienda Ccapana, also held Q'ero lands.

7. *Lloq'e pañamanta* describes a plying technique in which threads are spun to the right and to the left, creating alternating warped threads. These are found in the Inca quipu, as well as the Inca uncu, and have been recorded for pre-1950 Cuzco-area textiles. *Lloq'e pañamanta* refers to Inca practices of adding and subtracting, which are related to the personal pronouns *ñoqa*, "me," and *qan*, "you." See Silverman, in press, for a description of this technique.

8. Compare Rowe and Cohen 2002 with Heckman 2003.

9. My belt samplers have been exhibited throughout the years in exhibits in Cuzco and Lima (Silverman-Proust 1988a, 1990; Silverman 1995c, 1996, 2005b; Silverman, ed. 1991a, 1991b).

10. I taught these students fieldwork methodology, and they also underwent a weaving apprenticeship with me.

11. Compare this classification with Heckman 2003:16.

12. See Silverman, in press, for more drawings by Cuzco informants.

13. *Orqo* also means "male" (González Holguín [1608] 1989:449).

14. At the beginning of my fieldwork no one could pronounce my name, so I called myself María Quispe until everyone got accustomed to saying Gail.

15. I thank Javier Flores for these ideas.

2. Weaving the Book

1. Flores Ochoa (1978:1010) defines *alqa* as "a generic name given to a combination of colors in which the light tones predominate and occupy the greater part of the coat… dark colors do not occur on more than half the coat. The proportion is approximately two-thirds light coat and one-third dark." He identifies more than six different combinations of alqa: "manutusa alqa [white neck, the rest black], puruta alqa [white front leg and bottom], mut'u phata alqa [black face, back, and back legs], sewarillo alqa [one black eye and black back], yana simillu alqa [black mouth and bottom], and paru alqa [black face and neck]." Bertonio ([1612] 1984:10) defines *alqa* as "a mixture of diverse colors," and Lira (1982:28) describes it as "spotted of various colors." Flores 1978:1010 defines *muru* as "spotted" and *wallata* as "spots on their backs that remind them of the packs they carry."

2. There is no standardization of the terms for the spinning, plying, and weaving tools used in Cuzco.

3. See Dransart 1995 for spinning methods used in northern Chile.

4. See Silverman 2005b for an exhibit of Cuzco textiles dyed with plants, the cochineal insect, human fermented urines, and fireplace ashes.

5. A triangular loom formed with a forked tree branch is used in the Cotabambas-Tambobambas area. See Silverman, ed. 1995:36 for a photograph.

6. See Urton 1981 for the identification of the *ch'isin* star in Misminay. Cuzco weavers believe they have a star that guides them called *ch'isin ch'aska*.

7. This string is called *q'ullcha* in Parubamba and Willoq.

8. In 1980 I donated a considerable collection of Q'ero textiles to the University of Cuzco, and they can be seen in the Inca Museum.

9. My own Q'ero collection is documented as to ayllu (village) location.

10. Josefina Olivera generously shared her outstanding private collection with me. I also spent many nights in her San Pedro store learning about textile provenance from her.

11. As I spent more time in the field, I gathered different names for these panels which are related to the sacredness of cloth. See Silverman, in press.

12. Inesa Sayri died in 1982.

3. The Structure of Space

1. For the use of isosceles triangles in native art, see Nolte 1991 and Bastien 1978:75.

2. Lorenzo could be trying to say *co-lindero*, which also means "boundary." Lorenzo spoke some Spanish in 1979. Both terms, *co-lindero* and *colendero*, for *colindante*, have the idea of halving space, exactly what this line does in the hatun inti motif.

3. I asked Francisco this question using the word *ruway*, "to make," but he answered using the verb *away*, "to weave." For a description of cloth perceived as a living thing, see Cereceda 1978, Derosiers 1982, Arnold 2000, and Silverman 1994a, 1994c.

4. *Pata* also refers to the term *patapata*, which means "terrace" in Quechua. These terraces were made during Inca times; they had stone stairways, retaining walls, and sometimes motifs made with small stones decorating their walls. According to Barreda Murillo (2005), there are abandoned Inca terraces in Q'ero close to Hatun Q'ero.

5. I am describing Tandaña as it was during my stay in 1986.

6. On agricultural practices in Q'ero, see Flores 2005, Flores and Fries 1989, and Webster 1972.

7. Cusihuamán (1976a:63) defines *kinray* as "a closed site."

4. The Woven Shadow of Time

1. I purchased this lliklla from a middleman who lives in Kauri.

2. It took me more than twenty-five years of fieldwork to understand that each Q'ero motif has more than one meaning. See Silverman, in press, for the multiple meanings of the repeating diamonds.

3. These ideas of the sun moving toward me and benefiting me, and the sun moving toward you and benefiting you, are the basis of Inka ideas about addition and subtraction. See Silverman, in press.

4. *Lado* (side) is *laru* in Quechua, and like *vale*, Spanish for "value," is a mixture of Quechua and Spanish.

5. Prudencio is another example of a Quechua speaker learning Spanish. Note his use of *tarde* for "late afternoon," *doce* for "noon," *derecha* for "right," and the addition of *s* to pluralize a Quechua noun.

6. Benito is learning to write in Spanish. This is an exact transcription of what he wrote.

7. *Sonran* is Juliana's pronunciation of *sombra*, "shadow."

8. Sun motifs are also woven in Choquecancha, but they do not have the radiating lines of the Q'ero inti motifs.

9. See Silverman-Proust 1984 for descriptions of the Q'ero wayakos and these two inti motifs.

10. *Q'ellu* means "yellow," but here it is referring to the yellow rays of the sun, which will not lighten and, therefore, burn. The term *lliuw/lliw*, according to Cusihuamán (1976a:296), means *todo*, "everything." Here Benito is literally saying, "Everything, everything, everything…will not burn."

11. I thank Gary Urton for his comments on this section.

5. Para Tiempo and Osari Tiempo: Seasonal Time

1. Rosa pointed to each graphic element as she named it.

2. Benito uses the Spanish *estrella* for *ch'aska*, "star."

3. Benito is using the Spanish *veces*, "sometimes," here.

4. Benito should have said *Llamaq Ñawi*, in which the suffix *q* indicates possession. The quotation is an exact transcription.

5. Prudencio Hakawaya and Benito Nina died in 1985.

6. See Sullivan 1999 for the importance of animals in the Inca calendar.

7. In Silverman, in press, I identify the Inca tocapu that represents Llamaq Ñawi.

8. Prudencio is using the Spanish *estrella* for *ch'aska* (star).

9. The solstices occur on June 21 and December 21, but in Cuzco they are celebrated on the 24th.

6. Lista: A Color Classification for Goods

1. See Arnold and Yapita 2000 for descriptions of these stripes woven in textiles from Qaqachaka, Bolivia.

2. See Laurencich Minelli 2001 for a description of the pukllay quipu used by the Incas.

3. There is no standardization in the names of the different colors of corn, which change from village to village in the Cuzco area.

4. Interestingly, the color *yana* (black) is almost never used to describe tubers.

5. Lira (1982:65) defines *ch'iñiko* as "very small"; Bertonio (1984:83) defines the related word *chinquini* as "both sisters, older and younger."

6. *Mut'u* means "mutilated." Lira (1982:203) says "stub-horned, mutilated, chopped off." Bertonio (1984:225) defines it as "chopped off." The terms in quotations marks in Santiago's list are his exact words.

7. Cusihuamán (1976a:92) states that *muru* is "black color, white spots on a dark ground, or black or brown spots on a white ground."

8. *Cruzta* is Spanish for "cross."

9. Flores Ochoa (1978:1013) states that *chullumpi* is a male llama used for breeding.

10. *Sumaq* means "beautiful" in Quechua.

11. I could not find this term in any Quechua dictionary.

7. The Graphic Representation of the Myth of Inkarri

1. See Silverman-Proust 1987a for more interviews.

2. As of 2006, the Q'ero still had not created a new ch'unchu motif.

3. *Valin* (*valeqnin*) is a good example of the use of Spanish in Kauri, which increased when the Belaunde government stressed the learning of Spanish in Quechua communities.

4. Did the Q'ero belong to Hurin Cusco during Inca times?

5. *Abuela* (*abuelayqin*) is Spanish-Quechua for "grandmother."

6. *Tiempo* (*tiempuqa*) is Spanish for "time."

7. *Lado* is Spanish for "side" or "part."

8. I have seen these secondary motifs only on pre-1900 Q'ero textiles.

9. Corpus (Corpus Christi) is a Catholic festival that occurs in June.

10. I thank Parvati Staal, who gathered these drawings in K'allakancha when I came down with pneumonia and had to return to Cuzco for treatment.

Glossary

A

aksu skirt

allpa earth

alqa light colors predominating on the fleece of a llama

anqas blue

Antisuyu Inca region northeast of Cuzco

apu sacred mountain

Apu Wamanllipa sacred mountain of Q'ero

Apu Wayra Rumi sacred mountain of Q'ero Tandaña, lit. "windy stone mountain"

aysa till motif

awa k'aspi horizontal pole used for loom construction

awana loom

awapan border of the Q'ero lliklla

awasqa plain-weave cloth, thick and rustic, used by commoners during Inca times

awa watana braided rope used to tie the stake to the horizontal pole of the loom

ayllu lineage based on common descent, a common ancestor, and the exploitation of communal lands

Ayllu Pongo an ayllu of Chinchero

C

Calca village northwest of Cuzco

Cápac Raymi the December solstice, an important Inca festival

Casma pre-Inca culture

castilla chukcha azul patilla a blue thread similar to hair, said to be a kind of quipu

castilla chukcha panti patilla a pink thread similar to hair, said to be a kind of quipu

castilla chukcha puka patilla a red thread similar to hair, said to be a kind of quipu

ceque sightlines used by the Inca for organizing space and time in the Cuzco region

chaka bridge

chakra field

chapi plant that produces a red dye

chawpi center

chili pasture land, usually composed of ichhu and khunkuna

chili puka alternating white and red stripes woven in the Q'ero ceremonial poncho and wayako

Chinchasuyu Inca region northwest of Cuzco

chuño dried potato

coca native Andean plant used as an appetite suppressant and in sacred rituals

Corpus Christi Catholic festival around the time of the June solstice

Cotabambas area located southwest of Cuzco, known for a weaving technique and iconographic content that is different from Q'ero or qheswa pallay

Coyllur Rit'i Festival of the Snow

Cruz Southern Cross

cumbi the finest Inca cloth, woven with tocapu motifs, feathers, etc.

Cuntisuyu Inca region southwest of Cuzco

Cuzco the ancient Inca capital

CH'

ch'aska star

ch'isin ñawi night star

ch'umpi belt

ch'unchu general term for an anthropomorphic or geometric motif woven in the northeast/northwest of Cuzco before 1920

E

ese (Spanish) motif in the form of the letter S

estaca (Spanish) stake for weaving

G

guacamayo jungle bird whose feathers were prized by the Incas

guitarra (Spanish) recent motif in the form of the keys of any musical instrument

H

hakaku Chinchero motif in the form of an S
Hanan Cusco upper Cuzco, Inca nobility
hanan pacha upper world
Hanan Tandaña upper Tandaña
hanka sara roasted corn
hatun ch'illka plant that produces a yellow dye
Hatun Hapu Q'ero community
hatun inti large sun, midday sun, the sun at zenith
Hatun Kiko Q'ero community
hoq uya one-faced cloth woven with iskaymanta
Huancarani village northeast of Cuzco
hurin lower part; inferior; commoners
Hurin Cusco lower Cuzco
hurin pacha lower world
Hurin Tandaña lower Tandaña

I

ichhu pasture for alpacas
illawa heddles
illawa k'aspi heddle stick
inti sun
inti chinkapushan setting sun
inti lloqsimushan rising sun
intiq chakran fields of the sun
Inti Qhawa Valle the valley to watch the sun, lower Hatun Q'ero
intiwatana solar clock found at Machu Pichhu, Pisac, and Ollantaytambo
iskay inti two rising and setting suns
iskaymanta two-color supplementary warp technique that uses two threads, usually red and white, to create a one-faced (hoq uya) cloth, rarely found in precolumbian textiles
iskay uya two-faced cloth, made with kinsamanta, a three-color complementary warp weaving technique, found in precolumbian textiles
isqon chakran nine fields
isqon inti nine suns
isqon pupu nine origins

J

jara (Spanish) diamond motif

K

karana vertical cord that forms the Q'ero pukllay p'acha

Kauri village south of Q'ero

kawlla weaving tool ("sword") used to open the sheds

kay pacha this world

khunkuña pasture for alpacas

kinray organo horizontally aligned furrow motif

kinsamanta three-color, complementary warp weaving technique used in Q'ero, has precolumbian antecedents

kinsa pata three zones, three terraces

kinsa pupu three periods of time

kiru teeth

kiqwa a narrow motif

kunku neck

kuti hoe or farming tool motif

kuti loraypu motif in the form of a large diamond with an S in the center

K'

K'allakancha Q'ero village close to Paucartambo

k'anchay sunlight

k'aspi stick for weaving

k'ero Inca ceremonial drinking cup

k'iraqey puntas mountains motif

k'uchu k'uchu plant that produces a green dye

L

ley cruz (Spanish) law-cross motif; may refer to the Southern Cross

ley p'aki law-broken motif

lista (Spanish) multicolored stripes of various widths woven in Q'ero and qheswa cloth

Loran/lorayan stems and roots of plants

loraypu kuti motif in the form of a diamond with a hoe

luma ch'illka plant that produces a black dye

LL

llama sarsillu small, needle-knitted bag worn by the lead pack animal
llanthu shadow
lliklla woman's shawl
lloq'e left
lloq'e pañamanta from the left, from the right
Lloqlla Pampa Q'ero Totorani hamlet

M

maki maki hand-hand motif, many hands; related to ch'unchu motif
Mama Ocllo wife of Manco Cápac, founder of the Incas
Manco Cápac father of Inkarri
Markapata town southeast of Q'ero
maway planting period
mayu river
Mayu Milky Way
millma fleece
mini weft
misti foreigner
monte (Spanish) yunga, lowlands
moraya dehydrated potatoes

Ñ

ñan road
ñawi eye; hole made in the earth in order to plant
ñawpa ancient
ñawpa ch'unchu ancient ch'unchu
ñawpa churo ancient interior world
ñawpa inka ancient Inca
ñawpa silu (Spanish) ancient sky

O

oca tuber
Ocongate village south of Q'ero
Ollantaytambo town northwest of Q'ero
olluco tuber
oqe gray

organo field
orqo mountain
orqo puntas mountain peaks
osari tiempo cold and dry season, June solstice
otorongo jaguar

P

Pacha Mama Mother Earth
Palkabamba Q'ero village
pallay to pick up; motif
pampa qocha motif of a lake and uncultivated land
panti pink
papa wayko boiled potato
paqo man of knowledge, shaman
para tiempo rainy season, December solstice
pata high ground, terrace
patan border motif
Paucartambo town northwest of Q'ero
peliku spindle whorl
pili pasture
pinchinchu bird that announces rebirth
piñis white seed beads
Pisac village northwest of Q'ero
Pitumarka village south of Q'ero
puka pampa red uncultivated land
Pukara Q'ero village
pukllay p'acha type of quipu, braided belt, sling for dancing
pullto diamond motif
punku door
puntada mountain peaks
puntas (Spanish) mountain peaks
pupu origin, navel

P'

p'acha cloth
p'aki broken; motif
p'asñacha young girl

Q

qallu tongue; half of a lliklla or poncho
qheswa valley
qheswa ñawi mid-zone eye motif
qheswa pallay valley motif
qocha lake that forms the interior world
qocha ley lake-law motif
Qochamoqo Q'ero village
Qollari wife/sister of Inkarri
qolla sara queen corn
quellcani to engrave, paint, carve
quillca like tocapu and quipu, geometric motifs put on wood, ceramics, and
    cloth
quipu Inca knotted string device used for recording knowledge
quipukamayoq he who makes the quipu
Qulluyullu Q'ero hamlet

Q'

Q'achupata Q'ero village
q'ampo (Spanish) diamond motif, field
q'antiy to ply
Q'asa Apacheta mountain deity near Tandaña; Freezing Pass
q'ellu yellow
q'ellucha yellow-orange
q'enqo zigzag motif, furrows
q'enqo qocha diamond motif with zigzag furrows
Q'ero the name of a people and a region northeast of Cuzco
Q'ero Grande/Hatun Q'ero ceremonial center of Hanan Q'ero
Q'ero Totorani ceremonial center of Hurin Q'ero
q'ewe plied; motif
q'omer green
Q'oto Pleiades

R

rakhu q'aytu thickly spun thread
raymi solstice
rueda (Spanish) wheel motif
ruk'i potato

S

sani purple
saqas pallay diamond motif
sara wachu corn furrow
saya qocha diamond motif with diagonal furrows
sencillota (Spanish) small, rectangular, needle-knitted change purse
senqa nose
sillu (Spanish) sky motif
simi mouth
sonqocha little heart, center
so'qo thick stick used for making rope
suñkha beard
suri silky alpaca fleece
suyu region

T

Tandaña Q'ero village
Tandaña Mayu Tandaña River
tawa four
tawa inti qocha the sun at midnight (anti-zenith); motif
tawa pata four high parts
tawa pupu four navels, origins
tawa suyu four regions
tawa t'ika four flowers
tawa t'ika qocha four-flower-lake motif woven with two-color supplementary
    warp weave
taytanchis inti/sun
terenkas hair ribbons with pom-poms
tipana plain-weave panel
tissi spindle shaft
tocapu geometric motifs used by the Incas
tukuru multiple heddles made with bamboo sticks
tupu measuring string

T'

t'anta monica bread made with dehydrated chuño or moraya potatoes
t'ika flower
t'ika qocha flower-lake motif

U

uku pacha interior world
uma head
uma puriq flying head
uncu tunic
unkhuña carrying cloth
urpi bird
Urubamba town northwest of Q'ero
uya face

V

vara post
varayoq he who makes the vara, political official
vicuña most prized fiber of animal of the same name

W

wachu furrow
wachuchan small furrow
wallata llama
waqra t'ika horn flower
waqra waqra plant that produces a bright yellow dye
warak'a sling
warak'a tusuypaq sling for dancing
wasi house
wata year
watana a cord, a rope, something used for tying
wayako bag
waylla pasture
Wayna Cápac Inti/Sun

Y

yana black
yana orqo black mountain
yana pampa black uncultivated land
yawri needle
yunga lowlands
yuraq white
yuraq pampa white uncultivated land
yuraq paqocha white plain-weave panel

Bibliography

Acosta, José D.
1979 [1590]   *Historia natural de las Indias*. Mexico City: Fondo de Cultura Económica.

Adelson, Laurie, and Arthur Tracht
1983   *Aymara Weavings: Ceremonial Textiles of Colonial and Nineteenth Century Bolivia*. Washington, D.C.: Smithsonian Institution Press.

Aliaga, Francisco
1985   Tayta wamani: Pratiques et croyances religieuses dans les Andes centrales. Ph.D. dissertation. École de Haute Études en Sciences Sociales, Paris.

Allen, Catherine
1988   *The Hold Life Has: Coca and Cultural Identity in an Andean Community*. Washington, D.C: Smithsonian Institution Press.

Ansión, Juan
1987   *Desde el Rincón de los Muertos*. Lima: Gredes.

Araujo, Hilda
1998   Parentesco y representación iconográfica: Las "Tablas de Sarhua," Ayacucho, Perú. In *Gente de carne y hueso: Las tramas de parentesco en los Andes*, edited by Denise Y. Arnold, 461-524. La Paz: Ciase.

Archivos del Ministerio de Agricultura, Cuzco
1957   Folio de la comunidad de Q'ero.

Arellano Hoffmann, Carmen
1999   Kipu y tocapu: Sistemas de comunicación Inca. In *Los Incas: Arte y símbolos*, edited by Franklin Pease, 215-262. Lima: Banco de Crédito del Perú.

Arellano Hoffmann, Carmen, and Peer Schmidt
2002   Prefacio. In *Libros y escritura de tradición indígena*, edited by Carmen Arellano Hoffmann, Peer Schmidt, and Xavier Noguez, 11-26. Mexico City: El Colegio Mexiquense.

Arguedas, José María, and Josafat Roel Pineda
1973   Tres versiones del mito de Inkarri. In *Ideología mesiánica del mundo andino*, edited by Juan Ossio Acuña, 219-236. Lima: Ediciones Ignacio Prado Pastor.

Arnold, Denise, ed.

1997   *Parentesco y género en los Andes.* Vol. 1. La Paz: CIASE.

2000   Convertirse en persona el tejido: La terminología Aymara de un cuerpo
            textiles. In *Actas de la I Jornada Internacional sobre Textiles Precolombinos,*
            edited by Victoria Solanilla Demestre, 9-28. Barcelona: Server de Publica-
            ciones de la UAB.

Arnold, Denise, and Juan de Dios Yapita

1998   *El río de vellón, río de canto.* La Paz: Hisbol.

2000   *El Rincón de las Cabezas.* La Paz: UMSA.

Ascher, Marcia, and Robert Ascher

1978   Números y relaciones de los antiguos kipus andinos. In *Ideología mesiánica
            del mundo andino,* edited by Juan Ossio Acuña, 733-772. Lima: Ediciones
            Ignacio Prado Pastor.

1981   *Code of the Quipu.* Ann Arbor: University of Michigan Press.

Astvaldsson, Astvaldur

2002   Coming to Power: Knowledge, Learning, and Historic Pathways to Author-
            ity in a Bolivian Community. In *Knowledge and Learning in the Andes,* edited
            by Henry Stobart and Rosaleen Howard, 109-126. Liverpool: Liverpool
            University Press.

Aveni, Anthony

1981   *Sky Watchers of Ancient Mexico.* Austin: University of Texas Press.

Barreda Murillo, Luis

2005   Arqueología de Hatun Q'ero Ayllu. In *Q'ero, el último ayllu inka,* edited by
            Jorge Flores Ochoa and Juan Victor Núñez del Prado Bejar, 39-56. Lima:
            Universidad Nacional Mayor de San Marcos and Instituto Nacional de
            Cultura.

Barthel, Thomas

1971   Viracochas Prunkgewand. *Tribus* 19:91-96.

Bastien, Joseph

1978   *Mountain of the Condor: Metaphor and Ritual in an Andean Ayllu.* Long
            Grove, Ill.: Waveland Press.

Bertonio, Ludovico

[1612] 1984 *Vocabulario de la lengua aymara.* La Paz: Ceres, IFEA, MUSEF.

Betanzos, Juan de

[1551] 1987 *Suma y narración de los Incas.* Notes by Maria del Carmen Martín Rubio.
            Madrid: Ediciones Atlas.

Bird, Junius

1969   Fiber and Spinning Procedures in the Andean Area. In *The Junius B. Bird*
            Pre-Colombian Textile Conference, edited by Ann Pollard Rowe, Elizabeth
            Benson, and Anne Louise Schaeffer, 13-18. Washington, D.C.: Dumbarton
            Oaks.

Boone, Elizabeth Hill, and Walter D. Mignolo, eds.

1994   *Writing without Words: Alternative Literacies in Mesoamerica and the Andes.*
            Durham, N.C.: Duke University Press.

Bouysse-Cassagne, Teresa

1978   L'organisation de l'espace aymara. *Annales*, 33 année (5-6):1057-1080.

Brokaw, Galen

2005   Nuevas investigaciones sobre el khipu. *Identidades*, Año 4, no. 87:6-7. Lima:
            El Peruano.

Brown, Cecil

1991   Hieroglyphic Literacy in Ancient Mayaland: Inferences from Linguistic
            Data. *Current Anthropology* 32(4):489-496.

Burns, William Glynn

1981   *La escritura de los Incas: Una introducción a la clave de la escritura secreta de*
            los Incas. Lima: Editorial Los Pinos.

1990   *Legado de los Amautas.* Lima: Concytec.

2002   *Decodificación de kipus.* Lima: Banco Central de Reserva del Perú and Uni-
            versidad a las Peruanas.

Cahlander, Adele

1983   Understanding Some Complex Structures from Simple Andean Looms:
            Steps in Analysis and Reproduction. *Ars Textrina* 6:181-233.

Cahlander, Adele, and Susan Baizerman

1985   *Double Woven Treasures from Old Peru.* St. Paul, Minn.: Dos Tejedoras.

Casaverde Rojas, Juvenal

1976   El mundo sobrenatural en una comunidad. *Allpanchis* 2:121-244.

Cason, Majorie, and Adele Cahlander

1976   *The Art of Bolivian Highland Weaving.* New York: Watson-Gutpill.

Cehopu

1989   *La ciudad hispanoamericana: El sueño de un orden.* Madrid: Ministerio de la
            Cultura.

Cereceda, Verónica

1978   Semiologia de tissus andins: Les talegas d'Isluga. *Annales*, 33 année
            (5-6):1017-1035.

1987 Aproximaciones a una estética andina: De la belleza al tinku. In *Tres reflexiones sobre el pensamiento aymara*, edited by Javier Medina, 133-226. La Paz: Hisbol.

Cereceda, Verónica, Johnny Davalos, and Jaime Mejia

1993 *Una diferencia, un sentido: Los diseños de los textiles tarabucos y jalq'a*. Sucre, Bolivia: ASUR.

Champi Ccasa, Florentino

2005 Posibilidades de un etnodesarrollo en las comunidades de la "Nación Q'ero." In *Q'ero, el último ayllu inka*, edited by Jorge Flores Ochoa and Juan Victor Núñez del Prado Bejar, 427-436. Lima: Universidad Nacional Mayor de San Marcos and Instituto Nacional de Cultura.

Chirinos, Noemí

1999 Tintes en el Perú prehispánica, virreinal y republicana/Dyes in Pre-Hispanic, Viceregal and Republican Peru. In *Tejidos milenarios del Perú/Ancient Peruvian Textiles*, edited by Jose Antonio de Lavalle, 75-106. Lima: AFP Integra.

Cieza de León, Pedro

[1553] 1985 *Crónica del Perú: Primera y segunda partes*. Lima: Pontificia Universidad del Perú.

Cobo, Bernabé

[1653] 1956 *Historía del Nuevo Mundo*. Madrid: Ediciones Atlas.

Coe, Michael

1995 *Breaking the Maya Code*. New York: Thames and Hudson.

2001 *Reading the Maya Glyphs*. New York: Thames and Hudson.

Cohen, John

1957 An Investigation of Contemporary Weaving of the Peruvian Indians. Master's thesis. Yale University.

1986 Música de la sierra. In *Q'ero: Pueblo y música*, edited by Rodolfo Holzmann, 205-220. Lima: Patronato Popular y Porvenir Pro-Música Clásica.

1989 La música. In *Puna, qheswa, yunga: El hombre y su medio en Q'ero*, edited by Jorge Flores Ochoa and Anna María Fries, 72-74. Lima: Fondo Editorial, Banco Central de Reserva del Perú.

2005 Música de la sierra del Perú. In *Q'ero, el último ayllu inka*, edited by Jorge Flores Ochoa and Juan Victor Núñez del Prado Bejar, 363-374. Lima: Universidad Nacional Mayor de San Marcos and Instituto Nacional de Cultura.

Comisión Coordinadora Nacional del Concurso Nacional del Dibujo y Pintura Campesina (CNDPC)

1990 *Imágenes y realidad: A la conquista de un viejo lenguaje*. Lima: Gráficos S.R.

Crickmay, Lindsey

1997   Adentro, afuera y alrededor: Género y metáfora en la demaración del espa-
              cio textil. In *Parentesco y género en los Andes*, vol. 1, edited by Denise Y.
              Arnold, 531-546. La Paz: CIASE.

Cusihuamán, Antonio

1976a   *Diccionario Quechua: Cuzco-Collao*. Lima: Instituto de Estudios Peruanos.

1976b   *Gramática Quechua: Cuzco-Collao*. Lima: Instituto de Estudios Peruanos.

Daniels, Peter T., and William Bright, eds.

1996   *The World's Writing Systems*. New York: Oxford University Press.

Davalos, Johnny, Verónica Cereceda, and Gabriel Martínez

1992   *Textiles tarabucos*. Potosí, Bolivia: Qhorí Llama.

Davies, Paul

1988   *The Cosmic Blueprint*. New York: Simon and Schuster.

Dean, Carolyn

2002   *Los cuerpos de los Incas y el cuerpo de Cristo*. Lima: UNMSM and Banco
              Santander Hispano Central.

Dearborn, David, Katharine Screiber, and Raymond E. White

1987   Intimachay: A December Solstice Observatory at Machu Picchu, Peru.
              American Antiquity 52:346-352.

de la Jara, Victoria

1965   *La escritura peruana y los vocabularios Quechuas antiguos*. Lima: Imprenta
              Lux.

1967   Vers le dechiffrement des écritures anciennes du Peroú. *Science, Progrès,
              Nature* 3387:241-247.

Derosiers, Sophie

1982   *Metier à tisser et vêtement andins ou le tissu comme être vivant*. Paris:
              CETECLAM.

Dransart, Penny

1995   Inner Worlds and the Event of a Thread in Isluga, Northern Chile. In
              Andean Art: Visual Expression and Its Relation to Andean Beliefs and Values,
              edited by Penny Dransart, 228-242. Avebury, U.K.: Ashgate.

2000   Clothed Metal and the Iconography of Human Form among the Inca.
              In *Precolumbian Gold: Technology, Style, and Iconography*, edited by Colin
              McEwan, 76-91. London: Fitzroy Dearborn.

2002   Coloured Knowledge: Colour Perception and the Dissemination of Knowl-
              edge in Isluga, Northern Chile. In *Knowledge and Learning in the Andes*,
              edited by Henry Stobart and Rosaleen Howard, 56-78. Liverpool: Liverpool
              University Press.

Durbin, Marshall

1968   Linguistics and Writing Systems IV: The Incorporation of Linguistic Information into an Art Style. *Actes du XLIIe Congrès International des Américanistes* 42(4):13-36.

Escobar Moscoso, Mario

1983   Reconocimiento geográfico de Q'ero. In *Q'ero, el último ayllu inka*, edited by Jorge Flores Ochoa and Juan Núñez del Prado Bejar, 1-13. Cuzco: Centro de Estudios Andinos Cuzco.

Femenias, Blenda

1987   *Andean Aesthetics: Textiles of Peru and Bolivia.* Madison: Elvehjem Museum of Art, University of Wisconsin.

Fischer, Eva

2002a   Las categorías del tiempo y el concepto de temporalidad: El caso de Upinhuaya. *Revista Andina* 35: 167-190.

2002b   Textiles, historia y antropología cognitiva—Ejemplos andinos de tradición y cambio. In *Actas II Jornadas Internacionales sobre Textiles Precolombinos*, edited by Victoria Solanilla Demestre, 161-170. Barcelona: Grammagraf.

Flores Ochoa, Jorge

1973   Inkarri y Qollari en una comunidad del Altiplano. In *Ideología mesiánica del mundo andino*, edited by Juan Ossio Acuña, 301-338. Lima: Ediciones Ignacio Prado Pastor.

1978   Taxonomies animales. *Annales*, 33 année (5-6):1006-1016.

Flores Ochoa, Jorge, and Anna María Fries, eds.

1989   *Puna, qheswa, yunga: El hombre y su medio en Q'ero.* Lima: Fondo Editorial, Banco Central de Reserva del Perú.

Flores Ochoa, Jorge, Elizabeth Kuon Arce, and Roberto Samanez

1998   *Qeros: Arte inka en vasos ceremoniales.* Lima: Banco de Crédito del Perú.

Flores Ochoa, Jorge, and Juan Victor Núñez del Prado Bejar, eds.

1983   *Q'ero, el último ayllu inka.* Cuzco: Centro de Estudios Andinos Cuzco.

2005   *Q'ero, el último ayllu inka.* 2nd ed. Lima: Universidad Nacional Mayor de San Marcos and Instituto Nacional de Cultura.

Fossa, Lydia

2005   Guamán Poma, yupana y perspectiva. *Identidades*, Año 4(87):3-5. Lima: El Peruano.

Franquemont, Christine

1986   Chinchero Pallays: An Ethnic Code. In *The Junius B. Bird Conference on Andean Textiles*, edited by Ann Pollard Rowe, 331-338. Washington, D.C.: Textile Museum.

Franquemont, Edward

1986   Cloth Production Rates in Chinchero. In *The Junius B. Bird Conference on Andean Textiles*, edited by Ann Pollard Rowe, 309-330. Washington, D.C.: Textile Museum.

Franquemont, Edward, and Christine Franquemont

1987   Learning to Weave in Chinchero. *Textile Museum Journal* 26:54-78.

Franquemont, Edward, Christine Franquemont, and Billie Jean Isbell

1992   Awaq Ñawin: El Ojo del Tejedor; La práctica de la cultura en el tejido. *Revista Andina* 1(1):47-80.

Garcilaso de la Vega, El Inca

[1609] 1960 Comentarios reales de los Incas y historia general del Perú. In *Obras completas del Inca Garcilaso de la Vega*. Madrid: Biblioteca de Autores Españoles.

Gates, William

1931   *An Outline Dictionary of Maya Glyphs*. Baltimore: Johns Hopkins University Press.

Gayton, Anna

1961   The Cultural Significance of Peruvian Textiles: Production, Function, Aesthetics. *Kroeber Anthropological Society Papers* 25:111-128.

Gelb, Ignace J.

1963   *A Study of Writing*. Chicago: University of Chicago Press.

Getzels, Peter

1983   Los ciegos: Visión de la identidad del runa en la ideología de Inkarri-Qollari. In *Q'ero, el último ayllu inka*, edited by Jorge Flores Ochoa and Juan Victor Núñez del Prado Bejar, 170-201. Cuzco: Centro de Estudios Andinos Cuzco.

Girault, Louis

1969   *Textiles boliviens—Région de Charazani*. Paris: Musée de l'Homme.

Gisbert, Teresa

1980   *Iconografía y mitos indígenas en el arte*. La Paz: Gisbert y Cia.

1999   *El paraíso de los pájaros parlantes*. La Paz: Plural and UNSLP.

Gisbert, Teresa, Silvia Arze, and Martha Cajias

1987   *Arte textil y mundo andino*. La Paz: Gisbert y Cia.

Glave, Luis Miguel, and María Isabel Remy

1983   *Estructura agraria y vida rural en una región andina: Ollantaytambo entre los siglos XVI y XIX*. Lima: CBC.

González Holguín, Diego

[1608] 1989 *Vocabulario de la lengua general de todo el Perú llamada lengua Qquichua o del Inca*. Lima: UNMSM.

Goodell, Grace

1969   The Cloth of the Quechuas. *Natural History* 78(10):48-55.

Goody, Jack

1977   *The Domestication of the Savage Mind*. Cambridge: Cambridge University Press.

1987   *The Interface between the Written and the Oral*. Cambridge: Cambridge University Press.

Goody, Jack, and I. P. Watt

1963   The Consequences of Literacy. *Comparative Studies in History and Society* 5:304-345.

Gow, David

1974   Taytacha Qoyllur Rit'i. *Allpanchis* 7:49-100.

1976   The Gods and Social Change in the High Andes. Ph.D. dissertation. University of Washington.

Guamán Poma de Ayala, Felipe

[1615] 1980 *El primer Nueva Crónica y buen gobierno*. Edited by John V. Murra and Rolena Adorno, translations and textual analysis of Quechua by Jorge L. Urioste. México, D.F. : Siglo Veintiuno.

Gutiérrez de Santa Clara

[1556] 1963 Historia de las guerras civiles del Perú. In *Crónicas del Perú*. BAE Vol. 5. Madrid.

Haas, W., ed.

1976   *Writing without Letters*. Manchester: Manchester University Press.

Harris, Marvin

1968   *The Rise of Anthropological Theory*. New York: Crowell.

Harris, Olivia

1978   De l'asymetrie au triangle: Transformations symboliques. *Annales* 33 année (5-6):1108-1125.

Harris, Roy

1986   *The Origin of Writing*. London: Duckworth.

Havelock, E. A.

1976   *Origins of Western Literacy*. Monograph Series No. 14. Toronto: Ontario Institute for Studies in Education.

Heckman, Andrea M.

2003   *Woven Stories: Andean Textiles and Rituals*. Albuquerque: University of New Mexico Press.

Hugh-Jones, Stephen

1976   *The Palm and the Pleiades: Initiation and Cosmology in Northwest Amazonia*. Cambridge: Cambridge University Press.

Jackson, Donald

1981   *The Story of Writing.* New York: Taplinger.

Jansen, Maarten

1988   The Art of Writing in Ancient Mexico: An Ethno-iconological Perspective.
                Visible Religion 6:86-113.

Kauffmann-Doig, Federico

1969   *Manual de arqueología peruana.* Lima: Ediciones Peisa.

2005   *Machu Picchu: Tesoro inca.* Lima: CARTOLAN.

Larco Hoyle, Rafael

2001   *Los Mochicas.* 2 vols. Lima: Telefonica.

Laurencich-Minelli, Laura

1996   *La scrittura dell'antico Peru.* Bologna: CLUEB.

2001   Presentación del documento Exsul Immeritus Blas Valera Populo Suo. In
                Guamán Poma y Blas Valera: Tradición andina e historia colonial, edited by
                Francesca Cantù, 111-142. Roma: Antonio Pellicani Editore.

Laurencich-Minelli, Laura, and Paulina Numhauser Bar-Magen

2004   *El silencio protagonista: El primer siglo jesuita en el Virreinato del Perú, 1567-*
                1667. Quito: Abya Yala.

León Portilla, Miguel

1996   *El destino de la palabra.* Mexico City: Fondo de Cultura Económica.

Lira, Jorge A.

1982   *Diccionario Kkechuwa-Español.* Secretaría Ejecutiva del Convenio "Andrés
                Bello." Bogotá: Cuadernos Culturales Andinos.

Lizarraga, Karen

1988   *Identidad nacional y estética andina: Una teoría peruana del arte.* Lima: Con-
                sejo Nacional de Ciencia y Tecnología.

Locke, Leland

1923   *The Ancient Kipu or Peruvian Knot Record.* New York: American Museum
                of Natural History.

López, Jaime, Willer Flores, and Catherine Letourneux

1992   *Lliqllas chayantakas.* La Paz: Ruralter.

1993   *Laymi salta.* La Paz: Ruralter.

Lyons, Patricia

1979   Female Supernaturals in Ancient Peru. *Ñawpa Pacha* 16:95-104.

Mackey, Carol, Hugo Pereyra, Carlos Radicati, Humberto Rodríguez, and Oscar
                Valverde

1990   *Kipu y yupana.* Lima: Concytec.

Mamami Quispe, Cirilo

1978   Estudio preliminar de colorantes vegetales. Bachelor's thesis. Universidad Nacional San Antonio Abad del Cuzco, Cuzco.

Mangeot, Catherine

1975   Tissage Quechua contemporain, région du Cuzco. Master's thesis. Haute École en Sciences Sociales, Paris.

Mannheim, Bruce

1999   Poética Quechua y formación nacional. *Revista Andina* 17(1):15-45.

Marcus, Joyce

1992   *Mesoamerican Writing Systems: Propaganda, Myth, and History in Four Ancient Civilizations.* Princeton, N.J.: Princeton University Press.

Mariscotti, Ana María

1978   *Pachamama Santa Tierra.* Contribuciones al estudio de la religión autóctona en los Andes centro meridionales. Berlin: Gebr. Mann Verlag.

Martínez, Gabriel

1983   Los dioses de los cerros en los Andes. *Journal de la Société des Américanistes* 69:87-115.

Matos Mar, José, Alejandro Matos Ávalos, and Rosalia Matos Ávalos

1984   Tupe, pueblo tradicional en la provincia de Yauyos. *Boletín de Lima* 36:57-73.

Medlin, Mary Ann

1976   The Shape of the Sun: Selected Aspects of Designs in the Weavings of Q'ero, Peru. Master's thesis. University of North Carolina.

1983   Weaving, Social Organization, and Ethnic Identity. Ph.D. dissertation. University of North Carolina.

1986   Learning to Weave in Calcha, Bolivia. In *The Junius B. Bird Conference on Andean Textiles,* edited by Ann Pollard Rowe, 275-288. Washington, D.C.: Textile Museum.

1991   Ethnic Dress and Calcha Festivals, Bolivia. In *Textile Traditions of Mesoamerica and the Andes: An Anthology,* edited by Margot Blum Schevill, Janet Catherine Berlo, and Edward B. Dwyer, 261-279. New York: Garland.

Meisch, Lynn Ann

1988   The Living Textiles of Tarabuco, Bolivia. In *Andean Aesthetics: Textiles of Peru and Bolivia,* edited by Blenda Femenias, 46-59. Madison: Elvehjem Museum of Art, University of Wisconsin.

1991   "We are the sons of Atahualpa and we will win": Dress in Otavalo and Saraguro, Ecuador. In *Textile Traditions of Mesoamerica and the Andes: An Anthology,* edited by Margot Blum Schevill, Janet Catherine Berlo, and Edward B. Dwyer, 280-302. New York: Garland.

Millones, Luis

1988   *El Inca por la Coya*. Lima: Editorial Hipatia.

Ministerio de la Vivienda

1983   Censos nacionales, VII, de población de vivienda. Vol. A. Departamento de
       Cusco. Lima.

Molina (el Cuzqueño), Cristóbal de

[1575] 1943 Relación de las fábulas y ritos de los Incas. In *Las crónicas de los Molinas*.
       Los Pequeños Libros de Historia Americana. Serie 1, vol. 4. Lima: Librería
       Imprenta D. Miranda.

Morote Best, Efraín

1983   Un nuevo mito de fundación del imperio. In *Q'ero, el último ayllu inka*,
       edited by Jorge Flores Ochoa and Juan Victor Núñez del Prado Bejar, 158-
       169. Cuzco: Centro de Estudios Andinos Cuzco.

Mueller, Thomas, and Helga Mueller

1984   Mito de Inkarri-Qollari. *Allpanchis* 23(20):128-143.

Munsters, Martina

1986   Veranderend perspectief in de motieven en het wereldbeld van Chincheros,
       Ccachins, en Cusco, Peru. Master's thesis. Vrie University of Amsterdam.

Murua, Martín de

[1590] 1962 *Historia general del Perú*. Madrid: Biblioteca Americana Vetus.

Nolte, Rosa María Josefa

1991   *Qellcay: Arte y vida de Sarhua, comunidades campesinas andinas*. Lima: Tierra
       Nuova.

Núñez del Prado, Oscar

1970   *El hombre y la familia: Su matrimonio y organización político-social en Q'ero*.
       Cuzco: Garcilaso.

1973   Versión del mito de Inkarri en Q'ero. In *Ideología mesiánica del mundo
       andino*, edited by Juan Ossio Acuña, 275-280. Lima: Ediciones Ignacio
       Prado Pastor.

1983a   Una cultura como respuesta de adaptación al medio andino. In *Q'ero, el
       último ayllu inka*, edited by Jorge Flores Ochoa and Juan Victor Núñez del
       Prado Bejar, 14-29. Cuzco: Centro de Estudios Andinos Cuzco.

1983b   La vivienda inca actual. In *Q'ero, el último ayllu inka*, edited by Jorge Flores
       Ochoa and Juan Victor Núñez del Prado Bejar, 82-86. Cuzco: Centro de
       Estudios Andinos Cuzco.

1990   El kipu moderno. In *Kipu y yupana*, edited by Carol Mackey, Hugo Pereyra,
       Carlos Radicati, Humberto Rodríguez, and Oscar Valverde, 165-182. Lima:
       Concytec.

2005   El khipu moderno. In *Q'ero, el último ayllu inka*, edited by Jorge Flores Ochoa and Juan Victor Núñez del Prado Bejar, 169-198. Lima: Universidad Nacional Mayor de San Marcos and Instituto Nacional de Cultura.

Núñez del Prado Bejar, Juan Victor

1970   El mundo sobrenatural de los Quechuas del sur del Perú a través de la comunidad de Qotabamba. *Allpanchis* 2:57-119.

2005   Presentación. In *Q'ero, el último ayllu inca*, edited by Jorge Flores Ochoa and Juan Victor Núñez del Prado Bejar, i–viii. Lima: UNMSM and INC.

Ong, W. J.

1982   *Orality and Literacy: The Technologizing of the World*. London: Methuen.

Orlove, Benjamin

1991 Mapping Reeds and Reading Maps: The Politics of Representation in Lake Titicaca. *American Ethnologist* 18(1):3-38.

Ortiz, Alejandro

1973   *De Adaneva a Inkarri*. Lima: Retablod Papel Ediciones.

Ossio, Juan Acuña

1978   El simbolismo de agua y la representación del tiempo y el espacio en la fiesta de la acequia de la comunidad de Andamarca. *Actes du XLII Congrès International des Américanistes* 4:377-389.

1992   *Parentesco, reciprocidad y jerarquía en los Andes: Una aproximación a la organización social de la comunidad de Andamarca*. Lima: PUC.

2005   Los Q'ero de Cusco. In *Q'ero, el último ayllu inka*, edited by Jorge Flores Ochoa and Juan Victor Núñez del Prado Bejar, 245-264. Lima: Universidad Nacional Mayor de San Marcos and Instituto Nacional de Cultura.

Ossio, Juan Acuña, ed.

1973   *Ideologia mesiánica del mundo andino*. Lima: Ediciones Ignacio Prado Pastor.

Parssinen, Martti

1992   *Tawantinsuyu: The Inca State and Its Political Organization*. Helsinki: SHS.

Parssinen, Martti, and J. Kiviharju

2005   *Textos andinos*. Madrid: Instituto Iberamericano de Finlandia and Universidad Complutense de Madrid.

Pease, Franklin

1973   El mito de Inkarri y la visión de los vencidos. In *Ideología mesiánica del mundo andino*, edited by Juan Ossio Acuña, 439-460. Lima: Ediciones Ignacio Prado Pastor.

Pereyra, Hugo

1997   Los kipus con cuerdas entorchadas. In *Arqueología, antropología e historia en los Andes: Homenaje a María Rostworowski*, edited by Rafael Varón Gabai and Javier Flores Espinoza, 187-198. Lima: IEP and BCR.

Pérez-Galan, Beatriz

2002   Los alabados: Apuntes sobre el universo simbólico de la autoridad en comu-
            nidades del sur andino peruano. *Revista Andina* 35:247-264.

Phipps, Elena

2004   Garments and Identity in the Colonial Andes. In *The Colonial Andes: Tap-
            estries and Silverwork, 1530-1830*, edited by Elena Phipps, Johanna Hecht, and
            Cristina Esteras Martín, 16-41. New York: Metropolitan Museum of Art.

2005   Rasgos de nobleza: Los uncus virreinales y sus modelos incaicos. In *Los
            Incas, reyes del Perú*, edited by Natalia Majluf, 68-93. Lima: Banco de
            Crédito del Perú.

Pimentel, Nelson D.

2005   *Amarrando colores: La producción del sentido en khipus aymaras.* Oruro,
            Bolivia: Latina Editores.

Platt, Tristan

1978   Symetries en miroir: Le concept de yanatin chez les Macha de Bolivie.
            Annales 33 année (5-6):1081-1107.

Polo de Ondegardo, Juan

[1585] 1916 *De los errores y supersticiones de los Indios: Sacados del tratado y averiguación
            que hizo el Licenciado Polo.* Lima: San Martín.

Prefectura de Paucartambo

1957a   Expediente 81.

1957b   Informe del comandante de puesto de la Guardia Civil en Paucartambo al
            sub-prefectura.

Prochaska, Rita

1988   *Taquile: Tejiendo un mundo mágico/Weavers of a Magic World.* Lima: Arius
            S.A.

Quilter, Jeffrey, and Gary Urton, eds.

2002   *Narrative Threads: Accounting and Recounting an Andean Khipu.* Austin:
            University of Texas Press.

Quispe-Agnoli, Rocio

2002   Cuando Occidente y los Andes se encuentran: Qellqay, escritura alfabética,
            y tokapu en el siglo XVI. *Colonial Latin American Review* 14(2):263-298.

Radicati di Primeglio, Carlos

1979   *El sistema contable de los Incas.* Lima: Studium.

1990   El cromatismo en los kipus: Significado del Kipu de Canutos. In *Kipu y
            yupana*, edited by Carol Mackey, 35-50B. Lima: Concytec.

Randall, Robert

1982   Qoyllur Rit'i: An Inca Fiesta of the Pleiades; Reflections on Time and Space
            in the Andean World. *Bulletín de l'Institut Français d'Études Andines* 15:37-81.

Rasnake, Roger

1989   *Autoridad y poder en los Andes: Los Kuraqkuna de Yura.* La Paz: Hisbol.

Reinhard, Johann

1991   *Machu Picchu: The Sacred Center.* Lima: Nueva Imágenes.

Rivière, Gilles

1982   Sabaya: Structures socio-economiques et representations symboliques dans
            le Carangas-Bolivia. 2 vols. Ph.D. dissertation. École des Hautes Etudes en
            Sciences Sociales, Paris.

Roe, Peter

1982   *The Cosmic Zygote: Cosmology in the Amazon Basin.* New Brunswick, N.J.:
            Rutgers University Press.

Rosing, Iña

1990   *Introducción al mundo Callawaya.* La Paz: Editorial "Los Amigos del Libro."

1991   *Las almas nuevas del mundo Callawaya.* La Paz: Editorial "Los Amigos del
            Libro."

1997   Los diez géneros de Amarete, Bolivia. In *Parentesco y género en los Andes,*
            vol. 1, edited by Denise Y. Arnold, 77-93. La Paz: CIASE.

Rowe, Ann Pollard

1975   Weaving Processes of the Cuzco Area of Peru. *Textile Museum Journal*
            4(2):30-46.

1977   *Warp-Patterned Weaves of the Andes.* Washington, D.C.: Textile Museum.

Rowe, Ann Pollard, ed.

1986   *The Junius B. Bird Conference on Andean Textiles.* Washington, D.C.: Textile
            Museum.

Rowe, Ann Pollard, and John Cohen

2002   *Hidden Threads of Peru: Q'ero Textiles.* Washington, D.C.: Merrell in asso-
            ciation with the Textile Museum.

Rowe, John Howland

1946   Inca Culture at the Time of the Spanish Conquest. In *Handbook of South
            American Indians,* edited by J. H. Steward, 183-330. Bureau of American
            Ethnology, Bulletin 143. Washington, D.C.: Smithsonian Institution.

1999   Estandarización de las túnicas de tapiz inca/Standardization in Inca Tapes-
            try Tunics. In *Tejidos milenarios del Perú/Ancient Peruvian Textiles,* edited by
            José Antonio de Lavalle and Rosario de Lavalle de Cárdenas, 571-628. Lima:
            AFP Integra.

Rozas Álvarez, Washington

1983   Los paqos de Q'ero. In *Q'ero, el último ayllu inka*, edited by Jorge Flores
           Ochoa and Juan Victor Núñez del Prado Bejar, 143-157. Cuzco: Centro de
           Estudios Andinos Cuzco

1989   Los paqos. In *Puna, qheswa, yunga: El hombre y su medio en Q'ero*, edited by
           Jorge Flores Ochoa and Anna María Fries, 53-60. Lima: Banco Central de
           Reserva del Perú.

2005   Los paqos en Q'ero. In *Q'ero, el último ayllu inka*, edited by Jorge Flores
           Ochoa and Juan Victor Núñez del Prado, 265-276. Lima: Universidad
           Nacional Mayor de San Marcos and Instituto Nacional de Cultura.

Ruiz Durand, Jesús

2004   *Introducción a la iconografía andina.* Vol. 1. Lima: IKONO.

Ruiz Estrada, Arturo

1990   Notas sobre un kipu de la costa nor-central del Perú. In *Kipu y yupana*,
           edited by Carol Mackey, 191-194. Lima: Concytec.

Sallnow, Michael

1974   La peregrinación andina. *Allpanchis* 2:101-142.

Salomon, Frank

2004   *The Cord Keepers: Quipus and Cultural Life in a Peruvian Village.* Durham,
           N.C.: Duke University Press.

Santa Cruz Pachacuti Yamqui Salcamaygua, Juan de

[1613] 1959 Relacion de antigüedades de este reyno del Perú. In *Tres relaciones de anti-
           güedades peruanas*, edited by M. Jiménez de la Espada. Asunción, Paraguay:
           Editorial Guaranda.

Santo Tomás, Domingo de

[1560] 1951 *Lexicón o vocabulario de la lengua general del Perú.* Lima: UNMSM.

Sarmiento de Gamboa, Pedro

[1572] 1942 *Historia general llamada Inca.* Buenos Aires: Biblioteca Emece.

Schele, Linda, David Friedel, and Joy Parker

1999   *El cosmos maya: Tres mil años por la senda de los Chamanes.* Mexico City:
           Fondo de Cultura Económica.

Schevill, Margot Blum, Janet Catherine Berlo, and Edward B. Dwyer

1991   *Textile Traditions of Mesoamerica and the Andes: An Anthology.* New York:
           Garland.

Schmandt-Besserat, Denise

1990   Symbols in the Prehistoric Middle East: Developmental Features Preceding
           Written Communication. In *Oral and Written Communication: Historical
           Approaches*, edited by Richard Leo Enos, 16-30. Newbury Park, Calif.: Sage
           Publications.

1992 *Before Writing*. Vol. 1, *From Counting to Cuneiform*. Austin: University of
   Texas Press.

Seibold, Katharine

1992 Textiles and Cosmology in Choquecancha, Cuzco, Peru. In *Andean Cos-*
   mologies through Time: Persistence and Emergence, edited by Robert V. Dover,
   Katharine Seibold, and John H. McDowell, 167-201. Bloomington: Indiana
   University Press.

Seligmann, Linda

1978 The Role of Weaving in the Contemporary Andean Socio-Economic Formation. Master's thesis. University of Texas.

Sherbondy, Jeannette

1982 The Canal Systems of Hanan Cuzco. Ph.D. dissertation. University of
   Illinois.

Sillar, Bill

1997 Engendrar la vida y vivificar la muerte: Arcilla y miniaturas en los Andes. In
   Parentesco y género en los Andes, vol. 1, edited by Denise Y. Arnold, 513-530.
   La Paz: CIASE.

Silverblatt, Irene

1990 *Luna, sol y brujas: Género y clases en los Andes pre-hispánicos y coloniales.*
   Cuzco: CBC.

Silverman, Gail

1994a *El tejido andino: Un libro de sabiduría*. Lima: Banco Central de Reserva del
   Perú.

1994b La metáfora del cuerpo humano: Una nueva hipótesis en relación al significado de la iconografía de los textiles Q'ero. *Antropológica* Año 12(2):63-85.

1994c Iconografía textil Q'ero vista como texto: Leyendo el rombo dualista Hatun
   Inti. *Bulletin de l'Institut Français d'Études Andines* 23(1):171-190.

1995a La importancia de las investigaciones etnográficas de los textiles en la arqueología cusqueña. *Boletín de Lima* 17(99):39-48.

1995b *Leyendo el tejido cusqueño*. Exhibition catalog. Lima: Museo Nacional de la
   Cultura.

1995c Q'ero: Tierras, cultivos, y viviendas. *Boletín de la Sociedad Geográfica de Lima*
   5(108):105-118.

1996 *El tejido andino: La figura y la palabra*. Exhibition catalog. Lima: Biblioteca
   Nacional del Perú.

1997 Iconografía cusqueña. *La Casa de Cartón de OXY II Época* 10:72-79.

1998 *El tejido andino: Un libro de sabiduría*. 2nd ed. Mexico City: Fondo de Cultura Económica.

1999   Iconografía textil de Cusco y su relación con los tocapus inca/ Textile Ico-
            nography from Cusco and Their Relation to the Inca Tocapus. In *Tejidos
            milenarios del Perú/ Ancient Peruvian Textiles*, edited by José Antonio de
            Lavalle, 803-836. Lima: AFP Integra.

2001a   Leyendo el tejido andino: Historia y textualidad en el mundo de los Q'ero.
            In *Jornadas andinas de literatura latinoamericana*, edited by Enrique Rosas
            Paravicino, 245-250. Lima: Fondo Editorial Cronolibros.

2001b   La representación del tejido andino. *Boletín de Lima* 23(123):63-74.

2005a   Motivos textiles en Q'ero. In *Q'ero, el último ayllu inka*, edited by Jorge Flores
            Ochoa and Juan Victor Núñez del Prado Bejar, 349-362. Lima: Universidad
            Nacional Mayor de San Marcos and Instituto Nacional de Cultura.

2005b   *La "haute couture" andina: Tejiendo para un futuro mejor.* Exhibition catalog.
            Cuzco: Instituto Cultural Peruano Norteamericano.

In press   *Reading Inka Writing.* Salt Lake City: University of Utah Press.

Ms.a   La guía del tejido cusqueño.

Ms.b   Leyendo la escritura inka.

Silverman, Gail, ed.

1991a   *El léxico Gráfico del Cusco.* Vol. 1 of Awana Wasi del Cusco. Lima: Concytec.

1991b   *Chinchero Pallay.* Vol. 2 of *Awana Wasi del Cusco.* Lima: Concytec.

1993   *Ch'unchu Pallay.* Vol. 3 of *Awana Wasi del Cusco.* Lima: Pontificia Universi-
            dad Católica del Perú and Southern Peru Copper Corporation.

1995   *The Cusco Area Textile Tradition.* Vol. 4 of *Awana Wasi del Cusco.* Lima:
            Awana Wasi del Cusco.

Silverman-Proust, Gail

1983   Motivos textiles en Q'ero. In *Q'ero, el último ayllu inka*, edited by Jorge Flores
            Ochoa and Juan Victor Núñez del Prado Bejar, 87-105. Cuzco: Centro de
            Estudios Andinos Cuzco.

1984   Los motivos de los tejidos de Q'ero: La descripción de los motivos. *Revista
            del Museo e Instituto de Arqueología* 23:281-308.

1986a   Cuatro motivos inti de Q'ero. *Boletín de Lima* 46:61-76.

1986b   Representación gráfica del mito Inkarri en los tejidos Q'ero. *Boletín de Lima*
            48:59-71.

1987a   Le mode tissé du temps: Les textiles andins conçus comme un registre du
            savoir. Ph.D. dissertation. Université de Paris V, Rene Descartes, Sciences
            Humaines, Sorbonne, Paris.

1987b   The Woven Shadow of Time: Four Inti Motifs from Q'ero. *Dialogo Andino*
            6:107-126.

1988a   *Los tejidos Q'ero visto como un registro de sabiduría.* Exhibition catalog. Cuzco: Casa Cabrera and UNSAAC.

1988b   Significado simbólico de las franjas multicolores tejidas en los wayakos de los Q'ero. *Boletín de Lima* 57:37-44.

1988c   Weaving Technique and the Registration of Knowledge in the Cusco Area of Peru. *Journal of Latin American Lore* 14(2): 207-241.

1988d   Tawa inti qocha, símbolo de la cosmología andina: Concepción Q'ero del espacio. *Antropológica* Año 6(6):7-42.

1989   Textiles. In *Puna, qheswa, yunga: El hombre y su medio en Q'ero,* edited by Jorge Flores Ochoa and Anna María Fries, 75-80. Lima: Banco Central de Reserva del Perú.

1990   Representación gráfica del mito Inkarri en los tejidos Q'ero. In *Mitos universales, americanos y contemporáneos,* edited by Moisés Lemlij, 147-175. Lima: Sociedad Peruano de Psicoanálisis and UNSAAC.

1991   Iskaymanta/kinsamanta: La técnica de tejer y el libro de sabiduría en el Departamento del Cusco. *Boletín de Lima* 74:49-66.

Solari, Gertrude

1980   Signos simbólicos de un chumpi de Huanta. *Peru Folk* 7:1-2.

1982   Ideogramas en la textilería andina actual. *Boletín de Lima* 22:1-7.

1983   Interpretación de los signos de una manta de la isla de Taquile, Lago Titicaca. *Boletín de Lima* 24:1-29.

Squier, George

1877   *Peru: Incidents of Travel and Exploration in the Land of the Incas.* New York: Harper and Brothers.

Stobart, Henry

1998   Lo recto y lo torcido: La música andina y la espiral de la descendencia. In *Parentesco y género en los Andes,* edited by Denise Y. Arnold, 581-604. La Paz: CIASE.

Stone-Miller, Rebecca

1992   *To Weave for the Sun: Ancient Andean Textiles in the Museum of Fine Arts.* New York: Thames and Hudson.

Sullivan, William

1999   *El secreto de los Incas.* Barcelona: Ed. Grijalbo.

Taylor, Gerald

1981   Enonces exprimant la possession et l'obligation en Quechua. *Amerindia* 6:85-94.

Título Privado

1851   Instrumentos de Markachea y Totorani, Paucartambo. Cuzco.

Túpac Yupanqui, Demetrio

1955a   Expedición a Q'ero. *La Prensa*, 23 August, 1-2.

1955b   El misterio de los kipus resuelven etnólogos en Q'ero. *La Prensa*, 24 August, 1-2.

Ulloa, Liliana Torres, and Vivian Gavilán Vega

1992   Proporciones methodológicas para el estudio de los tejidos andinos. *Revista Andina* 10(1):107-134.

Urton, Gary

1981   *At the Crossroads of the Earth and the Sky: An Andean Cosmology.* Austin: University of Texas Press.

1986   Calendrical Cycles and Their Projections in Pacaritambo, Peru. *Journal of Latin American Lore* 212(1):45-64.

1997   De nudos a narraciones: Reconstrucción del arte de llevar registros históricos en los Andes a partir de transcripciones en español de los kipus incaicos. In *Saberes y memorias en los Andes,* edited by Terese Bouysse-Cassagne, 303-324. Paris: Institut des Hautes Études de l'Amérique Latine and IFEA.

2003   *Signs of the Inka Khipu: Binary Coding in the Andean Knotted-String Records.* Austin: University of Texas Press.

Valencia, Abraham

1973   Inkarri-Qollari dramatizado. In *Ideología mesiánica del mundo andino,* edited by Juan Ossio Acuña, 281-301. Lima: Ediciones Ignacio Prado Pastor.

1979   Nombres del maiz y su uso ritual por los K'anas. *Anthropologica Andina* 3:75-88.

Velázquez de la Cadena, Mariano

1974   *Spanish and English Dictionary.* Chicago: Folleto.

Wasserman, Tamara, and Jonathon Hill

1981   *Bolivian Indian Textiles: Traditional Designs and Costumes.* New York: Dover.

Wachtel, Nathan

1990   *Le retour des ancêtres: Les indiens Urus de Bolivie.* Paris: Gallimard.

Webster, Stephen

1970   An Indigenous Quechua Community in Exploitation of Multiple Ecological Zones. *Actes du XXXIX Congrès International des Américanistes* 39:174-183.

1972   The Social Organization of a Native Andean Community. Ph.D. dissertation. University of Washington.

1983   El pastoreo en Q'ero. In *Q'ero, el último ayllu inka,* edited by Jorge Flores Ochoa and Juan Victor Núñez del Prado Bejar, 48-81. Cuzco: Centro de Estudios Andinos Cuzco.

Wilson, Lee Anne

1991   Nature versus Culture: The Image of the Uncivilized Wild Man in Textiles from the Department of Cusco, Peru. In *Textile Traditions of Mesoamerica and the Andes*, edited by Margo Blum Schevill, Janet Catherine Berlo, and Edward B. Dwyer, 205-230. New York: Garland.

Wissler, Holly

2005   Tradición y modernización en la música de las dos principales festividades de Q'eros: Qoyllur Rit'i y Carnaval. In *Q'ero, el último ayllu inka*, edited by Jorge Flores Ochoa and Juan Victor Núñez del Prado Bejar, 363-420. Lima: Universidad Nacional Mayor de San Marcos and Instituto Nacional de Cultura.

Yabar, Américo

2005   Siguiendo las huellas de los Q'eros en el místico mundo de los Andes. In *Q'ero, el último ayllu inka*, edited by Jorge Flores Ochoa and Juan Victor Núñez del Prado Bejar, 277-286. Lima: Universidad Nacional Mayor de San Marcos and Instituto Nacional de Cultura.

Yabar, Américo, Orlando Vásquez, and Antonio Vásquez

1994   El ayllu de Qqeros-Paucartambo." *Revista Universitaria* 38:3-26.

Zorn, Elayne

1979   Warping and Weaving on a Fourstake Ground Loom in the Lake Titicaca Basin Community of Taquile, Peru. *Textile Museum Journal* 18:212-221.

1980   Sling Braiding in the Macusani Area of Peru. *Textile Museum Journal* 19-20:41-54.

1983   Tradition versus Tourism in Taquile, Peru. Master's thesis. University of Texas.

1986   Textiles in Herder's Ritual Bundles of Macusani, Peru. In *The Junius B. Bird Conference on Andean Textiles*, edited by Ann Pollard Rowe, 289-308. Washington, D.C.: Textile Museum.

2004   *Weaving a Future: Tourism, Cloth, and Culture on an Andean Island*. Iowa City: University of Iowa Press.

Zuidema, R. T.

1964   *The Ceque System of Cuzco: The Social Organization of the Capital of the Inca*. Leiden: E. J. Brill.

1973   La quadrature du cercle dans l'ancien Perou. *Signes et langages des Amériques: Recherche Amerindiennes au Quebec* 3(1-2):147-165.

1976   La imagen del sol y la huaca de Susurpuquio en el sistema astronómico de los Incas en el Cusco. *Journal de la Société des Américanistes* 63:200-230.

1982a   Catachillay: The Role of the Pleiades and the Southern Cross and A and B Centaurii in the Calendar of the Incas. In *Ethnoastronomy and Archaoastronomy in the American Tropics*, edited by Anthony Aveni and Gary Urton, 203-220. New York: Annals of the New York Academy of Sciences 385.

1982b   Bureaucracy and Systematic Knowledge in Andean Civilization. In *The Inca and Aztec States, 1400-1800: Anthropology and History*, edited by George A. Collier, Renato I. Rosaldo, and John D. Wirth, 419-457. New York: Academic Press.

1983   Hierarchy and Space in Incaic Social Organization. *Ethnohistory* 30(2):49-75.

Zumbuhl, Hugo

1979   *Tintes naturales usados en Huancayo, Perú*. Huancayo, Peru: Kamaq Maki.

Index

Cusihuamán, Sabino Ccuyro, 84

Damaso, Luis, 106
de Barry, Eduardo, 42–43
de Barry, Otto, 42
de la Jara, Victoria, xvii, 25, 54
Domestication of the Savage Mind, The
   (Goody 1977), 22
Dransart, Penny, 11, 180
Durbin, Marshall, 23
dyes, 30–31

Escobar, Mario, 120
Espinosa, Miguel Salas, 114

Fernández, Santusa, 15, 79
Fischer, Eva, 11
Flores Ochoa, Jorge, 54
Flores, Juliana, 35
Flores, Rosa Chura, 19, 35, 67, 95
Flores, Sebastian, 139–40
Flores, Willer, 11
Fossa, Lydia, 25
Franquemont, Christine, 11
Franquemont, Edward, 10

Gamboa, Sarmiento de, 96
Garcilaso de la Vega, El Inca, 96
garments, bags, and embellishments: aksu
   (skirt), 39; aymilla (jacket), 39; challina (scarf), 42; ch'ullu (knitted hat), 39,
   48–49; ch'umpi (belt), 39; ch'uspa (ceremonial bag), 42, 128–29; golon (skirt
   borders), 42; llama sarsilla (knitted bag),
   42; llaqolla (head covering), 8, 39; lliklla
   (shawl), 39, 42, 44–45, 53, 112, 128; poncho, 42, 46–47, 53, 112, 128; uncu, 7, 39, 42;

unkhuña, 42; warak'a (slings), 47; watana
   (hat straps), 42; wayakos (bags), 63–64,
   109–110, 117, 128
Gayton, Anna, 10
Girault, Louis, 10
Gisbert, Teresa, 10, 124
Goodell, Grace, 10
Goody, Jack, 22
graphic elements in textile motifs: circles,
   16; crosses, 51–52, 67–68, 77; diamonds,
   51–52, 67, 77, 79; functioning as word
   signs, 148–50; horizontal lines, 16; radiating lines, 16, 51–52, 63, 65–67, 88, 98–101;
   rectangle, 63, 77; representation of daily
   time, 83–91; representation of seasonal
   time, 97–107; triangles, 16, 53, 60–64,
   82–83; vertical lines, 16, 51–52, 63–64
Great Divide Theory, 22
Guamán Poma de Ayala, Felipe, 100
Gutiérrez, Berna, 66
Gutiérriz de Santa Clara, 177

Hakawaya, Prudencio, 17, 82, 103
Harris, Olivia, 73
hatun inti (midday sun): description of, 76;
   graphic elements of, 16, 51, 64–67, 87;
   literal translation of, 86; representation
   of time and space, 52, 75, 86–87
Havelock, E. A., 22
Heckmann, Andrea, 11
Holguín, González, 44, 178
Hoyle, Rafael Larco, 24
huacas, 178–79
Hugh-Jones, Stephen, 100

iconography, textile: functioning as nonalphabetic writing, 15, 22, 147, 180–81; and

quipus, 25; in Q'ero, 11–12, 14, 15. *See also* motifs, Q'ero; nonalphabetic writing; *specific motifs*

Incas: ceque system of time and space, 59–60; garments worn by, 7–8; motifs, 10, 54; nonalphabetic writing of, 1, 8; observation structures of, 80–81; quipus of, xvii, 6–7, 25, 109, 115–16, 183n7; representation of seasonal time, 96–98; representation of time and space, 79–80, 91–92, 140; story of first Inca, Inkarri, 123; study of astronomy, 104; types of cloth, 8; weaving techniques, 7–8, 38;

Inkarri, myth of, 123–24, 133–36, 140–42, 180–81

inti chinkapushan (sunset), 52, 76, 86

inti lloqsimushan (sunrise), 52, 75–78, 86–87

iskaymanta hoq uya (two-color supplementary warp weaving), 12–14, 38, 52, 175–79

Juárez, Filomena, 15, 78–79

Kauffmann-Doig, Federico, 139

kinsamanta iskay uya (three-color complementary warp weaving): iconographic content of, 175; and Q'ero pallay, 12, 52, 129; and relationship between two faces of cloth, 85–86; representation of spatial and temporal concepts, 13–14; trinary logic of, 177, 179; weaving technique of, 38

kinsamanta. *See* kinsamanta iskay uya

k'iraqey puntas (tooth points): in ch'unchu motif, 129, 136; description of, 52–53, graphic elements of, 82–83, 97; relationship to mountains, 60–62, 82; representation of time and space, 82–83; as secondary motif, 76–77

knitting, 47–48

Lara, Francisco, 17, 67–68, 89–91, 103

Laurencich-Minelli, Laura, 25

Letourneux, Catherine, 11

Lira, Jorge, 80

listas: colors used in, 110–12; multi-colored stripes of, 109, similarity to quipu, 113–16; symbolism of, 117; uses of, 110–13; weaving techniques of, 110–13

looms, 31–38, 111

López, Jaime, 11

Machaca, Jorge, 176

Mangeot, Catherine, 129

Martínez, Gabriel, 60

Medlin, Mary Ann, 11, 82

Meisch, Lynn Ann, 11

Meuller, Helga, 136

Meuller, Thomas, 136

Mignolo, Walter, 25

Minelli, Laura Laurencich, 115

Molina, Cristóbal de, 80, 91–92

motifs, Q'ero: chakran (his/her/its field), 66, 99–100; in design panels of llikllas, 44–45, in design panels of ponchos, 46–47, 112; dictionary of, 150–72; and gender, 15–18, 54, 124–25, 179–80; identification of, 15, 75; knowledge recorded in, 21, 23, 51, 91–93, 113–15, 176–77; named variations of, 11–12, 112; principal, 44–46; secondary, 44–46, 76–77; meaning of, 44, 51, 64, 77–78, 98–101; relationship to ceque system, 177; representation of time and space, 75–93; and similarity to drawings, 16–17, 61–62, 67; symbolic use of color, 82–85; trinary logic of, 177; vertical lines, 51–52, 63–64; weaving techniques use with, 85–86, 175–76; word signs of, 147–49; used in contemporary wayakos, 110. *See also* ch'unchu; graphic elements in textile motifs; hatun inti; inti chinka-pushan; inti lloqsimushan; k'iraqey puntas; listas; qheswa pallay; sonqocha; tawa inti qocha

Munsters, Martin, 11

Nina, Benito, 17, 83, 86

nonalphabetic writing systems: of Incas, 1, 25; and graphics, 22, 25; and knowledge recorded in cloth, 23, 75–78, 113; and quipus, 25; and relationship with textile iconography, 15

Numhauser, Paulina, 115

Núñez del Prado, Oscar: anthropological study of Q'ero, 6; and freedom of Q'ero people, 21; and myth of Inkarri, 123, 136; and the quipu, 109; and Q'ero motifs, 11–12, 61; textile collection, 43, 54

Ochoa, Jorge Flores, 27, 121

Olivera, Josefina, 43

Ondegardo, Polo de, 96

one-faced cloth. *See* iskaymanta hoq uya

Ong, W. J., 22

Orihuela, Manuel, 42

Ortiz, Alejandro, 135–36

Ossio, Juan, 84

Parssinen, Martii, 25

Pauccar, Benito Salas, 62, 81–91, 98–107, 114, 139–40

Pauccar, Felipa, 35

Pauccar, Juliana, 35

Pauccar, Ramón Salas, 67

Pauccar, Rosa, 63

Pauccar, Santiago Salas, 120

Pauccar, Tomasa, 17, 126

Paz, Percy, 131

Pimentel, Nelson, 25

Pineda, Josafat Roel, 136

Platt, Tristan, 73

plying, techniques of, 30

Poma, Guamán, 25, 80, 82, 179

Prochaska, Rita, 11

pukllay p'acha, 114–15

Q'ero: agriculture of, 3–4, 27, 73–74, 118–21; classifications of bodies of water, 119–20; classifications of corn, 118, 186n3; classifications of llamas and alpacas, 120–21, 184n1; classifications of potatoes, 118–19, 186n4; classifications of soil, 120; and colonialism, 20; communities of, 1–2, 4, 183n3; functional uses of textile motifs, 9, 82–85, 88–93, 117; garments of, 7–8; and Inca culture, 2–3, 5, 6–8, 20; Inkarri, myth of, 123; location of, 1; marriages, 6; meanings associated with colors, 116–21; modernization of, 21; plying techniques, 30; recording of goods and possessions, 117–18; religious culture of, 3, 5; spinning techniques, 28–29; symbolism of color, 117–21; textiles of, 10–12, 42; traditional dress of, 39; understanding of celestial space, 101–7; use of quipus, 6–7, 109, 117; weaving techniques of, 7–8, 12–13; wool production, 25. *See also* garments, bags, and embellishments; iconography, textile; listas; motifs, Q'ero; quipus

Q'ero pallay (Q'ero motif). *See* motifs, Q'ero

qheswa pallay (valley motif): binary logic of, 177; comparison with Q'ero pallay, 12–13;

graphic elements of, 175–77; knowledge
recorded in, 176–77; quartered diamond
motif, 54–55, 176; slings and knitted
items, 47–50; symbolism of, 14; weaving
techniques used in, 12–13, 175–77; word
signs of, 147

qocha, 88–91

quartered diamond motif. *See* tawa inti
qocha (four sun lake)

quipus, 6–7, 8, 25, 109–17

Quispe, Benino, 90–91

Quispe, Cipriana, 14

Quispe, Juana, 130

Quispe, Juliana, 142–43

Quispe, Lorenzo, 64

Quispe, Maria Pauccar, 6

Quispe, Paulina, 6

Quispe, Sabino, 106

Quispe, Serephino Samanta, 126

Quispe, Victoria, 33

Reinhard, Johann, 60

Rincón de las Cabezas, El (Arnold 2000)

Río de vellón, río de canto (Arnold and Yapita 1998)

Rivière, Gilles, 70

Rojas, Juvenal Casaverde, 84

Rosing, Iña, 180

Rowe, Anne Pollard, 10, 14, 54, 136

Rozas, Washington, 60

Ruiz Durand, Jesús, 11

Salas, Benito, 16, 74

Salas, Martin Pauccar, 106

Salas, Miguel, 20

Salas, Ramón, 16, 19

Salas, Santiago, 19, 27

Salomon, Frank, 25

Samanta, Cilio Apasa, 126

Samanta, Juliana, 83

Samanta, Marcelino, 74

Schmandt-Besserat, Denise, 147

Seibold, Katherine, 11

Seligmann, Linda, 11

Sequieros, Ana de, 117

Sera, Luisa, 68

Sherbondy, Jeannette, 59

Silverblatt, Irene, 180

Silverman, Gail P.: and ch'unchu motif, 124;
fieldwork, xvii, 14–15, 42, 78–79, 124; living in Tandaña, xvii, 17–20, 185n5; study
of textile iconography, xvii, 12, 14, 22, 117;
weaving, 12–14, 33, 78, 111–12, 142–43;

Skar, Sarah Lund, 81

Solari, Gertrude, 11

sonqocha (little heart): symbolism of, 52,
63–64, 86–88; representation of time and
space, 52, 86–88; literal translation of, 86

spinning, techniques of, 28–29

Stobart, Henry, 180

tawa inti qocha (four sun lake): and cosmological concepts, 51–52, 50–60; found
in other cultures, 54; function as word
signs, 148–50; graphic elements of, 51–52,
55–58, 76, 95–107, 147–48; representation
of dual social organization, 64–65; representation of time and space, 59–60, 63,
68–70, 76–78, 147–48; and similarities to
Inca ceque system, 59–60; variations of,
55–58; weaving technique used with, 52

textiles: collections of, 42–43; comparison
of, 42–44, 112–13; early studies of, 10–12;
knowledge recorded in, 17, 21, 60–61;
of Q'ero, 43–44; socioeconomic function of, 11–12; wool used in, 43. *See also*

garments, woven; iconography, textile; motifs, Q'ero;

three-color complementary warp weaving, *See* kinsamanta iskay uya

Tracht, Arthur, 131

two-color supplementary warp weaving. *See* iskaymanta hoq uya

two-faced cloth. *See* kinsamanta iskay uya

Ulloa, Liliana Torres, 11

Urton, Gary, 25, 73, 102, 105

Vega, Vivian Gavilan, 11

Vilabar, Salsaro, 140–41

Wachtel, Nathan, 70

Waman, Austina Flores, 68, 86, 99

Waman, Domingo Pauccar, 126

Warkasaya, Benito Nina, 99, 105–06

Warp-Patterned Weaves of the Andes (Rowe 1997), 14

warping, techniques of, 111–13

Watt, I. P., 22

weaving, techniques of, 32–38, 113–14. *See also* iskaymanta hoq uya; kinsamanta iskay uya; *specific motifs*; textiles

Webster, Stephen, 6, 12, 120

Wilson, Lee Anne, 11, 123, 131

Wissler, Holly, 21

wool, 27, 30, 43

writing systems, xvii, 22–24

Yabar, Luis Angel, 7, 42

Yapita, Juan de Dios, 11, 25, 117

Yupanqui, Demetrio Túpac, 109

Zorn, Elayne, 10, 121

Zuidema, R. T., 22, 59, 80–81, 100, 179